ACTA UNIVERSITATIS UPSALIENSIS
Studia Anglistica Upsaliensia
58

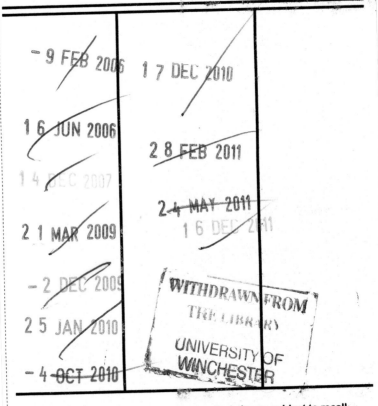

Michael Srigley

Images of Regeneration:

A Study of Shakespeare's *The Tempest* and Its Cultural Background

UPPSALA 1985

Distributor:
Almqvist & Wiksell International
Stockholm

Doctoral Thesis at Uppsala University 1985.

Abstract
Srigley, Michael, 1985. Images of Regeneration: A Study of Shakespeare's *The Tempest* and Its Cultural Background. Acta Universitatis Upsaliensis. *Studia Anglistica Upsaliensia* 58, 182 pp. Uppsala. ISBN 91-554-1734-5

This dissertation is a study of *The Tempest* in the context of the ideas and preoccupations of the early seventeenth century. By relating the imagery of the play to various images of regeneration drawn from the medical alchemy of Paracelsus and from Christian and pagan rites of initiation, it sets out to show that the traditional interpretation of *The Tempest* as an allegory of regeneration is substantially correct. The play is also related to the Protestant millenarian movement of the first two decades of the seventeenth century, and it is suggested that *The Tempest* is a highly topical allegory of the apocalyptic hopes and fears of this period. Contrary to the accepted view, it is argued that Shakespeare wrote *The Tempest* in anticipation of the wedding of Elizabeth Stuart and Frederick V. It is shown that negotiations for this match had started as early as 1610. The topicality of *The Tempest* in 1611 is also indicated by the similarities of Prospero to Rudolf II, Holy Roman Emperor, who in that year was being deposed by his brother for gross neglect of government and for his addiction to hermetic studies and magic. It is suggested in the final part of this dissertation that the standard view of Prospero as a white magician is incorrect. The "rough magic" that he finally abjures would have been regarded by James I as illicit, even when practised for good ends.

Michael Srigley, Engelska institutionen, Uppsala universitet, Box 513, S-751 20 Uppsala, Sweden.

ISBN 91-554-1734-5
ISSN 0562-2719

Printed in Sweden 1985
Textgruppen i Uppsala AB

Contents

Preface

The debts of gratitude accumulated in the course of writing a study like this are many and varied. They are owed to the many scholars, both living and dead, whose insights I have been able to use, as well as to the many individuals who over the years have helped to make this study possible. If I mention some in particular, it is as representatives of them all.

My gratitude goes above all to my wife, Ulla, not least for her suggestion that I terminate some two decades of note-taking on *The Tempest*, by actually writing on it. I am also especially grateful to my supervisor, Professor Gunnar Sorellius, not only for his detailed and helpful criticisms, but also for his firm support of my approach to *The Tempest*. This has steaded me much. My thanks also go to Dr Sven-Johan Spånberg for unfailing encouragement and help during and after the period he acted as my supervisor. My colleagues at the Department are to be congratulated for having listened with bemused patience to sudden harangues on such topics as the Eleusinian mysteries, the drinking habits of the Elizabethans or alchemical putrefaction; a special word of thanks goes to my friend and colleague, Mr Richard Glover, for our many valued colloquies on *The Tempest*. I would like to take this opportunity of thanking Mr Adam McLean of Edinburgh for providing me with a photocopy of Michael Maier's curious Christmas Card to James I, and Dr Sten Eklund and his colleagues of the Classics Department, Uppsala University, for their expert help in interpreting Maier's Latin. I would like to acknowledge the generous help given to me by Dr Marjorie Reeves of Oxford University in matters connected with Joachim of Fiore, and to thank Miss Molly Bennett of the Bodleian Library for prompt help in settling the original form of the phrase "Miranda sextae aetatis". The staff of the British Library and the Manuscripts Department are thanked for their usual efficiency and courtesy. For furnishing me with volumes that I prize above Prospero's dukedom, I am grateful to mine own library, Carolina Rediviva, and its helpful staff. A final word of gratitude goes to Dr Frank Kermode. It was his Introduction to the Arden *Tempest* that fired my enthusiasm for this play and prompted me to study it within the context of the ideas and events of its period.

To all these people, named and unnamed, I dedicate whatever may be of value in this study.

Uppsala, January 1985   M. B. S.

Chapter I
The Tempest as an Allegory

In a survey of criticism of Shakespeare's final group of plays, the Romances, covering the half century from 1900 to 1957, Philip Edwards came to the following gloomy conclusion:

It would be vainglory to suggest that recent criticism has succeeded in justifying the large claims it has made for Shakespeare's Romances. Though we may be convinced, because of the constant insistence, that the Romances are important, it is hard to point to the critic who has shown where the importance lies. At any rate, a retrospect of this century's work on the last plays has little progress to report.[1]

Although thirty years have passed since these words were written, the situation has not radically changed despite a number of excellent studies of these plays. The advice offered by Edwards at the end of his survey seems to have been followed: "criticism might for the moment ignore the illumination and the universality of the last plays."[2] Behind this bleak advice lies the realization that the grand allegorical approach of the nineteenth century and of this one has failed to deal adequately with the sensed richness of the Romances. It is therefore recommended that we lower our sights and begin afresh at a more modest level.

In view of this pessimistic recommendation, some justification is needed for undertaking the present type of study of one of the Romances. One justification is that there have been few full-length studies of *The Tempest*, which is somewhat surprising considering the high standing this play continues to have.[3] A further justification for this study lies in the fact that

---

[1] Philip Edwards, "Shakespeare's Romances: 1900—1957," *Shakespeare Survey* (Cambridge: Cambridge University Press), 11 (1958), 1. In his follow-up article, "Shakespeare's Romances since 1958: A Retrospect," *Shakespeare Survey*, 29 (1976), F. David Hoeniger draws attention to subsequent research into the topical allegory of the Romances, particularly of *Cymbeline*, but as far as I know such an approach has not been made to *The Tempest*. All quotations from this play are from the Arden *Tempest*, 6th ed. (London: Methuen, 1958), ed. Frank Kermode, unless otherwise stated.

[2] Edwards, "Shakespeare's Romances," p. 18.

[3] Full-length studies of *The Tempest* are Colin Still, *Shakespeare's Mystery Play: A Study of 'The Tempest'* (London: Cecil Palmer, 1921), and *The Timeless Theme* (London: Nicholson and Watson, 1936); A. D. Nuttall, *Two Concepts of Allegory: A Study of Shakespeare's The Tempest and the Logic of Allegorical Expression* (London: Routledge and Kegan Paul, 1967), and D. G. James, *The Dream of Prospero* (Oxford: Clarendon Press, 1967).

there have been a number of advances in our knowledge of the age in which Shakespeare lived that throw a new light on *The Tempest*. Chief among these is our increased knowledge of the hermetic tradition of the Renaissance and in particular of contemporary attitudes to the practise of various forms of magic. This knowledge has not yet been fully used to define the sort of magic practised by Prospero. Normally described as white magic, it is, as I shall try and show, by no means certain that a Jacobean audience would have seen it as such. Thanks largely to the researches of Professor Debus, another important aspect of Shakespeare's period has now come into focus. This is the impact on contemporary thought of the new alchemical medicine associated with the name of Paracelsus. Its importance for an understanding of Shakespeare has been brought out in a major study by Charles Nicholl.[4] Fortunately for the present writer he did not extend his treatment to *The Tempest*, although I believe that it is above all in this play that the imagery of Paracelsan regeneration through alchemy is to be found. Another related area of research that is relevant to an understanding of *The Tempest* concerns the mood of apocalyptic and millenarian expectation that prevailed during the period of Shakespeare's Last Plays. Scholars like Marjorie Reeves and Frances Yates have in their different ways revealed the extent to which belief in the Last Days and the imminent restoration of the Golden Age or establishment of the Millennium conditioned the thinking and politics of the early seventeenth century. As I shall show, James's two eldest children, Henry and Elizabeth, became the focus in Britain of these apocalyptic and millenarian beliefs from about 1609 onwards. Although the relationship of the Romances in general to the royal family has been increasingly recognized, *The Tempest* remains in modern criticism insulated from the contemporary world. I shall try and show that *The Tempest* too with its young lovers and its deposed royal magician was highly topical in 1611 when it was first performed.

A third reason for undertaking this study has to do with changes in our own times. Each generation will inevitably interpret a play like *The Tempest* in terms of its own assumptions and experience. It will respond more deeply to some aspects of the play and ignore others. In the 1980's we live under the constant threat of nuclear annihilation. Our world view is being changed by the discoveries and theories of quantum physics. There has been a marked rise in the interest in occultism, meditation and in altered states of awareness. There is a profound sense of crisis, comparable, as we shall see, to the apocalyptic mood that existed in the first two decades of the seventeenth cen-

---

[4] Charles Nicholl, *The Chemical Theatre* (London: Routledge and Kegan Paul, 1980).

2

tury. Then as now there was a belief that only a major change in human attitudes, a shift of paradigm as is now said, would bring peace and brotherhood to men. Out of this belief there arose and there arises today the question of how this change is to be brought about. How is human nature to be so changed that we avoid self-destruction? As the tensions that built up to the Thirty Years' War and all its devastation and violence mounted during the period when Shakespeare wrote *The Tempest*, the same question was being posed by Shakespeare's contemporaries throughout Europe in their own terms. By what means was the second Golden Age to be inaugurated? How was human nature to be so altered that the transition into the Millennium could be assured and hastened. *The Tempest*, with a topicality that has not been recognized, dramatizes and examines one answer made by some of Shakespeare's contemporaries. The means to be used was a form of magic, the magic that Prospero finally abjures as rough.

In order to understand the nature of the burning topical issues taken up in *The Tempest*, it is essential to grasp the terms in which they were expressed. Today we speak of a new world order, of the global village and of the establishment of right human relationships. Some speak of a dawning Age of Aquarius. In Shakespeare's day, the dream of a regenerated society was expressed in another terminology. As we shall see in this study, the theme of regeneration was understood and expressed in terms derived from the following spheres of thought: the symbolic or spiritual alchemy of the Paracelsan school of medicine, contemporary knowledge of pagan and Christian initiation, and regeneration as an apocalyptic and millenarian event. It is from these spheres of thought that the basic images of regeneration to be found in *The Tempest* take their source. In order to clear the ground for a discussion of these various but closely related images of regeneration and to show how they constitute the allegory of the play, it is first of all necessary to determine what the word allegory meant in the Renaissance.

The Stony Allegorist

During the nineteenth century *The Tempest* was treated as a simplistic allegory that was easily translatable into a clear meaning. John Ruskin provides one example of this type of allegoresis. In his *Munera Pulveris* he writes that he finds in *The Tempest* "an undercurrent meaning" which links the play with Plato's ideas on government. Miranda 'corresponds' to Homer's Arte; "Ariel and Caliban are respectively the spirits of faithful and im-

aginative labour, opposed to rebellious, hurtful and slavish labour. Prospero
. . . a true governor, is opposed to Sycorax, the mother of slavery.''[5] The
method is one of simple equivalence, with one character 'standing for' some
abstract concept. The other major type of nineteenth century allegory, the
biographical, can be represented by Dowden. For him, Prospero is "the
great artist", Miranda is his "Art", while Caliban stands for "the grosser
passions and appetites." Ferdinand, as the decoding system demands, must
be young Fletcher, Shakespeare's apprentice in the dramatic art, piling
thousands of logs (*logoi*?) in an effort to become worthy of Miranda who
is that art.[6] Again, allegory becomes a matter of simple equation. It was
against this form of biographical and reductionist allegoresis with its myth
of the wisely benevolent grey-haired Shakespeare returning to Stratford to
tend his mulberry bush that Lytton Strachey reacted in his waspish essay of
1906. Thereafter this type of allegorical interpretation of *The Tempest* in
terms of Shakespeare's life and thought declined.

But what might be called simplistic allegory continued to be applied to *The
Tempest*, but increasingly in terms of its themes. Furnivall's view of the play
as belonging to the fourth-period spirit of "Re-Union, of Reconciliation,
and Forgiveness,"[7] has survived down to recent times, and is found in its
best form in Wilson Knight's two works, *The Crown of Life* (1947) and *The
Shakespearean Tempest* (1932). Wilson Knight's thematic approach to the
Last Plays and his treatment of them as myths of immortality has deepened
our understanding of these plays, and yet his grand approach has the disad-
vantage of often soaring far beyond the detail of the text. *The Tempest* seems
to provoke a form of rhapsodic flight as in the following passage from his
The Shakespearean Tempest:

> *The Tempest* is Shakespeare's instinctive imaginative genius mapped into a universal
> pattern; not neglecting, but enclosing and transcending, all his past themes of loss
> and restoration, tempest and music.[8]

Criticism of *The Tempest* in the postwar period has recoiled from the
grand allegorical approach. It is characterized by a distrust of the very word
'allegory', and this has led to some odd results. In its extreme form this has
led to the idea that *The Tempest* is no more than its story. "I cannot believe

[5] John Ruskin, *Munera Pulveris* (1872), p. 126, cited in the New Variorum *Tempest*, ed.
H. H. Furness (New York: Dover Publications, 1964), p. 363.
[6] Cited in New Variorum *Tempest*, p. 364.
[7] Cited in New Variorum *Tempest*, p. 365.
[8] G. Wilson Knight, *The Shakespearian Tempest* (London: Oxford Univ. Press, 1932), p.
263.

that there is any allegory . . . or symbolism . . . or even 'veiled biography' ''
in *The Tempest*, writes E.E. Stoll.[9] The characters are what they are and
what they do and no more. Explaining Prospero's harshness of character,
Stoll says it "is mainly owing to the poverty of the plot."[10] Few critics have
followed Stoll so far in his total rejection of allegory in the play. Rather,
significances are found in the play, but it is denied that they are allegorical.
A few examples will serve to illustrate this distrust of the word 'allegory'.
Northrop Frye has written that "*The Tempest* is not an allegory, or a religious drama",[11] but he finds in it "an emphasis on moral and spiritual
rebirth—which suggests ritual initiation, like baptism or the ancient mystery
dramas, as well as of festivity".[12] Patrick Grant in his illuminating essay on
the play, "The Magic of Charity" writes:

At this point, I should say that I do not think *The Tempest* is allegorical; merely that
. . . we feel throughout the play some heightened significance which I am now at
pains to account for in Miranda.[13]

Both Frye and Grant find a heightened significance in the play, but deny
that allegory is involved. It is left unclear what we are to call an interpretation
that finds the theme of spiritual rebirth and ritual initiation in the play, or
investigates it, as Patrick Grant does learnedly, in terms of *caritas*, chastity
and castigation. One solution to this problem of terminology has been proposed by A. D. Nuttall, in his study of the play, *Two Concepts of Allegory*
(p. 160):

Is *The Tempest* allegorical? If I have done my work properly, the question should
have shrunk in importance . . . For the island, as for most of the elements of the
play, I should prefer to coin a rather ugly term—pre-allegorical.

The reasons for inventing this term—pre-allegorical—are interesting. Nuttall wishes to avoid the sort of allegoresis of the play that reduces it to a series
of statements about the play's meaning:

The minutely perceptive scepticism of *The Tempest* defeats the stony allegorist and
the rigid cynic equally. The mystery is never allowed to harden into an ontological
dogma to be reduced to symbols or rejected with contempt. Instead we have an ex-
traordinarily delicate and dramatic play, which, until the Last Day makes all things
clear, will never be anything but immensely suggestive (p. 160).

---

[9] E. E. Stoll, *The Tempest* (1940) in *Twentieth Century Interpretations of The Tempest*, ed.
Hallett Smith (Eaglewood Cliffs: Prentice-Hall, 1969), p. 25.

[10] Stoll in *Twentieth Century Interpretations*, p. 33.

[11] Northrop Frye, Introd. to the Penguin *Tempest* (Harmondsworth: Penguin Publications, 1959), p. 17.

[12] Northrop Frye, p. 24.

[13] Patrick Grant, "The Magic of Charity: A Background to Prospero," *Review of English
Studies*, 27 (1976), 10.

If I understand these words correctly Nuttall is anxious to avoid a certain form of allegorical interpretation that imposes limited meanings on a play that constantly goes beyond them by virtue of its immense suggestiveness. This leaves us in a critical cul-de-sac. The suggestiveness of *The Tempest* is so much in excess of our powers of comprehension or expression that, unless the Last Days are closer than we suppose, we must abide its mystery with long patience. Is the position quite so hopeless? Perhaps the answer would be to turn our attention to this rich suggestiveness of the play, and avoid any attempt to formulate the play's abstract meanings. It is possible that this suggestiveness adequately explored *is* the meaning, and that the more we are able to respond to the play in its verbal detail, the more will we approach its core of meaning as an experience. We may not be able to express this meaning in words, for that would be to compete with the play itself. But what is possible is to attend to what is said in the play line by line and so increase our sensitivity to its verbal suggestiveness. This is the approach that modern art historians have taught us to make to a Renaissance painting. The allegory of Botticelli's *Primavera* is dispersed in the detail, and to respond to it requires patience and study. If I will be forgiven a play on words, it is the approach and not the arrival that is the concern of criticism. The critic's task is to clear the approach, leaving the final act of comprehension, the moment of arrival, to each individual reader. Such an approach is in fact a return to the practise of Shakespeare's time, and was implicit in the very nature of Renaissance allegory. The meaning of an allegory was approached through the detail and not arrived at through a process of abstraction.

To Say One Thing and Mean Another

The Renaissance attitude to allegory was in large part a repetition of traditional attitudes that went back to the ancient world and had been enriched and elaborated during the Middle Ages. Central to it was the view, derived ultimately from the mystery religions and from Christianity, that certain high truths must be veiled in order to protect them from profanation, just as the inner sanctum of a temple was veiled to conceal the *sacra* from the uninitiated.[14] This association between religious and allegorical concealment is found, for example, in the statement of Demetrius the Rhetorician that:

[14] For the traditional association between religious and allegorical veiling, see James Norhnberg, *The Analogy of the Faerie Queene* (Princeton: Princeton Univ. Press, 1976), p. 90, n. 6.

6

The mysteries are revealed in allegorical form in order to inspire such shuddering and awe as are associated with darkness and light; allegory too is not unlike darkness and light.[15]

A similar justification for the concealment of allegory was also derived from Christianity. A key passage was Matthew 13: 10—13, where Christ explains why he spoke to the multitude in parables, but explicitly to his disciples:

Because it is given unto you to know the mysteries of the kingdom of heaven, but to them it is not given.

This passage was not only used in the Renaissance to justify a deliberate obscurity of style in philosophical discourse, but was cited to justify poetic allegory.[16] An example of this use is contained in John Harington's Preface to his translation of Ariosto's *Orlando Furioso* (1591):

But in the rest it is manifest that he [Christ] that was all holinesse, all wisdom, all truth, used parables, and even such as discreet Poets use, where a good and honest and wholesome Allegorie is hidden in a pleasaunt and pretie fiction.[17]

During the Renaissance it was above all the group of Platonists gathered round Marsilio Ficino in Florence at the end of the fifteenth century who transmitted the view of allegory as a means of concealing sacred truths. Continuing the classical and medieval belief that the works of such writers as Homer and Virgil were detailed allegories and that the pagan myths contained recondite truths, they produced new works of learned allegoresis. For example, Ficino's disciple, Christofero Landino, wrote an influential allegorical interpretation of Dante's *Divine Comedy* and of the first six Books of Virgil's *Aeneid*; we shall examine the latter in its relation to *The Tempest* at a later point in this study. Imitating what they believed to be the conscious method of the ancients, the Florentine Platonists cultivated their own form of allegorical obscurity when speaking of the "mysteries" of existence. Referring to his own allegorical interpretation of some poems, Pico della Mirandola, Ficino's most famous disciple, wrote in a letter: "If I am not mistaken, it will be intelligible only to a few, for it is filled with many mysteries from the secret philosophy of the ancients."[18] Edgar Wind has shown in his *Pagan Mysteries in the Renaissance* that such studied conceal-

---

[15] Cited by R. M. Grant, *The Letter and the Spirit* (London: Macmillan, 1957), p. 9.

[16] See Edgar Wind, *Pagan Mysteries in the Renaissance* (London: Faber and Faber, 1958), pp. 17 ff., for a discussion of Pico's calculated obscurity of style.

[17] John Harington, Preface to *Orlando Furioso* in *Elizabethan Critical Essays*, ed. G. Gregory Smith (Oxford: Oxford Univ. Press, 1904), II, 206.

[18] Cited by Wind, *Pagan Mysteries in the Renaissance*, p. 10.

ment was sanctioned for these thinkers by the belief that there was a core of teaching in pagan mysteries such as those of Eleusis and in the mysteries of the early Church which was rigorously concealed from outsiders. Hence during the Renaissance allegory in art and poetry continued to have an almost religious status as a method of concealing sacred truths from the gaze of the vulgar and the uninitiated. The proper manner for an official mystagogue, Pico suggested, was to speak in riddles, in words that "are published and not published," *editos esse et non editos.*[19] Influenced in part by this attitude to allegory of the Florentine School of Platonism, the artists and writers of the Renaissance saw themselves as the guardians of certain profound truths which they concealingly revealed to a worthy élite, while distracting the unworthy and profane with the surface fiction.

Behind such commendations of concealment through allegory is the complementary idea that not only is such veiling necessary but it is also inevitable. By its very transcendant nature, ultimate truths are unavoidably concealed when expressed in language derived from the phenomenal world. But because there is nevertheless some degree of correlation between what E. H. Gombrich has called "the two worlds" of the Renaissance, the physical and the spiritual, the former is able to hint at the latter.[20] There is nevertheless a disparity between the sign and the signified. For this reason "an allegorical work is not self-contained, but is part of an incomplete process. The process is only completed when the reader fully intuits the meanings which the author himself can only partly express."[21] The allegorical writer is therefore making a virtue of necessity in concealing his meaning. Such allegorizing is ultimately Platonic in inspiration. The Ideas and Archetypes of ultimate reality can only be evoked through their imperfect simulacra or images in the phenomenal world. The poet's function, therefore, becomes that of the image-maker or user of the imagination, bodying forth and yet concealing the formless.

These various ideas on the nature and function of allegory were well known in England, and are repeated with almost monotonous insistence. Thomas Nashe expresses the generally held view of poetry as "a more hidden & diuine kinde of Philosophy, enwrapped in blinde Fables and darke stories."[22] For George Puttenham, allegory was the principal device or fig-

---

[19] Wind, p. 11.
[20] E. H. Gombrich, *Symbolic Images: Studies in the Art of the Renaissance, II* (Oxford: Phaidon Press, 1972), p. 146.
[21] Isabel Rivers, *Classical and Christian Ideas in English Renaissance Poetry* (London: Allen and Unwin, 1978), p. 170. The section on allegory in this work contains a brief but informative survey of Renaisssance ideas on this subject.
[22] Thomas Nashe, *A General Censure* in *Elizabethan Critical Essays,* I, 328.

ure of "the Poeticall or oratorie science," and he called it "False Semblant" because it involved a species of dissembling on the part of the poet.[23] Representative of a cultivated Elizabethan reader of poetry at the end of the sixteenth century is Frances Meres who in his notes "Of Poetry and Poets" put down this standard passage from Plutarch on the nature of allegory:

As in a Vine clusters of grapes are often hidde under the broade and spacious leaves: so in deepe conceited and well couched poems, figures and fables, many things verie profitable to be knowne, do passe by a young scholler.[24]

For one of the fullest accounts of allegory as understood in the Elizabethan period we turn to Sir John Harington's Preface to his translation of *Orlando Furioso* (1591):

The ancient Poets have indeed wrapped as it were in their writings divers and sundry meanings, which they call the senses or mysteries thereof. First of all for the litterall sence (as it were the utmost barke or ryne) they set downe in manner of an historie the acts and notable exploits of some persons worthy of memorie: then in the same fiction, as a second rine and somewhat more fine, as it were nearer to the pith and marrow, they place the Morall sence profitable for the active life of man, approving vertuous actions and condemning the contrarie. Manie times also under the selfesame words they comprehend some true understanding of natural Philosophie, or somtimes of politike governement, and now and then of divinitie: and these same sences that comprehend so excellent knowledge we call the Allegorie, which Plutarch defineth to be when one thing is told, and by that another is understood.[25]

What emerges as central to the broad concept of allegory held during this period is the element of conscious dissimulation on the part of the allegorist. The surface fiction is deliberately used to conceal layers of deeper meaning, and to mislead the unwary or unworthy reader. This is in conformity with the definition of allegory derived from Plutarch in the case of Harington but often taken from Quintillian, that in it one thing was said and another meant.[26]

The same degree of care that went into allegorical concealment was required of the reader who would discover the truths concealed beneath the surface fiction. Advising the reader who would unwind the "intricate involutions" of poetry, Boccaccio wrote:

You must read, you must perservere, you must sit up at nights, you must inquire and exert the utmost powers of your mind . . . For we are forbidden by divine command to give that which is holy to dogs, or to cast pearls before swine.[27]

[23] George Puttenham, "Of Ornament" in *Elizabethan Critical Essays*, II, 169.

[24] Frances Meres, "Palladis Tamia" in *Elizabethan Critical Essays*, II, 309.

[25] John Harington, Preface to *Orlando Furioso* in *Elizabethan Critical Essays*, II, 201—2.

[26] Quintillian, *Institutio Oratoria* (Loeb ed.), VIII, vi, 44.

[27] Boccaccio, *Genealogia Deorum Gentilium* (1472), XIV, xii, cited by Michael Murrin, *The Veil of Allegory* (Chicago and London: Univ of Chicago Press, 1969), p. 15.

Speaking of the "highest and deepest mysteries" concealed within the *Faerie Queene*, Kenelm Digby explained that Spenser

hath done this soe cunningly, that if one heed him not with great attention, rare and wonderful conceptions will unperceived slide by him that readeth his works, and he will thinke that he hath mett with nothing but familiar and easy discourses, but let one dwell awhile upon them and he shall feele a straunge fulnesse in all he saith.[28]

The inattentive reader, said Thomas Lodge, will be misled by "the vanitie of tales", and yet "if we aduisedly looke into them they wil seme and proue wise."[29]

The same views are found in Edmund Spenser's Letter to Sir Walter Raleigh, appended to the *Faerie Queene*. The "continued Allegorie or darke conceit" which conveys "the general intention and meaning" of the poem is concealed within an historical fiction. He has chosen this fiction from the tales of Arthur "rather for variety of matter, then for the profite of the en-sample." The fiction gives pleasure, while the intention and meaning "thus clowdily enwrapped in Allegorical devises" gives instruction.[30] Here again we find the standard view of the surface fiction as a blind distracting the un-worthy reader from the concealed inner meaning. As Michael Murrin observes in his illuminating study of Renaissance allegory, *The Veil of Allegory* (p. 13), allegory is eclectic in its appeal: "the poet causes a division in his audience, separating the few from the many, those who understand from those who cannot." Only those with the requisite knowledge and in-sight, who were prepared to perservere, could make the transition from the surface to the allegorical depths. To aid such readers, certain pointers were placed in the text which, if properly heeded, would guide him to the true level of allegorical meaning. Spenser alludes to this aid in the *Faerie Queene*:

> Of Faerie lond yet if he more inquire
> By certaine signes here set in sundry place
> He may it find.[31]

[28] Kenelm Digby, "Concerning Spenser that I wrote at Mr Day's Desire," in *Spenser: The Critical Heritage*, ed. R. M. Cummings (London: Routledge and Kegan Paul, 1971), p. 150.
[29] Thomas Lodge, *A Defence of Poetry* (1579), in *Elizabethan Critical Essays*, I, 65.
[30] Edmund Spenser, Letter to Raleigh, in *The Faerie Queene*, ed. A. C. Hamilton (London: Longman, 1977), p. 737.
[31] *The Faerie Queene*, Bk. II, Proem 4:1—3.

Telltale Incongruity

Here again the Renaissance derived from the Ancients its ideas concerning the way in which a reader could be alerted to the presence of allegory. It was particularly among the Alexandrian school of Platonists that this aspect of allegoresis was developed. For them the presence of allegory was revealed by some incongruity in the text caused by a disparity between the surface meaning and the concealed meaning. The more absurd or grotesque the detail, the more likely was it to be a bearer of some hidden meaning. In his *In Rempublicum* Proclus attempted a full-scale vindication of Homer's use of the myths of the gods as vehicles for conveying spiritual mysteries. The very grotesqueness of some of Homer's stories of the gods, he argued, was an indication that hidden meanings were present:

Since therefore such myths arouse those naturally endowed to a longing for the knowledge hidden within them, and by their grotesque surface provoke a search for the truth which has been set within its shrine, while at the same time preventing prophane individuals from laying hands on what is forbidden them to touch, are they not, in an outstanding way, appropriate to the very gods whose substance they communicate to us.[32]

Dionysius the Areopagite, whose ideas were particularly influential during the Renaissance period, refers to the use of 'inappropriateness' in the Scriptures:

The holy authors of the revealed writings have deliberately used inappropriate symbols or similes so that we should not cling to the undignified meaning . . . To the prophane these enigmatic images conceal the holy arcanum of the supernatural; to the initiate, however, they serve as the first rung of the ladder by which we ascend to the Divine.[33]

As E. H. Gombrich has pointed out, this theory of "the apophetic way of mysterious monstrosity" of Dionysius is cited with approval by Torquato Tasso, author of the allegorical epic, *Jerusalem Delivered*, in his discussion of allegory in his *On The Heroic Poem*.[34]

This use of incongruity to indicate the presence of allegory was familiar to Renaissance writers and theorists. Edgar Wind has noted about Renaissance allegories that "as in the study of rituals, it is an almost unfailing rule that those allegories which seem the most ridiculous at first may prove in the end to be the most vital",[35] and in a footnote he adds that

---

[32] Cited by James A. Coulter, *The Literary Microcosm: Theories of Interpretation of the Later Platonists* (Leiden: Brill, 1976), p. 59.
[33] Cited by E. H. Gombrich, *Symbolic Images*, p. 151.
[34] Gombrich, p. 152.
[35] Wind, *Pagan Mysteries in the Renaissance*, p. 27.

Constructive absurdity is also at the root of the supposedly rational use of allegory by which an idea or image which has become objectionable is 'saved' through a figurative interpretation.[36]

To use Antonio's phrase in *The Tempest* (II.i.85), "impossible matter" in the text becomes an indication that we must seek a figurative interpretation. This is precisely what that most obscure of poets, George Chapman, recommends to his readers in his Preface to *The Odyssey* (1616):

If the Bodie (being the Letter, or historie) seems fictive, and beyond Possibilitie to bring into Act: the sense then and Allegorie (which is the soule) is to be sought.

We have seen that in the Renaissance allegory involved a form of deliberate concealment of meaning in which following Quintillian's definition one thing was said and another meant. There was the surface meaning carrying and concealing the true meaning within it. The literal story was the husk, rind or body, while the allegorical sense was the pith, marrow or soul. In origin the justification for allegorical concealment was religious: to conceal the secrets of ultimate reality from the profane. For the profane the 'delight' of the surface story was a decoy leading them astray so that they become lost in the maze of superficial pleasure, mistaking the truth entirely. For the worthy seeker, however, there existed signposts in the text guiding him towards the hidden meaning. A puzzle, riddle, incongruity, a seeming inconsequence were indications to the alert wayfarer that guidance was being offered which he must ponder and not ignore. These incongruities constituted the clew that would lead him safely through the forthrights and meanders of the surface fiction. To change the image, allegory was an extended metaphor which constantly offered the reader a choice between its literal term and its figurative term, a bifurcation of meaning which corresponds to what Gombrich calls the Renaissance "doctrine of the two worlds". It is in terms of this doctrine that we can understand the essential difference between allegory as understood in the Renaissance and allegory as understood from the eighteenth century onwards.

It is generally true to say that during Shakespeare's lifetime, the ancient view of the physical world and all that happened in it as a sign pointing beyond itself to a transcendant world still held sway. Human life was itself an allegory, an effect of an invisible cause. By studying the *visibilia* as signs, the causative *invisibilia* could be more easily understood:

The Universe in this conception is a vast symphony of correspondences in which each level of existence points to the level above. It is by virtue of this interrelated harmony

---

[36] Wind, p. 27, n. 3.

that one object can signify another and that by contemplating a visible thing we can gain insight into the invisible world.[37]

This concept of a hierarchy of correspondences means that there is always an organic relationship between the sign and the signified. It also implies that what is signified cannot be reduced to a single meaning, but that various levels of meaning are contained in the sign. We are therefore compelled to think polysemously and hold simultaneously a variety of meanings.

It was precisely against this sort of multivalent allegory that a reaction set in during the eighteenth century. It was a reaction, as E. H. Gombrich has shown, against "the open sign with its plenitude of meaning" (p. 182), in favour of limited signs that were accessible to rational explanation. Allegory thereafter becomes the equivalent of personified abstractions which are easily translatable into clear meanings. As I have suggested, the present uneasiness about the use of the word allegory to describe *The Tempest* arises from a sound recognition that this play is not an allegory in the eighteenth or nineteenth century meaning of the word. But in the sense in which it was used in Shakespeare's lifetime, *The Tempest* is, I claim, truly an allegory, richly suggestive, resistent to simplified, abstract interpretation, and approachable only through its detail.

There is one objection that could be raised against this claim. The theory of allegory we have been discussing applied to a certain type of poetry or prose. As far as I know there was no clearly defined critical concept of allegorical drama in England at this time. The general tendency in the second half of the sixteenth century was away from the allegorization of the old moralities to increasing realism of character and plot. However universal the themes of *Dr Faustus* or *Lear*, they are not concealed by the plot or the characters but arise organically from them. It is otherwise in the Last Plays, those "naive and impossible romances" as S. L. Bethell has called them.[38] Here, I would argue, the plots with all their improbabilities correspond to the surface fiction of poetic allegory, to what Thomas Lodge called "the vanitie of tales", providing entertainment for the more superficial sections of the audience, but concealing solid intellectual fare for the more perceptive members of the audience. In this respect the Romances and particularly *The Tempest* share features with the Court masque as developed by Ben Jonson.

[37] Gombrich, *Symbolic Images*, p. 152.
[38] S. L. Bethell, *The Winter's Tale: A Study* (London and New York: Staples, 1947), p. 20.

Allegoric Romance

It was above all Ben Jonson who fashioned the Jacobean masque into a vehicle for recondite, neoplatonic allegories. In his preface to *Hymenai*, he speaks of the need of an audience to "lay hold on more remoud'd mysteries" that are concealed within a masque.[39] It is made clear by Jonson that not everyone at Court was appreciative of the "more remou'd mysteries" in his masques, and he goes on to attack them for crying out against "all endeuour of *learning*, and sharpnesse in these *transitorie devices*." Jonson's attack on them betrays that elitist tendency of allegory to divide an audience, as Michael Murrin says, into those who understand and those who do not. A similar division is conveyed in *The Tempest* by the wrangling between Gonzalo on one side and Antonio and Sebastian on the other as to the meaning of their experiences on the island. This creates in turn a division in the play's audience between those who assume that there is meaning in Gonzalo's impossible matter, and those who do not. Those who do not believe that *The Tempest* with its masque-like elements contains any "remou'd mysteries" will at worst react to any suggestion that it does with the incredulity of an Antonio and a Sebastian. And yet the very presence in *The Tempest* of features borrowed from the Court masque increases the likelihood that allegory is present too.

In developing the dramatic form of what I have called Allegoric Romance, Shakespeare not only borrowed features from the Court masque but also from pastoral tragicomedy made fashionable from about 1605 onwards in such plays as Samuel Daniel's *Queenes Arcadia* (1605) and Fletcher's *The Faithful Shepherdess* (1608).[40] In 1610 the King's Men revived the old romance *Mucedorus*, and at about this time Beaumont and Fletcher wrote their successful play, *Philaster*, which was performed twice at Court in connection with the wedding of Princess Elizabeth and Frederick, the Elector Palatine, during the winter of 1612—13. It is sometimes suggested that Shakespeare's *Cymbeline* was influenced by *Philaster* or vice versa, but in one important respect they are totally unlike. *Philaster* is a romance pure and simple. Apart from some probable topical references to the subject of the marriages of the royal children, the play is innocent of allegory. Its thin, nerveless verse never points beyond the immediate dramatic situation. It is far otherwise with *Cymbeline* and the other Romances by Shakespeare. With them there is always the feeling that something is being said that transcends

---

[39] Ben Jonson, *Works*, ed. C. H. Herford and P. and E. Simpson (Oxford: Clarendon Press, 1938), VII, 209.

[40] See Frank Kermode's discussion of this revival in the Arden *Tempest*, pp. lix—lxi.

their improbable plots. We are in other words in the presence of romance being used for the purposes of allegory.

There is a third ingredient in Allegoric Romance that may have been decisive for Shakespeare's final phase as a dramatist. This is found in the general allegorical tradition of writing represented by Sidney's *Arcadia* and Spenser's *Faerie Queene*. The influence of Sidney's *Arcadia* on the Romances has been investigated by J. F. Danby in *Poets on Fortune Hill* and E. C. Pettett in *Shakespeare and the Romance Tradition*.[41] Concerning Spenser's *Faerie Queene*, Frank Kermode has drawn attention to the influence of above all Book Six on *The Tempest*, and has suggested that "it might be possible to argue that Spenser alone is sufficient to account for the pastoral situation in *The Tempest*."[42] I shall suggest that Book One has also strongly influenced *The Tempest*. A partial explanation for this belated influence of Spenser may lie in the circumstance that in 1609, some thirteen years after its first publication, Books One to Six of the *Faerie Queene* were republished along with the newly printed *Mutabilitie Cantos*. In 1611, the year when *The Tempest* received its first performance, a folio edition of Spenser's collected works was published. Would it be far-fetched to imagine that Shakespeare reread Spenser perhaps in 1609, and that fired above all by the *Faerie Queene* he conceived the idea of a dramatic form of allegorical romance?

He may have been encouraged to experiment in this direction by a revival of interest in Spenserian chivalry and romance that has not received the attention it deserves. This revival took place at the court of James's eldest son, Prince Henry. As Graham Parry has shown in his chapter on Henry's court in his *The Golden Age Restor'd*, from about 1605 onwards it came to rival even that of his father.[43] It was Henry's militant Protestantism and his patronage of learning that gave his court a special lustre and made it a focal point for all those who yearned for a revival of the buoyant Elizabethan spirit. Among those patronized by Henry were that dark allegorist, George Chapman, the poet Michael Drayton and John Florio, translator of Montaigne's *Essays*, one of which, "On Cannibals", Shakespeare probably consulted when writing *The Tempest*. Henry befriended Sir Walter Raleigh then

---

[41] J. F. Danby, *Poets on Fortune Hill: Studies in Sidney, Shakeseapre, and Beaumont and Fletcher* (London: Faber and Faber, 1952); E. C. Pettett, *Shakespeare and the Romance Tradition* (London: Staples, 1949).

[42] Kermode, Arden *Tempest*, p. lx.

[43] See Ch. 3, "The Court of Henry, Prince of Wales," in Graham Parry, *The Golden Age Restor'd: The Culture of the Stuart Court, 1603—42* (Manchester: Manchester Univ. Press, 1981), pp. 64—94.

in the Tower carrying out alchemical experiments and working on *The History of the World*, with Henry's encouragement. Inigo Jones was one of the servants of his household, and from 1610 onwards he employed Jonson in composing masques for him. It was in this court that the new vogue for romance and chivalric themes received a powerful impulse. Its character is indicated by the challenge issued late in 1609 by Prince Henry for a "feat of arms to celebrate the chivalric eminence of Great Britain",[44] and at the Tournament that followed "Henry feasted his comrades-in-arms like a prince from the *Faerie Queene*".[45] For the occasion Jonson wrote *Prince Henry's Barriers*, basing it on the Arthurian matter and presenting Henry as a new Red Cross Knight of the *Faerie Queene*.[46] The same Arthurian and Spenserian themes are taken up in Jonson's *Oberon, The Faerie Prince*, a masque performed for Prince Henry on January 1st, 1611. The figure of Oberon is taken from Spenser's *Faerie Queene*, Book II, Canto X. The theme of the *Barriers* and of the masque were suggested to Jonson by Henry himself. It would require a separate study to investigate the relationship of this revival of Arthurian and Spenserian themes centring on Prince Henry's court and the general revival of interest in romance reflected in Shakespeare's Last Plays. One thing is, however, reasonably clear. As commentators have noted the Romances as a whole are in some way linked with the royal children, above all with Henry and Elizabeth. I shall be discussing this connection and its bearing on *The Tempest* in Chapter Six. Here I would like to suggest the possibility that Shakespeare, like his fellow writers, had also responded to the growing cult of Henry and his sister, to the revival of chivalry associated with them and to the millenarian hopes which, as we shall see, they increasingly came to represent. He may have also have responded to Henry's personal interest in allegory. This interest is indicated by his patronage of George Chapman, by the active interest he took in the two masques Jonson wrote for him, and by the fact that it was Henry who suggested the allegorical themes of the two entertainments performed on the Thames at his sister's wedding to the Elector Palatine in 1613.

It is, I suggest, against this background of revived interest in Spenserian allegory and themes and the development of the allegorical Court masque in Jonson's hands, that we should place *The Tempest*. In this play Shakespeare fuses elements of pastoral tragicomedy, popular at Court, with the

[44] Parry, *The Golden Age Restor'd*, p. 70.
[45] Parry, p. 70.
[46] Parry, p. 71.

recondite suggestiveness of the Court masque. Ben Jonson in his reference in the Induction to *Bartholomew Fayre* (1614) to "those that beget *Tales, Tempests,* and such like *Drolleries,* to mix his head with other mens heeles", seems to have objected to Shakespeare's confusion of genres in the Last Plays.[47] But, as I believe, it was rather a creative fusion that is perfected in *The Tempest.* It resulted in a new dramatic genre, what I have called allegoric romance.

Impossible Matter

By what tokens would *The Tempest* have been recognized by its original audience as an allegory calling for the same sort of close attention that Kenelm Digby demanded of the reader of the *Faerie Queene*? The first, I suggest, is the very improbability of its plot, a feature it shares with the other Romances. S. L. Bethell has expressed the problem of the Last Plays in this way:

Why does Shakespeare in the last phase of his dramatic activity turn to these naive and impossible romances? And why is his dramatic technique apparently crude and incoherent? Was his interest waning—in the drama, or in life? Was his technical ability deserting him? These are questions which every critic of the last plays must attempt to answer.[48]

If we do not accept that Shakespeare was losing his creativity or that his interest in life and art was waning, we must seek another explanation for his choice of "these naive and impossible romances" at the end of his career. The explanation lies, I believe, in the fact that their very naivety and impossibility provided him with a welcome freedom from verisimilitude. By its very nature, romance allows the miraculous, the absurd, the improbable, to invade normal life. This enabled Shakespeare, as E. M. W. Tillyard suggested, to explore "planes of reality" other than those of the senses, shimmering behind the surface of the phenomenal world.[49] It seems that in his final phase as a creative writer, Shakespeare wished to explore recurring pat-

---

[47] Induction to *Bartholomew Fayre* in Jonson's *Works*, VI, 16.
[48] S. L. Bethell, *The Winter's Tale*, p. 20.
[49] See E. M. W. Tillyard's excellent discussion of this aspect of the Romances in *Shakespeare's Last Plays* (London: Chatto and Windus, 1962), pp. 59—80. S. L. Bethell makes much the same point in his Introduction to the New Clarendon *The Winter's Tale* (Oxford: Clarendon Press, 1938), where he argues that the old tales of the Romances, "However silly and inconsequential on the surface," enabled Shakespeare to "subordinate plot and character to the main function of conveying an inner meaning."

terns of human behaviour that underlie all the surface variety of detail, certain archetypal rhythms that we refer to feebly as loss and restitution, death and rebirth. The romance-fictions that he chose enabled him to do this with a new freedom, much as Spenser chose the tales of Arthur "rather for variety of matter" and because they provided the best vehicle for complex allegory. Guided by the example of the *Faerie Queene*, the presence of naive and impossible matter in a play like *The Tempest* would have alerted a courtly audience to the fact that they were watching an allegory.

The original audiences of *The Tempest*, suspecting that its true import was something other than its surface plot, would have been on the look-out for the second main token that they were witnessing an allegory—what I have called telltale incongruity. These would appear in the form of anomalies, puzzles, improbabilities in the dialogue or in the events of the play. These would be indications to the alert members of the audience that they were to leave the surface meaning and that "the sence . . . and Allegorie (which is the soule) is to be sought," as George Chapman advised.

The Tempest has its share of incongruities which may or may not be indicative that allegory is present. It was to some of these that Lytton Strachey objected when he spoke of the "dreary puns" that punctuate the various exchanges between Gonzalo, Antonio and Sebastian. But there are also a number of remarks made by Gonzalo that puzzle the understanding. They are referred to contemptuously by Antonio as "impossible matter" (II.i.85). They include his repeated statement that their clothes have become fresher after being soaked in salt water, which is a palpable absurdity. He suddenly introduces Dido and Aeneas into the conversation without explanation, and asserts that Tunis and Carthage are the same. He makes a speech about a second Golden Age in which he would be king, although he has stated that there would be no sovereignty in it. All the time he is mocked and interrupted by Antonio and Sebastian. What is any audience to make of this "impossible matter"? Frank Kermode is almost persuaded that in part of it at least there is more than meets the eye:

This line [II.i.74] begins a series of apparently trivial allusions to the theme of Dido and Aeneas which has never been properly explained; if we take them at their face value one must allow that Lytton Strachey's strictures on this scene are perfectly justified . . . But we must not take them at their face value. *The Tempest* is far from being a loosely built play; and nowhere in Shakespeare, not even in his less intensive works, is there anything resembling the apparent irrelevance of lines 73—97. It is a possible inference that our frame of reference is badly adjusted, or incomplete, and that an understanding of this passage will modify our image of the whole play.[50]

[50] Kermode, Arden *Tempest*, note to II.i.74.

I believe this is true, and that by an adjustment of our frame of reference we can come to an understanding of Gonzalo's allusions to Dido and Aeneas. They provide the key to the riddle of the strange nature of the island on which the whole action of the play unfolds. If these allusions can be made to yield good sense, the same is probably true of Gonzalo's other "impossible matter." This matter is not to be taken at face value, but rather pondered and investigated until the frame of reference that makes sense of each conundrum or seeming absurdity is recovered.

The meaning or intention of any Renaissance allegory lay in its detail, and the method I have chosen in this study of *The Tempest* is to try and elucidate some of the more cryptic details of its allegory by discovering their concealed frame of reference. This is the way I believe that a John Harington or a Kenelm Digby would have approached a play like *The Tempest*. We have to discover and interpret the various "signes" as Spenser called them that are set in the text of this play as guides to the reader. We discover them by their telltale incongruity, and we interpret them by searching for the appropriate frame of reference. In so far as an allegory is in the Renaissance definition an extended metaphor or image,[51] our task becomes one of discovering the underlying metaphors or images of the play which will make sense of the many cryptic details of the play. I shall attempt to show that these images are variants of a central image of death and regeneration *as understood in the early seventeenth century.*

The most inclusive of the images of regeneration to be found in *The Tempest*, providing its principal frame of reference, is the image of human life as an alchemical process of dissolution and regeneration as taught by the Paracelsan school of medicine that arose in the second half of the sixteenth century and became dominant in England during the period when *The Tempest* was written. This I shall deal with in the following chapter. In Chapter III I shall examine the image of human life as an initiatory ordeal in terms of Renaissance interest in and knowledge of the pagan mysteries. Chapter IV is devoted to the image of human life as the experience of baptismal purgation and regeneration. Closely related to this image is the image of human history as a long purgative experience leading to the apocalyptic renewal believed to be imminent in the early years of the seventeenth century. This I take up in Chapter V. In Chapter VI I relate these various images of purgative regeneration to the European crisis of 1611 focussed on the Holy

---

[51] Quintillian's definition of allegory as *continua metaphora* became a commonplace of the period, and is found for example in Erasmus' text-book, *De Copia* (I, xviii): "Allegory has the same force as metaphor. For allegory is nothing but a continuous metaphor."

Roman Emperor, Rudolf II, about to be deposed by his brother for gross neglect of government and for addiction to magic and alchemy. In the final chapter I take up the all-important subject of how we are to regard the project of human purgation and regeneration undertaken by Prospero, and this involves an assessment of the "rough magic" he uses and finally abjures.

Let us now begin by examining the first of the images of regeneration present in *The Tempest*, the image of human life as a process of alchemical dissolution and regeneration. As I have suggested, this is the most inclusive image of them all in that the alchemists of the period were in the habit of describing the changes wrought in "the furnace of affliction" in imagery borrowed from pagan initiation, Christian baptism and apocalyptic renewal.

Chapter II
The Furnace of Tribulation: *The Tempest* and Alchemy

Of the various metaphors of regeneration available to Shakespeare in the early 17th century there is one that I have suggested is basic to *The Tempest*. This is the metaphor of life as an alchemical *fornax tribulationis* or furnace of tribulation in which sinful human nature is purged of its defects through a species of death and rebirth and finally restored to its original purity. I would like to suggest that this alchemical metaphor is to be found not only in Act V as commentators have noted, but runs through the entire play. Prospero's project is also an alchemical projection, carried out primarily on the Three Men of Sin with the aid of a mercurial spirit. As I shall suggest, Prospero with his books, utensils and the great pile of logs outside his cave, is a mage-physician of the sort exemplified by Paracelsus and his many followers, using alchemy to bring about changes in the minds and bodies of human beings. In using imagery derived from contemporary alchemy, Shakespeare was able to rely on the enormous interest of his contemporaries in the subject. In order to provide a framework for an interpretation of *The Tempest* as an alchemical allegory, I shall give an account of this pervasive interest and of the sort of medical alchemy that is associated above all with the name of Philip Theophrastus Bombastus von Hohenheim, known for short as Paracelsus. It is his brand of alchemy as used in medicine that provides, as I believe, one key to the understanding of *The Tempest*.

Born in 1493, Paracelsus received his early training in *adepta philosophia* from Trithemius, author of the cabalistic work on ciphers, the *Steganographia*. In 1527 he marked his break with the traditional medicine of his time by publicly burning the works of Galen, Hippocrates and Avicenna. Throughout the 1530's he produced his major works on the new spagyric or iatrochemical medicine, but only one of them was published during his lifetime. What was new in his ideas concerning medicine can be briefly summarized here. The four pillars of the new medicine, according to Paracelsus, were Philosophy, Astronomy, Alchemy and Virtue. Medicine concerned the whole man, both mind and body. As the microcosm, he lived under the incessant influence of the macrocosm, and health or illness arose from the interplay of the two. In curing a patient, the Paracelsan doctor sought to isolate the influence or 'virtue' stamped on a herb or mineral by a related heavenly body. This was achieved by alchemical extraction of the active 'virtue'. In treating the patient, the Paracelsan doctor differed fundamentally from the Galenist in that he cured like by like. One ill expelled another. This homaeopathic therapy as was noted by its opponents was violent in its effect, frequently making the patient worse in order to bring about a final cure. The effect of the alchemically extracted medicine was to stimulate the alchemical activity of the various bodily and mental organs so that the poison in the system was released, broken down and then expelled. In addition to studying philosophy, astronomy, alchemy and virtue (in the sense of an active, quintessential power), the Paracelsan physician was also required to be knowledgeable about the various spirits that constantly surrounded men and could have good or bad effects on them. In other words, he must also be a goetist able to control and use invisible entities. Also present in Paracelsus's teachings was the idea of the universe as an alchemical creation, and of history as an alchemical *processus* during which man's nature was slowly purged and then transmuted in preparation for the establishment of a Golden Age or the Millennium. These are some of Paracelsus's main ideas, and they will be dealt with in more detail in the rest of this chapter.

After Paracelsus's death in 1541, his ideas spread throughout Europe as his works appeared either singly or in collected editions. From the 1580's onwards there is evidence of a renewed interest in alchemy in the increased number of works published on the subject. In 1589 Paracelsus's collected works were published. In 1593 the *Artis Auriferae* containing a total of twenty-three separate alchemical works was published. In 1602 the first three volumes of the *Theatrum Chemicum*, comprising twenty-nine separate alchemical works, were brought out. It is indicative of the mounting interest in the spagyric or alchemical medicine of Paracelsus that nine of the alchemical tracts in the first volume are by Gerard Dorn, the foremost disciple of Paracelsus. Dorn's works mark the emergence of a new type of alchemy concerned as much with mental as with physical healing. It is this type of alchemy, as we shall see, that Donne utilized in his poetry, which Ben Jonson satirized, and which I argue is to be found in Shakespeare's *The Tempest*.

The volume of works published on alchemy is matched by the large numbers who attempted to carry out in practise the obscure directives for obtaining the Philosopher's Stone or Elixir given in these works. It is probably true to say that there was no town in Europe, no court of any pretension that did not have its resident alchemist. It is said that the Holy Roman

Emperor, Rudolf II employed over a hundred alchemists in his large laboratory in Prague during the first decade of the seventeenth century. Many of
the foremost alchemical writers of the period, such as Heinrich Khunrath,
Gerard Dorn, Oswald Croll, Martin Ruland and Michael Maier, belonged
to Rudolfine Prague and were patronized by Rudolf. As we shall see, it is
Maier who provides the link between the Paracelsan physicians of Prague
and a group of Paracelsians in London.

The practise of alchemy in England at this time was no less common. An
early figure worth mentioning because of a possible connection with Shakespeare is Thomas Moffett (1553—1604). His *De Jure et Praestantia
Chemicorum Medicamentorum* (1584, 1602, 1613) is one of the earliest
presentations of the iatrochemistry of Paracelsus by an Englishman, and
paved the way for its final acceptance during the second decade of the seventeenth century. During the last decade of his life, Moffett worked for Mary,
Countess of Pembroke, in her alchemical laboratory at Wilton House,
Wiltshire, along with one Bolton, an alchemist from Salisbury, and Adrian
Gilbert, half-brother to Sir Walter Raleigh. We learn from Aubrey in his
Brief Lives that the Countess of Pembroke "was a great Chymist and spent
yearly a great deal in that study".[1] If as Dover Wilson and others have
argued the Young Man of Shakespeare's Sonnets is her son, William
Herbert, third Earl of Pembroke, and Shakespeare began the Sonnets at the
instigation of the Countess, it is well possible that Shakespeare knew of the
alchemical experiments at Wilton and may have met or watched her team
of chemists. But there were others experimenting in England at this time.
In about 1600 the Paracelsan physician, Francis Anthony (1550—1623), produced an elixir known as *aurum potabile* or potable gold and began using
it on his patients, despite the protests of the Royal College of Physicians.
To meet their criticism, Anthony published in 1610 his *Medicinae Chymicae*.
In the autumn of the same year, Ben Jonson in his attack on Paracelsan
alchemy, *The Alchemist*, refers both to Anthony's *aurum potabile* and to
his claim that it could cure the plague.[2] The controversy aroused by Anthony's claims for his elixir was long-lasting. In 1616 he published a further
defense in English and Latin. This Latin work, *Apologia veritatis illuscentis
pro auro potabili* contains a dedication to James I.[3] Another interesting

---

[1] See *Aubrey's Brief Lives*, ed. O. L. Dick (London: Secker and Warburg, 1949), under
"Mary Pembroke".
[2] Ben Jonson, *The Alchemist*, ed. F. H. Mares (London: Methuen, 1967), II.i.67—9, III.i.
41.
[3] In his dedicatory epistle Anthony asks James to take him under his protection and
patronage. Anthony also prints a letter from Alexander Gill to Michael Maier, alchemical writer
and physician to Rudolf II, commending his potable gold.

alchemist working in London at this time is that somewhat maligned figure, Simon Forman.[4] Often described as a quack, Forman was in fact a fairly typical medical practitioner of the time with an extensive practise. He possessed a laboratory for the preparation of medicines, but also used it from time to time to try and produce the medicine of medicines, the Philosopher's Stone. He consulted with the Elizabethan mage, John Dee, on these matters, and had a valuable collection of alchemical manuscripts. At his death in the early autumn of 1611, these manuscripts passed to his pupil, Richard Napier who took them off to his vicarage at Great Linford in Buckinghamshire. There he maintained a laboratory and like Forman used it both for preparing chemical medicines and the elixir itself. As Michael Macdonald has shown in his facinating study of Richard Napier, *Mystical Bedlam: Madness, Anxiety and Healing in Seventeenth Century England*, Napier became something of a specialist in psychological disorders, using both traditional medicines and Paracelsan ones such as tincture of laudanum for violent or sleepless patients. It is possible that the translator of an alchemical work by Jean Baptista Lambye, published in 1623 as by R.N.E. under the title *A Revelation of the Secret Spirit declaring the most concealed secret of Alchymie* was the same Richard Napier of Great Linford.[5] This work is dedicated to another well-known alchemist of the period, John Thornborough, Bishop of Worcester, whose palace at Hartlebury Castle is described as "an Apollonian retreat, a living library, a flourishing Academy, or a religious Abbey".[6] It seems to have been a major centre of alchemical research during the early decades of the seventeenth century. Two alchemical treatises by Thornborough are known. One is a manuscript Letter on Chemistry sent to Lady Knowles in 1614 (B.M. Sloane MS 1799 fols. 74—104), and the other published in 1623 is a theoretical work on alchemy which draws on the writings of Paracelsus, *Lithotheorikos, sive Nihil, Aliquot, Omina.* Thomas Fuller records that Thornborough had presented James I with "a precious extraction . . . reputed a great preserver of health and prolonger

---

[4] For a full account of this colourful figure, see A. L. Rowse, *Simon Forman: Sex and Society in Shakespeare's Age* (London: Weidenfeld and Nicolson, 1974). In his youth Forman had been servant to John Thornborough, later Bishop of Worcester and a prominent Paracelsan alchemist. In his turn Forman was teacher to the Paracelsan physician, Richard Napier, and a friend of John Dee.

[5] A note in the B.M. copy of this work identifies its author, "R. N. E." as Robert Napier of Murchiston. It seems more likely that the initials stand for this Richard Napier, who was also related to the mathematician and alchemist, John Napier of Murchiston.

[6] This description from R. N. E.'s dedication to Thornborough in *A Revelation of the Secret Spirit*, is cited by Allen G. Debus, *The English Paracelsans* (London: Oldbourne, 1965), p. 104.

of life''.[7] Among visitors to the Bishop's Apollonian retreat was perhaps the most important hermetic figure of the period, Robert Fludd.[8]

Fludd's importance in the hermetic tradition of the Renaissance is now well established, thanks mainly to the researches of Frances Yates. Here I would like to concentrate on Fludd as an alchemist. It is often stated that from about 1600 onwards alchemy became increasingly speculative and symbolic and more and more divorced from work in the laboratory. But this is to ignore the fact that many alchemists of the period were also practising doctors interested in Paracelsan medicine. Examples are Simon Forman, Francis Anthony and Robert Fludd. The alchemical extraction of essences and tinctures from metals and plants was an intrinsic part of their medical practise. It was but a short and natural step from this to attempts to produce the Elixir. This was undertaken less to produce gold than to find the universal medical panacea. "This single spagyric medicine", as Gerard Dorn wrote, would perfectly cure all diseases of body and mind.[9]

However misguided we might think this search for a universal medicine there was a certain logic to it. If the quintessence of a plant or a mineral extracted and fixed in the laboratory was specific against a certain disease, it was logical to believe that there was a fundamental quintessence underlying all manifestation which if it could be isolated and fixed or coagulated would cure all diseases under the sun. It is clear that Francis Anthony's *aurum potabile* and Bishop Thornborough's "precious extraction" were thought to be identical with or close to Dorn's all-curing single spagyric medicine. It was by the same sort of logic that Robert Fludd, grand theoretical hermetist of the period, undertook in 1611 to extract the elixir from putrefied grains of wheat.

Fludd's detailed account of this experiment exists in a manuscript that has now been beautifully edited by Professor Debus.[10] It is a fascinating document not least for the insight it provides into the mind of a well-educated Jacobean alchemist working in London in the same year that Shakespeare wrote *The Tempest*. Where a modern chemist sees a series of explicable chemical reactions inside a retort, Fludd witnessed with amazement a

[7] See Thomas Fuller, *The History of the Worthies of England* (1639; rpt. ed. P. Austin Nuttall, 1840).

[8] Fludd states in his *Mosaicall Philosophy* (1659), p. 118, that he once stayed at Hartlebury Castle, and in his *Anatomiae Amphitheatrum* (1623) he addresses the Bishop as "amico meo singulari".

[9] Gerard Dorn, *Physica Trismegisti* in *Theatrum Chemicum*, I (1602), p. 433. F. H. Nollius, another Paracelsan physician and an admirer of the "excellentissimus Crollius", states in his *Systema Medicinae Hermeticae Generale* (1613), A², that the purpose of alchemy is not the transmutation of metals but the eradication of serious illnesses.

[10] Allen G. Debus, *Robert Fludd and the Philosophicall Key* (New York: Science and History Publications, 1979). Debus dates the m.s. of this work to 1618—20.

duplication in miniature of the creation of the universe as described in Genesis. The rationale for the experiment was the biblical statement that unless a grain of wheat rots in the soil it will not grow (John, 12:24), a passage often cited by alchemists to explain the basic alchemical processes of putrefaction and regeneration.

In the *Philosophical Key* Fludd appeals to James I to be "my best Patron and worthyest Maecenas", and speaks of certain enemies who have been attacking him, above all the "Calumniator" who is described as ever ready to "slubber over whole lines to produce the ridiculous subject of thy scoffing vein."[11] It is possible that the Calumniator is none other than Ben Jonson who attacked Paracelsan physicians in his *The Alchemist* (III.iii.229—233), and returned to the attack in the Court masque, *Mercurie Vindicated from the Alchemists at Court* in about 1616. This contains an open attack on a group of alchemists who are described as followers of "Bombast of Hohenhein" or Paracelsus and as practising alchemy in a cellar of one of the Court buildings. This masque may be the "ridiculous subject of thy scoffing vein" mentioned by Fludd. His reference to the Calumniator slubbering over whole lines may allude to Jonson's well-attested habit of composing while inspired by Canary wine.[12] Included in the attack would have been Fludd's colleagues and friends, Sir William Paddy and Sir Theodor Turquet de Mayerne, both royal physicians and supporters of Paracelsan medicine. It can be mentioned that Paddy was a friend of the alchemical writer and Paracelsan physician, Michael Maier, whose *Arcana arcanissima* (c. 1614) is dedicated to Paddy. I shall return at a later point to these contacts between the Continental and English Paracelsians.

From this brief survey of alchemy and Paracelsan medicine at about the time *The Tempest* was written and performed, it is clear that both were the focus of considerable attention and heated controversy. Alchemy was being practised both in London and in the Provinces.[13] James was interested in the work of the alchemists, and may have patronized practitioners such as

[11] Debus, *Robert Fludd and the Philosophicall Key*, p. 76.
[12] See *Aubrey's Brief Lives*, ed. O. L. Dick, p. 253, and Jonson's *Works*, ed. Herford and Simpson, I, 179 ff: "Mem: I laid ye Plot of my Volpone, and wrote most of it, after a present of 10 dozen of (palm) sack." One thinks of Shakespeare's Rival Poet in Sonnet 86: "Was it his spirit, by spirits taught to write, / Above a mortal pitch, that struck me dead?"
[13] From 1606 onwards both Raleigh and the "Wizard Earl", Henry Percy, ninth Earl of Northumberland, were carrying out alchemical experiments in the Tower. Raleigh's elixir was used in a last, unsuccessful bid to save the life of Prince Henry in 1612. See E. J. Holmyard, *Alchemy* (Harmondsworth: Penguin Books, 1957), pp. 58—9.

Fludd. Two of the royal physicians were confirmed Paracelsians. When *The Tempest* was performed, alchemy, especially of the Paracelsan sort, had just been attacked in Jonson's *The Alchemist* in a production by Shakespeare's own company, the King's Men. What might be called literary alchemy was therefore in the air. Shortly after Jonson's attack, Shakespeare could also have read a poem in which the same type of alchemy is used with much greater sympathy. This is John Donne's *Anatomie of the World* written to commemorate the death of Elizabeth Drury late in 1610 and printed in 1611. Surely Shakespeare would have appreciated Donne's perfect assimilation of alchemical imagery in the following passage:

> Shee in whom vertue was so much refin'd,
> That for Allay unto so pure a minde
> Shee tooke the weaker Sex; shee that could drive
> The poysonous tincture, and the staine of *Eve*
> Out of her thoughts, and deeds; and purifie
> All, by a true religious Alchymie.
>   (ll. 177—182)

As Charles Nicholl has shown in his important study, *The Chemical Theatre*, Shakespeare had been making use of imagery derived from Paracelsan alchemy in a way comparable to Donne for some fifteen years by the time he came to write *The Tempest*. Nicholl has analysed *Lear* in terms of alchemical imagery, but does not deal with *The Tempest*. And yet it is in this play above all that I believe Shakespeare displays most clearly his grasp of "true religious Alchymie". Let us now turn to *The Tempest*, and see to what extent the spagyric alchemy of Paracelsus and his followers will aid us to a deeper understanding of its language and incidents.

The Tempest

Why in the first place is the play called *The Tempest*? It is obvious that in part the name derives from the spectacular opening scene in which a full tempest is simulated by the magic of Jacobean theatrical technique. But in addition to the opening tempest, there is a second tempest that occurs at the end of Act III when Ariel delivers judgement on the Three Men of Sin. He enters to "Thunder and lightning", and Alonso hears him through the sound of the billows, wind and thunder, reminding him of his crime against Prospero. Shortly afterwards as the poison of reawakened guilt courses through their veins, he and his two confederates in crime become temporarily mad. The outer tempest that opened the play now becomes, like Lear's, a psychological one, "a tempest in my mind". The function of Ariel's long speech of judgment at the end of Act III is to bring out the significance of the tempest that caused their ship to founder. It is Destiny that has caused "the never-surfeited sea" to belch up the Three Men of Sin on the island (III.iii.53—56). Because of their foul deed,

> The powers delaying, not forgetting, have
> Incens'd the seas and shores, yea, all the creatures,
> Against your peace
> (III.iii.72—75).

It was of course a commonplace of the period that natural disasters such as storms, floods, severe winters, outbreaks of the plague, or failures of crops, were expressions of divine displeasure at human sin,[14] but for the specific idea that meteorological and psychological tempests could be compared because they arose from the same causes we must turn to Paracelsus and his followers.

For Paracelsus a tempest was the outer effect of an invisible and spiritual cause. In Chapter 10 of his *Occult Philosophy* he writes:

The original of tempests is certainly nothing else, but the appearance of Spirits; and lightning or corruscations preceeding is the presence of them. . . These Spirits do not appear unto us without speaking first. But their voice is thunder, which as we see immediately follows every flash of lightning.[15]

A little later Paracelsus speaks of "such tempests as are caused by Magicians inchantments by reason of the Spirits by them raised in the Aire".[16] In both of the tempests in Shakespeare's play, the spirit causing them, Ariel, manifests as thunder and lightning, in conformity with Paracelsus' description. It is implicit in all Paracelsus' thinking that what happens in the great world is reflected in the little one, man. The analogy between the great tempest at the beginning of the play and the tempest of the mind in Act III is explicitly worked out by one of Paracelsus' most influential followers, Oswald Croll (c. 1550—1609).[17]

---

[14] See Keith Thomas, *Religion and the Decline of Magic: Studies in Popular Beliefs in Sixteenth- and Seventeenth Century England* (London: Penguin Books, 1973), pp. 560—563, and *passim*.

[15] Paracelsus, "Occult Philosophy", Ch. 10 in *The Archidoxes of Magic*, trans. R. Turner (1656); rpt. (London: Askin, 1975), p. 78. This connection between *The Tempest* and Paracelsus was noted by J. E. Hankins, *Backgrounds of Shakespeare's Thought* (Hassocks: Harvester Press, 1978), p. 44.

[16] Paracelsus, "Occult Philosophy", p. 79.

[17] For Croll's connections with Rudolf II, and with Christian of Anhalt, adviser to Frederick, the Elector Palatine, see Frances Yates, *The Rosicrucian Enlightenment* (London and Boston: Routledge and Kegan Paul, 1972), pp. 52—3, and Debus, *The Chemical Philosophy* (New York: Science and History Publications, 1977), I, 115.

28

Croll's main work, the *Basilica chymica*, was published in 1609 with a dedication to Christian of Anhalt and a privilege from Rudolf II. The previous year he had published a small treatise entitled *Tractatus de Signaturis Internis Rerum*, dedicated to the Bohemian alchemist, Peter Wok. This deals with the Paracelsan doctrine of signatures or specific stellar influences stamped, as it were, on each plant and metal, and making them the vehicles of curative forces. One section of this tract is of particular interest. It traces the correspondences between a tempest and a fit of epilepsy in a human being. Croll begins by saing:

What causes tempests and thunder in the macrocosm, also causes epilepsy in the microcosm; and, as a tempest alters and weakens the animal sense and intellect, apparent in the unusual crowing of cocks, and also in the unexpected singing and noise of other birds and beasts, and in the more vehement stinging of flies and other insects, so in like manner it is with epileptics.[18]

Croll then goes on to list the correspondences between the course of a tempest and the cycle of an epileptic fit. The change in the air as the tempest approaches corresponds to the change in the faculty of reason at the onset of epilepsy. Clouds follow and there is a corresponding obscuring of vision or sleep. The blowing of the wind is matched by the dilation of the neck and stomach. The flashes of lightning are reflected in the fiery, bright eyes of the epileptic. Rain corresponds to foaming at the mouth. A thunderbolt manifests in the human being as a contraction of spirits causing intense pain in the limbs. Finally calm weather indicates a return to consciousness and sane discourse. Just as the muddy, rain-drenched roads are dried again by the sun, so the human being returns to himself, and after loss of peace, the microcosmos, man, with his mind and other bodily functions, is restored to its former state by the sun.[19]

As Croll states, what causes tempests, causes the loss of consciousness known as epilepsy. For Croll there were two forms of epilepsy, hereditary and acquired.[20] The 'fits' and 'distraction' suffered by the Three Men of Sin at the end of Act III, Scene iii, would therefore be the type of induced and temporary epilepsy. When we compare the sequence of states accompanying a fit of epilepsy as described by Croll with the two tempests in

---

[18] Oswald Croll, *Tractatus de Signaturis Rerum* (1608, 1635 ed.), p. 81; author's translation.

[19] Paraphrased from Croll, p. 83.

[20] See Croll, *Basilica chymica* (1609), p. 225, where he speaks of 'epilepsiam non haeriditatam . . . sed aliunde infectam.'' Nollius in his *Systema Medicinae Hermeticae Generale* (1613), p. 61 claimed that unlike the Galenists, the Paracelsians were able to cure diseases like leprosy and epilepsy.

the play, we find that in both cases the height of the tempest corresponds to a state of madness. When asked by Prospero:

> Who was so firm, so constant, that this coil
> Would not infect his reason?

Ariel replies that

> Not a soul
> But felt a fever of the mad, and play'd
> Some tricks of desperation.
> (I.ii.207—210).

But it is above all in the lead up to the second tempest in Act III, Scene iii, that Croll's sequence can be clearly followed. The change of air and the gathering of clouds corresponding to the approach of the tempest of the mind and to an obscuring of vision or to sleepiness is conveyed by Shakespeare in Act II, scene i, at the point when Gonzalo and Alonso suddenly feel "very heavy" and go to sleep (II.i.189). "What a strange drowsiness possesses them", Sebastian exclaims, and Antonio explains, "It is the quality o'th'climate" (II.i.194—5). When we next meet the King's Party in Act III, Scene iii, the equivalent of Croll's epileptic fit takes place. Ariel's speech of judgement leaves them "all knit up / In their distractions" (III.iii.89—90), and Prospero leaves them "in these fits". Gonzalo notes Alonso's "strange stare", and as the Three Men of Sin rush away, he sends men after them to

> hinder them from what this ecstasy
> May now provoke them to.
> (III.iii.108—9).

Throughout Act IV they are in state of coma, unable to budge, "all three distracted", until finally they are restored to their jostled senses by the rising sun that melts the darkness and drives away the ignorant fumes that mantle their clearer reason. This corresponds to the aftermath of Croll's tempest and epileptic fit when the sun dries the wet roads and "homo ad se redit", the man returns to himself. After the tempest comes "serenum tempus" (calm weather), just as Prospero promises Alonso "calm seas, auspicious gales" (V.i.313).

According to Croll the way in which a tempest and epilepsy are related is shown by the effect of a tempest in altering and weakening the animal sense and intellect, "apparent in the unusual crowing of cocks, and also in the unexpected singing and noise of other birds and beasts, and in the more vehement stinging of flies and other insects". This seems to be a seventeenth century equivalent of the modern idea that animals and insects are sensitive to atmospheric changes and can be used to predict approaching electric storms and earthquakes. But for Croll, a storm, a fit of epilepsy and the unusual behaviour of animals and insects arise from the same cause. I do not wish to push the analogies between Croll's little treatise and *The Tempest* too far, but it is a fact that even in this detail of unusual behaviour in the animal kingdom there seems to be agreement between them. As the opening tempest of the play is allayed by Ariel's song, we hear in the refrain the barking of watchdogs, and "the strain of strutting chanticleer, Cock a diddle dow" (I.ii.384—387). The explanation of the barking of the watchdogs as "probably derived from James Rosier's account of a ceremonial Virginian dance", even if correct, does not account for the mid-afternoon crowing of cocks.[21] It is more plausible to believe that the crowing and the barking are phenomena that accompany tempests and arise from the same cause, as Croll states. Shakespeare may be alluding to the same phenomena in the "crowing" wager of Antonio and Sebastian:

> Ant. Which, of he or Adrian, for a good wager, first begins to crow?
> Seb. The old cock
> Ant. The cockerel.
> (II.i.27—30)

The same explanation may also hold for the "hollow burst of bellowing / Like bulls, or rather lions", which Sebastian claims to have heard (II.i.306—7). Supporting him Antonio adds:

> O, 'twas a din to fright a monster's ear,
> To make an earthquake! sure, it was the roar
> Of a whole herd of lions.
> (II.i.309—311)

The island is indeed "full of noises" (III.ii.133), and some of them as I have just suggested can be taken as signs of that altering and weakening of the animal sense and intellect which in the human being manifests as an induced fit of epilepsy or distraction, leading to loss of consciousness. This state, reached by the Three Men of Sin at the end Act III, is the equivalent of the alchemical stage of *solutio* or dissolution.

Dissolution

The effect of the tempest at the beginning of the play is to initiate a process of psychological death in the Three Men of Sin which is completed by the

---

[21] Kermode, Arden *Tempest*, note to I.ii. 384.

end of Act III. In alchemical terms they undergo *solutio* or dissolution, prior to the *regeneratio* of the final act. The term "spagyric" coined by Paracelsus to describe alchemy is derived from two Greek words meaning to divide and unite. The substance to be transmuted must first be divided into its constituent parts, that is, dissolved or separated, until it reaches a stage known as *nigredo* or *mortificatio*. Thereafter the stages of reunification take place; the poisons that have been released during *solutio* are driven off by gentle boiling, and a new inner harmony created.

In *The Tempest*, the *solutio* commences with the plunging of the passengers of the ship into the salt sea. As Carl Jung states in his *Mysterium Coniunctionis*, alchemical Mercurius, the primary agent of transmutation, is constantly equated with salt.[22] In the *Turba philosophorum*, printed in the alchemical collection *Artis Auriferae* (1593), the transforming arcane substance is equated with saltwater and sea-water (p. 183). It was the *sal amarum* or bitter salt of the alchemists which brought about dissolution.

The vessel with the ingredients should be immersed in saltwater, and then the divine water will be perfected. It is, so to speak, gestated in the womb of the sea-water (p. 237).

For Heinrich Khunrath, salt was the philosophical stone itself (p. 246). One of the terms for dissolution was *salsatura* or marination (p. 201). The bitter, poisonous quality of alchemical salt was thought to act as a dissolvent, reducing the substance in the retort to a 'chaos' or undifferentiated state, to the "prima materia".

Alchemically speaking the plunging of the King's party in the sea is the equivalent of *salsatura* or marination in which they will undergo a transformation that is foreshadowed in Ariel's song that Ferdinand hears:

> Full fadom five thy father lies;
>   Of his bones are coral made;
> Those are pearls that were his eyes:
>   Nothing of him that doth fade,
> But doth suffer a sea-change
>   Into something rich and strange.
>   (I.ii.399—405)

The significance of their immersion in sea-water is also indicated by Shakespeare in the repeated references to the effect of brine on the colours of their

---

[22] Carl Jung's *Mysterium Coniunctionis*, Bollingen Series XX (Princeton: Princeton Univ. Press, 1963, 1977 ed.), is a learned study of the symbolism of alchemy based on a large number of alchemical texts, mainly from the 16th and 17th centuries. In this section I have made extensive use of this work and of others by Jung dealing with alchemy. The following page references in the text are to Jung's *Mysterium Coniunctionis*.

clothes. It is Ariel who first mentions this in his report to Prospero on the tempest:

> On their sustaining garments not a blemish,
> But fresher than before.
>   (I.ii.218—9)

Gonzalo remarks on the strange phenomenon four times:

> But the rarity of it is—which is indeed almost beyond credit,— . . . that our garments being, as they were drenched in the sea, hold, notwithstanding, their freshness and glosses, being rather new-dyed than stained with salt water
>   (II.i.56—62)

On three more occasions, at II.i.66—7, II.i.92—4, and II.i.98—9, Gonzalo tries to draw the attention of Alonso to this "rarity". Kermode following Colin Still, thinks it might refer to "a ceremonial cleansing",[23] but this does not explain the specific action of salt water in new dyeing their clothes and restoring their former glosses. Gonzalo's observation does, however, make sense alchemically, as we have seen. He is the only one to realize that the *amaritudo* or bitterness of their experience is the prelude to a profound renewal of their beings. It is the "excellent, harsh, and bitter acid" that is the agent of transmutation.[24] Like Ariel's song concerning the "sea-change", Gonzalo's observation about the new-dyed clothes foreshadows the eventual restoration of colours known as the *cauda pavonis* or peacock's tail that follows the alchemical stage of *nigredo*. But first the Three Men of Sin must undergo the extreme stage of *solutio* or *nigredo* before this alchemical restoration of colour can take place.

Mortificatio

It has already been suggested that the state of complete dissolution is reached at the end of Act III when the Three Men of Sin are "knit up / In their distractions" (III.iii.89—90). Alchemically speaking this has been brought about by the action of a poison—in this instance the poison of the "great guilt" that the second tempest of the play has revived in them.

To understand what happens to these three characters at this point in the play, it is necessary to remember that for Paracelsus and his followers the

---

[23] Kermode, Arden *Tempest*, note to II.i. 59—62.
[24] Jung, *Mysterium Coniunctionis*, p. 193.

task of the physician was to stimulate the alchemical processes within the patient so that the poison causing the ailment was separated and then dispelled. On the principle that like cured like, poison was administered to combat poison, and therefore the Paracelsan patient had to get worse to get better.

In order to get better, therefore, there must first occur what the Paracelsan physician, Gerard Dorn, called *distractio*, a separation or sundering of mind and body, which he compared to "a voluntary death". The "distractions" (III.iii.90) which the Three Men of Sin suffer correspond technically to this state of dissociation of mind and body. This *distractio* endures throughout Act IV of the play, during which time the Three Men of Sin can neither move nor speak. In the language of alchemy they ave been dissolved into the *materia prima* by the action of the tincturing poison, the *sal amarum*. If we are to locate them during the period of their *distractio*, it would be in an alchemical hell, the "Tartarus of the greater world" as Heinrich Khunrath called it in his *Von hylealischen Chaos* (1597).[25] It is the darkness of the state of *nigredo* and the poisonous remorse of *mortificatio* that the alchemists related to the descent into hell in Christian baptism and to the sufferings of evil-doers in the classical Hades. It is in this alchemical Tartarus that the Three Men of Sin undergo a psychological purging, until prompted by Ariel's pity for their suffering, Prospero decides to release them. At the beginning of Act V, they have reached what was called in alchemy the stage of *proiectio*. Prospero's project is almost complete.

Proiectio

When the stages of dissolution and purgation have been carried out, the final main stage of the alchemical work when the Stone is projected has been reached. It is now time to reunite what has been sundered, coagulate and fix what has been dissolved and separated. Traditionally this was the most difficult phase of the work. The fierce cleansing fire has to be reduced to a gentle heat, and care taken that the vessels do not crack, as Subtle pretends they do in Jonson's *The Alchemist* (IV.v. 57—62). It is to this difficult task that Prospero now turns.

It is above all in this Act that the alchemical imagery of the play becomes most explicit. As H. H. Furness pointed out in the New Variorum edition of the play, the word "crack" in Prospero's words "My charms crack not"

---

[25] Jung, p. 250.

(V.i.2) contains a reference to "the crucibles and alembics of magicians."[26] Frank Kermode agrees with Furness, and suggests that when Prospero says "Now does my project gather to a head", the word project might carry the meaning of alchemical projection.[27] The reference to time going "upright with his carriage" (V.i.1) might also be alchemical. The moment for the final projection was often determined by astrological factors, and in Prospero's case it is important to complete his "project" within the three hours when the influence of the "auspicious star" is available.

The Three Men of Sin are brought from their place of confinement, and Prospero calls for some "heavenly music . . . To work mine end upon their senses" (V.i.52—3). This too conforms to the traditional use of music in alchemy. Plate IV in Heinrich Khunrath's *Amphitheatrum sapientiae* (1609) depicting an alchemist's laboratorium, his place of *labor* and *oratorium* combined, shows in the foreground a long table piled with musical instruments, a book of music, and carrying the inscription *Musica Sacra*. Michael Maier's *Atalanta Fugiens* (1618) was printed with words and music to accompany the description of the alchemical work. In Johan Valentin Andreae's *Chemical Wedding* (1616), the final alchemical projection takes place on a remote island reached after a sea-voyage. At one stage a Moor's head is placed in a kettle and boiled to the accompaniment of a "delicate noise of Musick."[28] This scene provides an illuminating parallel to what next happens to the Three Men of Sin. To the sound of "solemn music", Prospero proceeds to boil their brains:

> A solemn air, and the best comforter
> To an unsettled fancy, cure thy brains,
> Now useless, boile within thy skull.
> (V.i.58—60)

I have restored the original F reading "boile" in place of the usual emendation "boil'd". In making this emendation insufficient attention has been paid to the alchemical imagery of this episode. Prospero is now in the process of curing the brains of the three men, and this involves driving off "the ignorant fumes that mantle / Their clearer reason" (V.i.67—8). Alchemically this is achieved by boiling their brains within their skulls.

In the preparation of the arcanum or elixir within the receptacle, repeated

[26] New Variorum *Tempest*, ed. H. H. Furness, note to V.i. 4.
[27] Kermode, Arden *Tempest*, note to V.i. 1—2.
[28] Johan Valentin Andreae, *The Chemical Wedding of Christian Rosenkreutz* (1616), in *A Christian Rosenkreutz Anthology*, ed. P. M. Allen (Blauvelt: Rudolf Steiner Publications, 1968), p. 141.

heating and boiling of the substance was necessary so that the poisonous vapours could be separated and driven off until only the stone or tincture was left. As Carl Jung has pointed out, in alchemical literature "the round vessel . . . is the skull,"[29] containing within it the divine principle or philosopher's stone. "The vessel necessary in this work must be round in shape, that the artifex may be the transformer of this firmament and of the brain-pan."[30] Perhaps the most remarkable example of this alchemical theme is found in the Gnostic treatise of Zosimos, dating to the third century A.D. The alchemical *opus* is here described in terms of participation in a pagan mystery cult like that of Eleusis. The climax of "these terrible mysteries" involves the boiling of the severed heads and chopped-up bodies in a bowl-shaped altar.[31]

In the light of these alchemical parallels, it seems that Prospero is about to boil the brains of the three men and so bring about their cure. Despite its awkwardness, the Folio reading "boile", with an implied relative before it, makes better sense than "boil'd". It is the boiling of their brains that serves to drive off the fumes that have previously obscured them:

> The charm dissolves apace;
> And as the morning steals upon the night,
> Melting the darkness, so their rising senses
> Begin to chase the ignorant fumes that mantle
> Their clearer reason . . .
>   (V.i.64—68)

The underlying imagery is again probably alchemical. Kenneth Muir has drawn attention to a parallel passage in *Macbeth*:

> memory, the warder of the brain,
> Shall be a fume, and the receipt of reason
> A limbeck only
>   (I.vii.67—69)

Muir cites an article by E. Schanzer that examines the alchemical imagery of this passage from *Macbeth*.[32] Prospero's speech is a similar evocation of

[29] Jung, *Mysterium Coniunctionis*, p. 514.
[30] Jung, p. 435, n. 248. In the same work that Croll traces the parallels between a tempest and a fit of epilepsy, he also provides the prescription for an anti-epileptic medicine made up from the boiled skulls of men who have died a violent death (*De Signaturis Internis Rerum*, p. 231). In boiling the skulls of the Three Men of Sin, Prospero is therefore using a standard, if gruesome, Paracelsan procedure.
[31] For the text of *The Treatise of Zosimos* and commentary on it, see Jung, *Alchemical Studies*, Vol. 13 in Collected Works (London: Routledge and Kegan Paul, 1967, 1983), pp. 59—108.
[32] See E. Schanzer, "Notes on Macbeth", in *Modern Language Review*, 52 (1957), p. 224, cited by K. Muir in the Arden *Macbeth*, App. E, p. 202.

the final stages of the projection in alchemy when by a process of gentle boiling the fumes of ignorance are driven off. It is possible too that the word "dissolves" used by Prospero to describe the ending of the charm he has cast on the Three Men of Sin was chosen because of its rich alchemical associations.

The image of light melting the darkness is of such universal character that it cannot be said to be exclusively alchemical. Nevertheless the alchemists made extensive use of this image, as for example in the appeal of the "infirm and weak old man" shut up in the dark cave of ignorance to see the light:

My soul and spirit depart; a terrible poison, I am likened to the black raven, for that is the wages of sin; in dust and earth I lie, that out of Three may come One. O soul and spirit, leave me not, that I may again see the light of day, and the hero of peace whom the whole world shall behold arise from me.[33]

Like him, Alonso, Sebastian and Antonio have been consumed by "a terrible poison", the poison of reactivated guilt. In the scene we have been examining we see this poison being driven off. Their *distractio* comes to an end. And for Alonso primarily the long purgative ordeal which he has undergone issues in the restoration of that which he has lost. This high moment in the play occurs when a curtain is drawn back to reveal Ferdinand and Miranda playing chess.

Sponsa and Sponsus

In any valid interpretation of the play as an alchemical allegory we would expect this scene to be fraught with alchemical significance. In accordance with the basic alchemical maxim, *solve et coagule*, we would expect the stage of dissolution to be followed by the stage of coagulation, symbolized so often by the alchemists as the union of the bride and bridegroom. In the 16th century *Rosarium philosophorum* this union of opposites is depicted as the copulation of a naked prince and princess. In other alchemical texts the union is represented by a hermaphroditic figure.[34] The alchemists frequently identified the *sponsa* and *sponsus* with the bride and bridegroom in Solomon's *Song of Songs*, treating the whole text as an allegory of the alchemical work. This is referred to in the *Hydrolithicus Sophicus seu Aquarium Sapientum* (1619):

[33] This passage from *Aurelia Occulta* which was reprinted in vol. 4 of the *Theatrum Chemicum* (1613), is quoted by Jung in *Mysterium Coniunctionis*, p. 515.
[34] See, for example, plates nos 21, 41, 42 in Stanislas de Rola, *The Secret Art of Alchemy* (London: Thames and Hudson, 1973).

37

The body of the Sun is gradually dissolved . . . and the one is blended in the other smoothly and gracefully, like ice in cold water. This has been investigated by the philosophers, and compared to the Sponsus and Sponsa of Solomon's *Song of Songs.*[35]

Are there any signs that Miranda and Ferdinand stand in the play for the alchemical bride and bridegroom? At first sight such an idea seems unlikely. When Prospero draws back the curtain to reveal the young couple in the cave, they are seen playing chess. This is the "wonder" (V.i.170) that Prospero has just promised to bring forth for Alonso. Charming as this scene is with Miranda good-humouredly accusing Ferdinand of having played her false, it is somewhat surprising. It is the highpoint of the play in which the King's supposedly dead son is restored. When the curtain is drawn and they are "discovered", we are not presented with something hieratic, as Colin Still believed, corresponding to the sacred marriage of Kore at Eleusis, but with a royal couple playing chess. Is this an example of telltale incongruity?

We are not told in what way Ferdinand has played false, but it seems reasonable to assume that he has just won the game and Miranda is surprised but not displeased. Would it disturb "the context of high-born and romantic love"[36] to suggest Miranda has been "mated"? Critics have investigated the traditional association between chess-playing and dalliance, and in itself it is not impossible that there is a sexual innuendo in this exchange between the two lovers.[37]

But there is another possibility that I would like to discuss. From an early date resemblances have been detected between the opening storm of *The Tempest* and the storm described in Chapters XVIII—XXII of the Fourth Book of Rabelais' *Pantagruel.*[38] There are other interesting points of contact between *The Tempest* and the Fourth and Fifth Books of *Pantagruel* that I shall mention later. Here I would like to draw attention to an episode during Pantagruel's voyage to the Oracle of the Bottle that links alchemy and chess. In the course of this voyage Pantagruel and his companions meet with a ship carrying Henry Cotiral, alias Henri Corneille Agrippa, author of the celebrated compendium on Renaissance magic, *De Occulta*

---

[35] Siebmacher, *Hydrolithus sophicus, seu Aquarium sapientum* (1619), in *Musaeum Hermeticum* (1677), p. 90; author's translation.

[36] Frank Kermode's phrase. See Arden *Tempest*, p. 123, for his long note on this passage.

[37] For a full discussion of the possible allegorical significance of this scene for the whole play see Bryan Loughrey and Neil Taylor, "Ferdinand and Miranda at Chess", *Shakespeare Survey*, 35 (1952), 113—118.

[38] Attention to these similarities was drawn by Gray in 1754 and by Maginn in 1839. See New Variorum *Tempest*, note to I.i. 43.

Philosophia (1533).[39] Cotiral shouts across to Pantagruel that he has discovered the 'vray Algamana', the true fusion of mercury and metal, "le vray Elixir", and reveals that he has just come from "La Quinte, en Touraine, Alchimie", inhabited by musicians, poets, astrologers, geomantists, alchemists and watch-makers, all of whom have the Quintessence.[40] Pantagruel immediately sets sail for the Isle of the Quintessence, and on arrival there he is entertained by Dame Quintessence herself. He watches her cure illnesses by means of music, and rejuvenate the aged. He then witnesses three games of chess, all performed by living pieces which move to the accompaniment of music. These games are an allegory of the alchemical *opus*.

In the first two games the silver King wins, but in the third game it is the gold King that wins, indicating the difficulty of achieving the final transmutation of the White Stone to the Red Stone. During the game emphasis is placed on the practise of dissimulation on both sides. We read that "a thousand subterfuges, assaults, retreats were made on both sides" and there is mention of "the subterfuges and sleights that they used to surprise each other."[41]

Here then we find a clear association between chess with its sleights and subterfuges and the *opus alchymicum* and its tricky operations, typified by the duplicity of Mercurius, his shape-shifting and his deceptions, which were the despair of alchemists and which, as we shall see, are the pre-eminent qualities of the tricksy spirit, Ariel. It is this duplicity that is also stressed in the game of chess that Miranda and Ferdinand have just completed. Miranda accuses him of having played her false (V.i.171), and yet she will accept his wrangling as "fair play" (V.i.175). As I have suggested this whole episode takes on a fuller meaning when it is related to Rabelais' games of alchemical chess. Rabelais' description of these games is taken almost verbatim from Prospero Colonna's famous allegory *Poliphili Hypnerotomachia*, published in 1499, but it was Rabelais who gave it an alchemical interpretation. Rabelais may have influenced Béroalde de Verville's translation and commentary of Colonna's work published in 1600 under the title *Le Songe de Poliphile*, where de Verville gives the whole work an alchemical interpretation.[42]

---

[39] Frank Kermode has said of Prospero that "he exactly resembles white magicians like Agrippa himself" (Arden *Tempest*, App. B, p. 143). But as I shall show in Chapter VII, Agrippa was regarded primarily by his contemporaries as the archetypal black magician.

[40] Rabelais, *Oeuvres Complètes: Le Cinquième Livre*, ed. J. Plattard (Paris: Société de Belles Lettres, 1959), pp. 63—4.

[41] Rabelais, pp. 88, 91.

[42] The title-page of *Le Songe de Poliphile*, reproduced in Jung, *Psychology and Alchemy*, Bollingen Series XX (Princeton: Princeton Univ. Press, 1953), p. 37, is a visual allegory of the alchemical work from the original "chaos" of the *prima materia* to the final projection of the "phoenix."

If Miranda and Ferdinand are seen as the alchemical *sponsa* and *sponsus*, their revelation to the King's Party in the final act of the play represents the completion of Prospero's project or projection. After alchemical separation, there comes reunion. Echoing this fundamental alchemical idea, Alonso gazing at Miranda says:

> Is she the goddess that hath sever'd us,
> And brought us thus together?
> (V.i.187—8)

Severing and bringing together, *solve et coagule*, form the twin operations of the spagyric art. The *separatio* of the castaways into scattered groups on the island, and of Alonso from his son, is now resolved in a dramatic as well as alchemical reunion at the end of the play. This reunion and restoration of what has been lost is the theme of Gonzalo's celebratory speech in which he speaks of them all having found

> ourselves
> When no man was his own
> (V.i.212—3).

Lacking only from this reunion are Caliban, Stephano and Trinculo. And yet even these three undergo a form of alchemical transformation, as we shall see.

Lingering Pickle

The change these three undergo is induced by drink. Stephano has come ashore astride a barrel of sack. It is this "celestial liquor" as Caliban calls it, a liquor "that is not earthly" (II.ii.118,127), that brings about those strange transformations of behaviour and even appearance that we call intoxication. The method of distilling wines into alcohol, discovered in Europe in the 12th century was basically an alchemical process, and the spirit of wine was regarded as a form of the elixir and was used in the form of alcoholic tinctures as a medicine. It was apparently only in the last quarter of the sixteenth century that strong spirits began to be used for "convivial purposes" as well.[43] In calling the sack, "celestial liquor" of an unearthly origin, Caliban suggests this association between alcoholic spirits and the elixir. This association is reinforced in another way in this scene. The bottle they drink

---

[43] See F. Sherwood Taylor, *The Alchemists* (London: Heinemann, 1952; Paladin Paperback, 1976), pp. 99—100.

the sack from and which Stephano has made from the bark of a tree is twice referred to as a book (II.ii.131, 142), and Caliban is made to kiss it and swear by it. Once again we are reminded of Rabelais' description in Book Five of Pantagruel's voyage to the Oracle of the Bottle. When finally they reach the Oracle, they discover that it lies in an underground mystery temple. On the altar is a large book shaped like a bottle. It is read by drinking from it, and when they do this they hear one oracular sound: TRINCH, meaning 'Drink'. As they drink the word of the book-cum-bottle they are filled with the poetic fury of the god Bacchus.[44]

Not only does this final episode of the Fifth Book remind us of Stephano's bottle-book, and the Bacchic intoxication it induces, but it would explain the element of parody or travesty in the scenes involving the two clowns and Caliban. In the language of the Renaissance Platonists, their vulgar, sublunary intoxication is a travesty of divine intoxication, just as the Bacchic drunkeness of Alcibiades in the *Symposium* is a profanation of the mysteries of love that Socrates had been unfolding before the intrusion of Alcibiades.[45] Like Alcibiades and his companions, the three Drunkards in *The Tempest* almost destroy the whole project on which Prospero is engaged. In terms of alchemical allegory, their pickled state stands for that false alchemy that the 'true' alchemists of the Renaissance period were never tired of condemning, the alchemy whose object was to produce solid material gold, rather than what Robert Fludd calls "the spiritual stone" which changes "dead stones into living philosophical stones."[46]

In Act V Stephano, Trinculo and Caliban, all having imbibed from their book-like bottle, finally rejoin the main group. They enter bedraggled, stinking from the foul water they have been plunged in, and roaring drunk. Alonso asks how this transformation has come about:

> And Trinculo is reeling ripe: where should they
> Find this grand liquor that hath gilded 'em?—
> How cam'st thou in this pickle?
> (V.i.279—281).

It was Warburton who first suggested that by "grand Liquor" (as it stands in the Folio text) was meant "the grand Elixir of the alchymists."[47] They are "gilded" both alchemically and alcoholically. The word "pickle" has

---

[44] Rabelais, *Oeuvres Complètes: Le Cinqième Livre*, ed. Plattard, chs. 43—47.
[45] On the distinction between spiritual and crude intoxication, see Edgar Wind, *Pagan Mysteries in the Renaissance*, pp. 60 ff.
[46] Robert Fludd, *Summum Bonum* (1629), Ch. 4, in *A Christian Rosenkreutz Anthology*, p. 359, 377.
[47] New Variorum *Tempest*, note to V.i. 333.

a variety of meanings that are played on in the succeeding dialogue. To be in a pickle is to be both in a plight and drunk.[48] It can also mean "steeped in preservative brine". It is partly in this sense that Trinculo uses the phrase when he says:

I have been in such a pickle, since I saw you last, that, I fear me, will never out of my bones: I shall not fear fly-blowing.
(V.i.282—4)

Finally pickle can mean to be in pain. When Stephano mutters:

O touch me not;—I am not Stephano, but a cramp
(V.i.286)

we realize that all three are in pain from having been driven through "tooth'd briars, sharp furzes, pricking goss, and thorns" and set on by Prospero's hell-hounds. They are here "pickled" in the sense of having salt or vinegar applied to the back after flogging, a punishment meted out in the navy in this period.[49] It is the same punishment that Cleopatra threatens to inflict on the messenger of bad news in *Antony and Cleopatra* (II.v.64—5):

Thou shalt be whipp'd with wires, and stew'd in brine,
Smarting in ling'ring pickle.

Through all this mercurial word-play Shakespeare preserves the idea of alchemical transformation, or rather a travesty of it. In their case the *sal amarum* of true alchemical transmutation has become the *aqua vitae* distilled in Shakespeare's London from stale beer, brutalizing instead of refining them.[50]

A word must be said about Caliban's role in the alchemical allegory of the play. Prospero calls him "Thou earth" (I.ii.316) and "this thing of darkness" (V.i.275). Nevertheless, he is in some ways indispensable to Prospero:

We cannot miss him: he does make our fire,
Fetch in our wood, and serves in offices
That profit us.
(I.ii.313—314).

We recall also the thousands of logs that Ferdinand has to move and pile up (III.i.10). If *The Tempest* is an alchemical allegory, the fuel collected by

---

[48] See Eric Partridge, *A Dictionary of Slang and Unconventional English* (London: Routledge and Kegan Paul, 1937), under "pickle, in", for a seventeenth century use of this phrase to mean drunk.

[49] N.E.D. under "pickle", 2.

[50] Jonson refers to this practise in *The Alchemist*, I.i. 53.

42

both Caliban and Ferdinand and the fire that Caliban tends are to enable Prospero to carry out his alchemical experiment. The same would also be true of the "utensils" that Caliban reports Prospero keeps in the cave. These are alchemical utensils. But Caliban serves in other ways. As "earth" and as "this thing of darkness", he is the equivalent of the *prima materia* or crude raw material without which the Stone cannot be produced. Caliban is the *elementum primordiale* of the alchemist which shaped and purified can be transmuted into gold by the alchemist. This primal material was thought of as dark, chaotic, misshapen, slow and leaden, just as Caliban is a thing of darkness, earthy, a misshapen mooncalf, a tortoise slow of response. Alchemically then Caliban can be seen as primordial matter, containing the potentiality of growth and development, by virtue of that inner spark of fire which according to Paracelsus drives all things towards completion. This hidden fire is stimulated by a celestial fire attracted and mediated by the alchemist and the Paracelsan physician alike to the raw material or to the patient. In *The Tempest* this celestial fire flaming amazement on all it encounters is the mercurial spirit of Ariel.

Ariel as Mercurius

No figure has greater importance in alchemy than Mercurius. He is at once the Philosophers' Stone, the Balsam, the Elixir, the spiritual essence locked within any substance awaiting release, the Work in all its stages, the bitter salt that dissolves and poisons, the purgative fire that purifies, the agent of death and rebirth. In character Mercurius is elusive and volatile. Because of his endless shape-shifting, Heinrich Khunrath calls him in his *Amphitheatrum sapientiae* (1609) "Proteus, the sea-god of the ancient pagan sages, who hath the key to the sea and . . . power over all things."[51] He is at home in all the elements, but as the fifth element, the quintessence, he is distinct from them.

When we study in detail the character and attributes of Ariel, it becomes clear that he is identical with the Mercurius of the alchemists. At his first appearance, as we saw, he is a spirit of fire, manifesting as lightning during the tempest and as St Elmo's fire. He appears here as the *ignis elementaris* or *ignis mercurialis* of the alchemists, "the secret, infernal fire, the wonder of the world, the system of the higher powers in the lower".[52] As Jung

---

[51] Jung, *Mysterium Coniunctionis*, p. 56. G. Wilson Knight has drawn attention to Ariel's mercurial nature in *The Crown of Life* (Oxford: Oxford University Press, 1947), p. 209.
[52] Jung, *Alchemical Studies*, Ch. 4, Part II, "Mercurius as Fire", pp. 209—10.

points out, this mercurial fire is related to hell-fire, the purgative flames of the lower world.[53] This enables us to understand that the opening tempest is experienced by "the fraughting souls" aboard the ship as a descent into hell: "Hell is empty,/And all the devils are here" (I.ii.214). Henceforth, these souls are in a purgatorial realm, and are subject to the transmuting effect of mercurial Ariel in his many forms.

Fire is not his only element. He is at home in all of them:

> be't to fly,
> To swim, to dive into the fire, to ride
> On the curl'd clouds
> (I.ii.190—3)

This is seemingly contradicted by his description in the "Names of the Characters" as "an ayrie spirit". But the word "ayrie" is used in a special sense. During his alchemical experiment of 1611, Fludd described a condensation of moisture as "a universall spirit of brightness wch was the soule of the world, or a universall spirituall & volatill ayre contayning in it a Chaos wch did embrace and possess in it the five particular elements to wit Aether, Fier, Ayer, Water, Earth."[54] Later he refers to it as "the ayery spirit", "the ayre of heaven", and "the universall aery spirit of the world."[55] In describing Ariel as an "ayrie spirit", then, Shakespeare is referring to quintessential air and not ordinary air, and is using the phrase in its strict Paracelsan sense.[56]

This mercurial "ayrie spirit" was notoriously difficult to control. Mercurius "evades every grasp—a real trickster who drove the alchemists to despair."[57] He is described by Gerard Dorn as "inconstant", "duplex", "full of duplicity."[58] Ariel shares these characteristics. For example, when Ariel asks for a year of his service to be abated, he gives one curious reason:

> I prithee,
> Remember I have done thee worthy service;
> Told thee no lies
> (I.ii.247—9).

---

[53] Jung, p. 210.

[54] Debus, *Robert Fludd and His Philosophicall Key*, p. 119.

[55] Debus, pp. 120, 123.

[56] As Professor Debus notes, "the concept of an aerial spirit of life was of great antiquity. It occurs frequently in the writings of sixteenth century Paracelsians." See *Robert Fludd and His Philosophicall Key*, p. 46.

[57] Jung, *Alchemical Studies*, p. 203.

[58] Jung, p. 217.

Telling no lies is odd self-praise until we recall the habitual duplicity of Mercurius. This deceptiveness extends to Ariel's skill as a trickster and illusionist throughout the play. He is praised by Prospero for the "trick" of making the banquet disappear before the eyes of the hungry castaways (IV.i.37). Prospero calls him "my tricksy Spirit" (V.i.226). He is tricksy too in his ability to shift shape from a spirit of fire to a nymph of the sea, to a harpy, to the figure of Ceres. It was the same shape-shifting that earned Mercurius the title of "versipellis", skin-changing and shifty.[59] One of the many shapes that Mercurius could appear in was as a bird, the *avis Hermetis* or bird of Mercury. The *Rosarium* (1555) instructs the artist to "sublime with fire, until the spirit which thou wilt find in it goeth forth from it, and it is named the ash or the bird of Hermes."[60] The alchemical work was compared to a germinating egg. The *Consilium coniugii* (1566) says that the alchemical egg contains the four elements and "the red sun-point in the centre, and this is the young chick." In his *Philosophia reformata* (1622), Mylius interprets "this chick as the bird of Hermes."[61] In its final perfected form the *avis Hermetis* was depicted as the Phoenix rising from its own ashes.[62] It is interesting that Prospero twice refers to Ariel as a bird. Praising him for misleading the Three Drunkards, he says: "This was well done, my bird" (IV.i.184), and at the end of the play when he promises to release Ariel, he calls him "My Ariel; my chick" (V.i.316). Even in the small detail of pet-names, Shakespeare continues to display an intimate knowledge of alchemical language.

Released from a pine tree just as "the mighty spirit Mercurius" was released from a tree in Grimm's famous fairy-tale, quicksilver Ariel is seen to preside over the whole alchemical *processus* in the play.[63] Like Mercurius, he too is 'the beginning, middle and end of the work'', and acts as "the healer of all imperfect bodies."[64] He is used by Prospero in the spirit of Paracelsan medicine to bring about an inner transformation in the human beings who are in his power. In this respect Ariel closely resembles the spirits that Paracelsus taught must be brought under control by the physician and used to cure those sick in mind or body. Prospero in employing this spirit

---

[59] Jung, p. 217.

[60] Jung, *Mysterium Coniunctionis*, p. 194.

[61] Jung, *Alchemical Studies*, p. 152.

[62] Note Sebastian's reference in III.iii. 21—4 to Arabia, the tree which is "the phoenix throne" and to the "one phoenix / At this hour reigning there." The symbol of the phoenix being reborn from its own ashes was, inevitably, a favourite one with the alchemists.

[63] See Jung, *Alchemical Studies*, pp. 193—9, for an analysis of this tale as an alchemical allegory.

[64] Jung, *Alchemical Studies*, p. 235.

is dealing with one of the most potent spirits known to the hermetic and cabalistic magic of the sixteenth century. He is mentioned by Agrippa,[65] and Reuchlin in his *De arte cabalistica* (1517) lists Ariel among the seventy-two most powerful spirits in the universe.[66]

If Ariel is Mercurius, Prospero emerges as a Paracelsan mage-physician of the sort represented in Jacobean London by Robert Fludd or at royal level by Rudolf II of Prague, the hermetic Holy Roman Emperor. With his magical and alchemical books and his laboratory utensils, with the great pile of logs outside to keep the fires going, Prospero begins to look and act like a typical alchemist of the period. He is under pressure. He is compelled to work rapidly while the influence of his "auspicious star" lasts. He is on edge and betrays signs of irritation, and even desperation. The transmutation of human nature is not easy. He is haunted too by a growing awareness that in some way his whole project is contaminated by the motives that have led him to undertake it, and by a final doubt about the rightness of forcibly changing the natures of the Three Men of Sin without their permission. Can human nature be rightfully subjected to imposed alchemical transmutation, or, to use the terms investigated in the next chapter, compelled to undergo the purgative experience of ritual initiation?

[65] See Kermode, Arden *Tempest*, App. B., p. 142, for this connection of Ariel with Agrippa's *Occult Philosophy*.
[66] Johannes Reuchlin, *De arte cabalistica* (1517; 1561 ed.), p. 517.

Chapter III
The Tempest as a Mystery Drama

Of the various allegorical interpretations of *The Tempest*, perhaps the most controversial is that offered by Colin Still in his *Shakespeare's Mystery Play* (1921) and *The Timeless Theme* (1936). Still's thesis was that *The Tempest* was based on the initiation rites enacted at the city of Eleusis outside Athens from about 1000 B.C. to about 300 A.D., the so-called Eleusinian mysteries. In this interpretation Prospero becomes the hierophant leading the initiations. The Three Men of Sin are undergoing initiation into the Lesser Mysteries. As at Eleusis they wander on a maze-like journey, they fast, they are confronted by frightening phantasmal spectacles, and are finally rewarded with the vision of the goddess and her consort, Miranda and Ferdinand, standing for Proserpina and the male god in the Eleusinian mysteries. Miranda and Ferdinand enact the rituals of the Greater Mysteries. The basic myth of Eleusis—the seizure of Proserpina by Pluto, the search for her by her mother Ceres, and the final restoration to her of Proserpina—is echoed, according to Still, in the basic situation of *The Tempest* with its theme of loss and recovery. As he points out, the principal goddess of Eleusis, Ceres, appears in the masque of goddesses in the play, and by implication Miranda becomes her daughter, Proserpina, finally restored. This summary account of Still's interpretation of *The Tempest* does no justice to the ingenuity with which he develops it.

Still's interpretation has been warily received by most commentators. Frank Kermode finds them "improbable", but occasionally quotes him in his Arden edition of the play. He puts his finger on the crucial weakness of Still's presentation of his ideas when he says:

His book fascinates; but anyone who does not share Still's own view that the author's responsibility for very detailed allegorical statement may be merely subliminal, will ask for some better account of the provenance of these ritual patterns which might explain their presence in Shakespeare.[1]

This criticism is justified. Still makes no attempt to show where Shakespeare could have found the "ritual patterns" he detects in the play. His failure

---

[1] Kermode, Introd. to Arden *Tempest*, p. lxxxiii.

to indicate just how much was known about the Eleusinian mysteries in Shakespeare's day explains the present-day neglect of his ideas. And yet, as I hope to show in this chapter, there was considerable interest in the pagan mysteries during the sixteenth and seventeenth centuries, and information about them had been largely systematized by about 1550. Had Shakespeare wished to write a play that follows the pattern of pagan initiation such as occurred at Eleusis, the relevant information was available, and Shakespeare's Latin was adequate to the task of reading the Latin works in which it was to be found. It has recently been suggested that Shakespeare's small Latin was superior to that of a modern university graduate in classics.[2]

Available first of all were the mythographic manuals of the sixteenth century which contained the basic factual information concerning the pagan mysteries. Equally important was the information to be gleaned from contemporary works of alchemy in which the alchemical *opus* was equated with ritual purgation and initiation. A further source of information was Virgil's *Aeneid*, especially Book Six, regarded in the sixteenth century as an allegory of Eleusinian and Platonic initiation. Finally there was Plato's own use in the Dialogues of the Eleusinian mystery rites to describe the journey of the human soul to a final visionary experience, known during the Renaissance as the *mysteria platonica*. I shall discuss these various sources of information about the pagan mysteries one by one and relate them to *The Tempest*.

Factual Sources of Information

Like Ben Jonson and other writers of the period, Shakespeare might well have consulted one of the mythographic handbooks of the period for information about the ancient mysteries. As Jean Seznec has shown, these handbooks were widely used by writers and artists of the period, as for example, George Chapman.[3] Much of Ben Jonson's ostentatious learning can be traced to such handbooks.[4] The earliest and most learned of them was Gyraldus' *De deis gentium* (1548). Here Shakespeare could have found had he wished "a sober account of the actual sources available in the Renaissance

---

[2] See J. Binns, "Shakespeare's Latin Citations: The Editorial Problems", in *Shakespeare Survey*, 35 (1982), 119.

[3] Jean Seznec, *The Survival of the Pagan Gods: The Mythological Tradition in Renaissance Humanism and Art*, Bollingen Series, 38 (New York: Pantheon, 1953), pp. 313 ff.

[4] See De Witt T. Starnes and E. W. Talbot, *Classical Myth and Legend in Renaissance Dictionaries* (North Carolina: University Press, 1955), for a comprehensive study of the use of dictionaries and mythographic manuals in education and in the creative arts of the time.

for reconstructing the ritual of Eleusis."[5] In the section dealing with the Eleusinian mysteries, Gyraldus cites eleven classical authors.[6] He relates that the mysteries were kept secret, and that they involved a reenactment by torchlight of the search of Ceres for her lost daughter Proserpina. For further information on the rites, Gyraldus directs the reader to the full but hostile account of them given by the Church Father, Clement of Alexandria. Gyraldus' description of the Eleusinian mysteries was taken over and amplified by Natale Conti in his *Mythologia* (1551).[7] It is worth mentioning that the earliest scholarly studies of the Eleusinian mysteries appeared during the decade following the first performance of *The Tempest*. The first of these is contained in *de Festis Graecorum Syntagma in que plurima Antiquitatis ritus illustratur* (1617), written by Petrus Castellanus of Leiden University. The chapter headed *Eleusinia* (pp. 657—663) assembles in summary all the known references to the Eleusinian mysteries. In his preface Catellanus mentions his gratitude to the classical scholar, Johannes Meursius, also of Leiden University, and it is likely that Castellanus had had access to the material collected by Meursius for his own work which is devoted entirely to the Elusinian mysteries. This is his *Eleusinia, sive de Cereris Eleusinia Sacra, ac Festo*, published in 1619. It was this work that Bishop Warburton consulted when he wrote the section of *The Divine Legation* in which he argues that Virgil's *Aeneid* is an allegory of the Eleusinian mysteries. In his turn Colin Still was inspired by Warburton's work in his studies of *The Tempest*. Obviously Shakespeare could not have consulted these two scholarly works on Eleusis, and they are significant only in that they show the continuing interest in the ancient mysteries. This interest can, however, be traced back a few years to the time that *The Tempest* was written. In the preface to the *Eleusinia* Meursius refers to the great European classical scholar, Isaac Casaubon, as *hic vir magnus*. It is known that Meursius was among the learned circle of friends with whom Casaubon corresponded in the early years of the seventeenth century, and it was Meursius who edited Casaubon's notes after the latter's death in England in 1614. Meursius' tribute to a great scholar and friend suggests that the inspiration for his own *Eleusinia* may have come from Casaubon's final work, completed in 1614 at the command of James I, his *Exercitationes de rebus sacris et ecclesiasticis*.

This work will be dealt with more fully in the next chapter, but something can be said here about its possible significance for the ritual theme in *The*

---

[5] Wind, *Pagan Mysteries in the Renaissance*, p. 7, n. 23.
[6] Gyraldus, *De deis gentium* (1548), Syntagma XIV, pp. 589—591.
[7] Natali Conti, *Mythologia* (1586), pp. 515—526.

Tempest. Casaubon had been invited to settle in England late in 1610 with the express purpose of writing a history of the early Christian Church in refutation of the Catholic version of its history given in the *Annales* of Baronius. Part of Casaubon's reply to Baronius deals with the profound influence of the rites and terminology of the pagan mysteries, particularly those of Eleusis, on the ritual and liturgy of the early Church. He shows in particular how the pagan mysteries influenced the early Church rite of adult baptism. Although Casaubon did not start the actual writing of the *Exercitationes* until about two months after the first performance of *The Tempest* in November, 1611, he had been speaking freely about his forthcoming work throughout 1611 when he was frequently at Court in attendance on James. James I was inordinately interested in such matters, and if, as I believe, the themes of pagan and Christian adult initiation are present in *The Tempest*, James would certainly have recognized them and responded to them. I shall return to the significance of Casaubon's work in the following chapter. Let us now see what information about the pagan mysteries Shakespeare could have derived from various alchemical works of the period.

Alchemical Initiation

The parallels between the 'death' and 'regeneration' of substance in alchemy and ritual initiation also involving a symbolic death and rebirth were noted and exploited by alchemists from an early date. The Gnostic alchemical text, *The Treatise of Zosimos the Divine concerning the Art* from the third century A.D. describes, as we saw, the production of the Stone in terms of a pagan ritual initiation involving a descent into the darkness, the boiling of the heads and limbs of the candidates for initiation, until they are transmuted into silver and then gold.[8] We were reminded of the alchemical boiling of the brains of the Three Men of Sin in *The Tempest* preparatory to their regeneration. The motif of the ritual entrance into darkness corresponding to the stage of *nigredo* or *mortificatio* reappears in one of the major alchemical works of the Renaissance, the *Amphitheatrum sapientiae aeternae* of Heinrich Khunrath, published in 1609. This work contains eleven engravings designed by Khunrath himself. The third of these shows the entrance to a large cave. Two persons are shown climbing the seven steps at the entrance, while one person is shown making his way down a dark tunnel towards a distant light. Three people outside the cave gaze up at the inscriptions that

---

[8] The text of the *Treatise of Zosimos* is given in Jung, *Alchemical Studies*, pp. 59—65.

surround the entrance. These indicate that the scene depicted is one of initiation into the ancient mysteries. One reads, for example: "The holy rituals whose Mysteries you are about to practise shall be open to the worthy but closed to the profane." This is echoed in the hieratic warning inscribed over the cave: *PROCUL HINC ABESTE PROFANI*, let the profane be far distant from this place.[9] These words are taken from Book Six of the *Aeneid* as the Sybil is about to conduct Aeneas into the cave that leads down into the darkness of the Underworld. Here Khunrath reflects the standard Renaissance view of Book Six of the *Aeneid* as an allegory of initiation. At the same time he is likely to have known that the Sybil's injunction that the profane depart was derived from the formula pronounced at the commencement of the Eleusinian mystieries.[10] The engraving following that of the Cave of Initiation shows an alchemist's laboratory. It is possible that Khunrath meant the viewer to understand that the Cave of Initiation with its inner glow of light led to this sanctum which is both a place of *labor* and an *oratorium*. The alchemist is seen kneeling before a tent that resembles the tent of the tabernacle of the Israelites in the Wilderness. In the centre of the picture is a table piled high with musical instruments symbolizing *musica sancta*, while the scene to the right depicts an alchemical workshop and its equipment. Thus for Khunrath the alchemical work involved both an inner and outer process, achieved in seven stages or steps "which leads us to the inner sanctum (*penetralia*) of the throne of true, eternal wisdom."[11]

The same association between alchemy and ritual initiation is also found in the writings of the Paracelsan physician, Michael Maier, already mentioned as an important figure at the court of Rudolf II at Prague and subsequently a defender of the Rosicrucians. In his *Silentium post Clamores* (1617) Maier claims that the Rosicrucians are the inheritors of the ancient secret of alchemical transmutation once possessed by the Eleusinians who "were very familiar with the art of making gold which they preserved and practised so secretly that no one learned the name of the process."[12] I have already referred to Maier's connections with a group of Paracelsan physi-

---

[9] The engravings of Khunrath's *Amphitheatrum Sapientiae Aeternae* are reproduced in *A Christian Rosenkreutz Anthology*, pp. 332—340.

[10] See for example Isaac Casaubon, *Exercitationes* (1614), p. 555, where he states that the formula *procul este profani* of the pagan mysteries was taken over by Christians in the form: *omnes Catechumeni foras discedite, omnes possessi, omnes non initiati.*

[11] Khunrath, *Amphitheatrum Sapientiae Aeternae* (1609), p. 50.

[12] Cited by Christopher McIntosh, *The Rosy Cross Unveiled*, p. 56. In his *Arcana arcanissima*, published in London with a dedication to Sir William Paddy, c. 1614, Maier treats all the ancient myths and the related mystery cults as allegories of alchemy.

cians in London, and in Chapter Five I shall give an account of two strange documents sent by Maier to James I and to Prince Henry during the Christmas season of 1611, shortly after the first performance of *The Tempest*. In view of Maier's contacts in London at such an early date, it is interesting that he makes the connection between alchemy and the Eleusinian mysteries that I believe is also present in *The Tempest*.

An allusion similar to Khunrath's to the descent of Aeneas in Book Six of the *Aeneid* is found in one of the illustrations in the *Splendor Solis* (1598) of Salomon Trismosin. This shows a figure in black on a ladder plucking the Golden Bough from the alchemical tree and passing it down to the figure of Aeneas. It is this Golden Bough that will make it possible for the alchemist to undertake the perilous journey into Hades, easy to enter but hard to leave as the Sybil warns.[13] The same link between ritual initiation and descent into the Virgilian Underworld is found in the most elaborate and sophisticated alchemical allegory of the period, *The Chemical Marriage of Christian Rosenkreutz*, written in 1605 by the Lutheran divine, Johan Valentin Andreae and published in 1616. Like *The Chemical Marriage*, the two principal Rosicrucian pamphlets, the *Fama* (1614) and the *Confessio* (1615), also contain information concerning the eponymous founder of the Rosicrucian Fraternity, Christian Rosenkreutz, but their exact relationship to *The Chemical Marriage* is in dispute.[14] The Chemical Wedding described in Andreae's work takes place at Easter and, as we shall see in the next chapter, follows the basic pattern of adult initiation into the Christian mysteries that took place at Easter in the early Church. But Andreae like so many other alchemists of the time also relates this symbolic wedding to the pagan mysteries. Like Khunrath he does this by alluding to the initiatory journey of Aeneas into the Underworld. When the narrator arrives at the Royal Palace where the wedding is to take place, he sees inscribed above the main entrance a variant of the Virgilian formula: *Procul hinc, procul ite profani*, a formula deriving as we saw from the Eleusinian mysteries.[15] This again is a clear indication that the alchemical allegory that follows and which is worked out in great detail includes the ordeals and testing of pagan ritual initiation.

[13] This illustration is reproduced in S. Klossowski de Rola, *Alchemy The Secret Art*, Plate 17.

[14] In his study of Andreae's *The Chemical Marriage* in *The Cross and The Crucible*, 2 Vols (The Hague: Nijhoff, 1972), J. W. Montgomery denies that Andreae was a Rosicrucian, while Frances Yates in her *The Rosicrucian Enlightenment* argues for the probability that he was.

[15] See *A Christian Rosenkreutz Anthology*, p. 342.

The Allegorized Aeneid

The comparison made by the alchemist between the stages in the production of the Philosopher's Stone and the descent of Aeneas in the Underworld may also help to explain why *The Tempest* is so strongly Virgilian in character. Kermode mentions "its strong echoes of the *Aeneid*."[16] Because of these echoes Colin Still suggested that "Shakespeare followed in a sense the example of Dante in taking Virgil as his guide."[17] Still is here repeating the view of Bishop Warburton that "the descent of Virgil's Hero into the infernal regions, I presume, was no other than a figurative description of an initiation; particularly, a very exact picture of the spectacles in the Eleusinian mysteries."[18] Another scholar who has detected the powerful influence of the *Aeneid* in *The Tempest* is J. M. Nosworthy.[19] He relates the opening storm in the play to *Aeneid*, I. 81—91, and Prospero's island to the island in the Bay of Carthage in *Aeneid* I. 159—68. The supernatural preservation of the mariners and the rescue of the ships has "a strong Virgilian parallel" in *Aeneid*, I, 390—1, 399—400. Nosworthy comes to the conclusion that "Shakespeare was familiar with a considerable part of the original *Aeneid*" and that he "boldly refashions Virgil's narrative so that it conforms to the requirements of his effectual plot" (pp. 288, 291). But concerning the most overt Virgilian reference in the play, the reference to Dido and Aeneas in Act II, Scene i, Nosworthy oddly interprets this as "a deliberate device to detach the rest of *The Tempest* from the Virgilian theme" (p. 293). I believe, on the contrary, that the parallels drawn between the marriage of Claribel to the King of Tunis and the meeting of Dido and Aeneas at Carthage serve to stress the Virgilian theme. In identifying Carthage and Tunis (II.i.80), Gonzalo (*pace* Frank Kermode) is not making a mistake.[20] In Shakespeare's day the exact location of Carthage was unknown, only that it lay somewhere near Tunis.[21] In any case, the point that Gonzalo is trying to make in the face of the gibes and facetiousness of Antonio and Sebastian is that their experiences in Africa and subsequently on the island parallel

---

[16] Kermode, Introd. to Arden *Tempest*, p. xxxiv, and note 2, where he points out that "the voyage of Alonso's party was, like that of Aeneas, from Tunis to Naples, with a purgatorial interruption."

[17] Still, *Shakespeare's Mystery Play*, p. 33.

[18] Warburton, *The Divine Legation*, I, 270.

[19] See Nosworthy's article "The Narrative Sources of *The Tempest*", in *Review of English Studies*, 24 (1948), 281—294.

[20] See Kermode, Arden *Tempest*, note to II.i. 78.

[21] See Donald Harden, *The Phoenicians* (Harmondsworth: Pelican Books, 1971), pp. 28—9.

53

those of Aeneas in Africa and his subsequent descent into the Underworld at Cumae near Alonso's city Naples. Like the repeated references to the new-dyeing of their clothes that come just before, Gonzalo is attempting to draw attention to the inner significance of what is happening to them. I believe that it is indeed true that "an understanding of this passage about Dido and Aeneas will modify our image of the whole play."[22] I suggest that Gonzalo is telling the King that their arrival on the island is comparable to the entry of Aeneas into the Underworld, and that they are now undergoing the ordeals of initiation. At the same time the audience watching the play is being alerted to these Virgilian parallels, and in the case of Shakespeare's original audiences their attention was being directed to a version of Virgil's *Aeneid* with which we are no longer familiar.

The *Aeneid* known during the Renaissance period was an epic poem heavily overlaid with allegorical interpretation. The most influential of such interpretations during the sixteenth century was the *Quaestiones Camaldulenses* of the Platonist and disciple of Ficino, Cristofero Landino. This work, which builds on the twelfth century commentary of Bernard of Silvester,[23] was published about 1480 and was reprinted four times during the sixteenth century and once early in the seventeenth.[24] In it Landino interprets the first six books of the *Aeneid* as an allegory of the Platonic search for truth culminating in the ritual initiation of Book Six. This approach to the *Aeneid* goes back to the second century commentator, Servius, who specifically relates the descent of Book Six with the performance of the rites of Proserpina.[25]

For Landino, "Virgil himself becomes one of a long line of seer-philosophers who made their secret truth available under a poetic veil" (p. 3). It was the function of such poetry, according to Landino, to reawaken memories of the prenatal state, obscured by the descent into matter at the moment of birth. "The mysteries of Aeneas' wanderings" are hidden in the

---

[22] Kermode, Arden *Tempest*, note to II.i. 74.

[23] See *The Commentary of the First Six Books of the Aeneid of Virgil, commonly attributed to Bernardus Silvestris,* ed. J. W. and E. F. Evans (Lincoln: Univ. of Nebraska Press, 1977).

[24] The following account is based on S. J. Stahel's translation and study, *Cristofero Landino's Allegorization of the Aeneid: Books III and IV of the Camaldolese Disputations* (Diss. Johns Hopkins Univ., 1968). Page references are to this work.

[25] Servius, *Commentarii in Virgilii* on *Aeneid*, VI, 136: *ad sacra Proserpinae accedere nisi sublato ramo non poterit inferos autem subire hoc dicit, sacra celebrare Proserpinae* (it is not possible to approach the rites of Proserpina without carrying the Golden Bough. To descend into the Underworld is the same as to celebrate the rites of Proserpina). Servius' commentary was often published with Virgil's *Aeneid* during the sixteenth century.

poem so as to keep "the profane away from holy and sacred matters" (pp. 51, 45). What Landino then goes on to discover in the first six books of the *Aeneid* is an allegory, consciously intended by Virgil, of the Platonic journey from a state of immersion in the realm of human passion to a state of spiritual enlightenment achieved when Aeneas descends into the Underworld. Let us now consider the maze-like wanderings of the Three Men of Sin in *The Tempest* in the light of Landino's commentary, adding references to Plato's own works where necessary.

The Storm

The sea voyage of Aeneas and his companions from Troy to Italy is treated by Landino in the traditional way as a voyage through the seas of human appetite (p. 74), which remain calm when not stirred by the wind of inordinate desire, but

Trouble it [appetite] with violent disturbances, then what waves and what tempests will be seen. Then in a most fickle way it fluctuates with an erratic boiling violence (p. 74).

The great storm raised by Juno in the *Aeneid* signifies the raising of human passion in which many may be wrecked (p. 119). Commenting on Virgil's line, *apparent rari nantes in gurgite vasto* (a few are seen swimming in the vast surge), Landino explains that "very few among the vast multitude who are plunged into such a storm of appetitive disquiet are able to survive" (p. 119). We are reminded of the opening storm of *The Tempest* and of the apparently few survivors who are able to stay afloat in the high seas, of the storm in *Lear* which objectifies Lear's own "tempest in my mind" and Clarence's "tempest to my soul" in *Richard III*.[26] As J. N. Nosworthy has pointed out, Prospero's island and the island in the inlet near Carthage in the *Aeneid* have a number of features in common. Their resemblance is increased when we turn to Landino's interpretation of the Virgilian island. Human beings, he says, would be overwhelmed by the vicissitudes of fortune

unless there were an island for us in the midst of the waters; and although this island may be beaten about on all sides by the sea, it is nevertheless strengthened by virtues and is not submerged.[27]

---

[26] Clarence's whole speech in which drowning, an inner tempest and a Virgilian descent into the Underworld are combined shows how closely entwined these elements were in Shakespeare's mind from an early date. For a study of the sources of this speech, see Harold F. Brooks, "Richard III: Antecedents to Clarence's Dream" in *Shakespeare Survey*, 32 (1979), 154 ff.

[27] Stahel, p. 133.

Such an island of refuge is fended, he says, by the cliffs of fortitude and temperence. It is to a similar island amidst a raging sea of human passion that the Three Men of Sin come to learn the virtues of fortitude to combat despair and of "subtle, tender and delicate temperance" (II.i.41—2) to moderate passion. Behind them lies the realm of Tunis which was Carthage, signifying according to Landino preoccupation with civic life (p. 139), and Aeneas' passion for Dido signifying that he has succumbed to wordly ambition (p. 153). Before them lies the experience on Prospero's island that corresponds to Aeneas' descent into the Underworld.

In Hades

Landino follows Plato and the Neoplatonists in regarding the Underworld as symbolic of the soul in incarnation:

the underworld for the soul is nothing other than the body itself in which it has been placed as if in a prison (p. 198).

Once it enters the body, the soul endures a state that is variously described as "imprisonment", "a falling asleep", "drunkeness", "a drowning", or "forgetfulness". Landino writes that "once it is drawn into matter, it drinks in the new drunkenness of that which is material—it is submerged, as it were, in a river" (p. 202). It drinks of the river Lethe, and suffers a forgetfulness of its true nature. The consequences of this amnesia are symbolized for Landino by the four rivers of Hades. Having drunk first of the waters of Lethe, the worldly human being suffers a loss of joy symbolized by the river Acheron which Landino derives from *a-chairon*, or joylessness. This in turn leads to the *tristicia*, the moroseness and despair that Gonzalo tries to combat in Alonso, symbolized by the river Styx. This deepens into the state of deep mourning represented by the river Cocytus:

From extended mourning we usually fall into the flames of frenzy and madness; and it is this heat that they call Phlegethon . . . and so from one river of matter all these evils eventuate (pp. 202—3).

It is to this state of frenzy and madness that Alonso and his two companions in crime are progressively reduced, reaching a climax at the end of Act III when Ariel in the shape of the Harpy delivers his speech of judgement on them. They are now in the section of the purgatorial realm of the Underworld reserved for criminals and evil-doers of their sort. With the aid of Book Six of the *Aeneid* we can locate them exactly: they are in Tartarus along with Tantalus and others of similar evil nature. Here is Virgil's description of the torments of Tantalus (VI. 603—607) that exactly parallels the torments of the Three Men of Sin:

For Tantalus there gleam golden supports upholding high banquetting seats, and before the sinner's eyes is laid a royal and sumptuous feast; but close to it reclines the most terrible of the Furies who allows no hand to touch the fare, but leaps up, torch on high, and shouts like thunder.

This corresponds to the moment in *The Tempest* when Ariel appears as a harpy to the accompaniment of "Thunder and lightning", and prevents the Three Men of Sin from enjoying the banquet. They are undergoing the purgative experience of the type of men that Virgil associates with Tantalus. They include

those who hated their brothers while life was theirs or struck a parent or entangled a dependent in deceit, or, having found riches, gloated over them alone . . . or took part in an unrighteous war, shamelessly betraying their liege-lords (VI. 608—614).

It is to this group that Alonso, Sebastian and Antonio belong, and at this point in the play they begin the Tartarean punishments appropriate to their crimes against their liege-lord, Prospero.

This way of reading the *Aeneid* as an allegory of Platonic philosophy is inseparable from the belief of Florentine Platonists such as Ficino and Landino that Plato's philosophy contained a description of ritual initiation into the pagan mysteries. The so-called *mysteria platonica* were regarded as a philosophical version of pagan mysteries such as those of Eleusis. As Edgar Wind has pointed out, "both Ficino and Pico professed to know that in the pagan initiatory rites of love the first stage was a purge of the sensuous passion, a painful ritual of purification by which the lover was prepared for his communion with the god."[28] The mystery rites of love reconstructed by the Platonists of the Renaissance were derived both from the writings of Plato and those of the Alexandrian Platonists. In the preface to his translation of Plato's *Charmides*, Politian praises the use of fables and riddles to convey philosophical truths *ne religiosa quodammodo Eleusinarum dearum mysteria profanarentur*—lest the religious mysteries of the Eleusinian goddesses be profaned in any way.[29] Rightly or wrongly, then, it was believed during the Renaissance that the *mysteria platonica* were modelled on the mysteries of Eleusis. We can now examine a number of Plato's dialogues and see what light the ritualistic elements in them will throw on *The Tempest* as a mystery drama.[30]

[28] Wind, *Pagan Mysteries in the Renaissance*, p. 146.
[29] Cited by Wind, p. 164. Politian (1454—1494), Renaissance scholar and poet, had studied under Landino in his youth.
[30] The influence of Plato's thought on Shakespeare has been investigated by John Vyvyan in his *Shakespeare and the Rose of Love* (London: Chatto and Windus, 1960), and *Shakespeare and Platonic Beauty* (London: Chatto and Windus, 1961).

Mysteria Platonica

Plato's *Phaedrus*, with its famous setting under a plane tree on the banks of the Ilissus near Athens, deals in its central parts with what the Renaissance Platonist, Pico della Mirandola, called "the mystery rites of love". Close to the setting of the Dialogue lay Agrai, the site of the sanctuary where the lesser mysteries were performed which qualified a person to take part in the greater mysteries of Eleusis. Socrates' instructions to the young man, Phaedrus, can therefore be regarded as a verbal initiation into the lesser mysteries of love.

In Socrates' second speech on love he resorts to the language of the mysteries. After death the soul rises to a region where pure truth is contemplated. There the soul beholds "the Plains of Truth" and the "Meadow", corresponding to the Rarian Plain and the meadow at Eleusis where the first grain of corn had been sown and harvested by Ceres. This is the first of a series of "transpositions" of the mystery-rites of Eleusis in the *Phaedrus* that scholars have noted.[31] Socrates goes on to relate that the clarity of vision of the soul between lives varies according to the degree of purity attained in the preceding life. The clearer this vision, the stronger the memory of it will be when the soul next incarnates. A little later Socrates again echoes the languages of the mysteries to describe the experience of the pure soul after death:

Then we were all initiated into that mystery which is rightly accounted blessed beyond all others; whole and unblemished were we that did celebrate it (250 C).

Here the state of the enlightened soul after death is compared to the high moment in the Eleusinian mysteries when the candidates witnessed a great light glowing from the inner sanctum in the vast telesterion at Eleusis and experienced an epiphany of the gods, including the restored Proserpina and her consort. In the postmortem state it is the vision of transcendent Beauty that most impresses itself upon the human soul, and it is the memory of this Beauty that causes a lover to behold his beloved with shuddering and awe. Socrates explains that it is this residual memory of perfect Beauty that makes the lover "offer sacrifices to his beloved, as to a holy image deity" (251 A). Mortal beauty arouses the memory of eternal Beauty.

It is in this way that Ferdinand responds to Miranda when he first catches sight of her. He perceives her inner divinity:

> Most sure the goddess
> On whom these airs attend.
> (I.ii. 424—5)

[31] *Plato's Phaedrus*, ed. R. Hackforth, p. 82.

Echoing Virgil's *dea certe* (*Aeneid*, I. 328), Ferdinand here recognizes the archetype behind the human form, just as Aeneas recognizes Venus in the girl he meets near Carthage. The lover, Socrates goes on to relate, now becomes intent on the beloved to such a degree that he wishes to become her slave:

All the rules of conduct, all the graces of life, of which aforetime she [the soul of the lover] was proud, she now disdains, welcoming a slave's estate (252 A).

Ferdinand likewise welcomes "a slave's estate":

> The very instant that I saw you, did
> My heart fly to your service; there resides,
> To make me slave to it; and for your sake
> Am I this patient log-man
> (III.i. 64—7).

The slavery of love leads paradoxically to enlargement from what Socrates calls the prison-house of the body (250 D). Ferdinand expresses the same paradox when he says that all the tribulations he is undergoing

> are but light to me
> Might I but through my prison once a day
> Behold this maid: all corners else o'th'earth
> Let liberty make use of; space enough
> Have I in such a prison.
> (I.ii. 492—496).

He is being tested, and part of the training he undergoes involves demonstrating control of lust.[32] This corresponds to the trials of Platonic love that Socrates describes in the *Phaedrus* where the driver of the chariot of the soul must subjugate the horse of lust (253 C ff.). When the lover has fully achieved this control he is then granted the "blessed vision" that crowns initiation into the mystery-rites of love.

The equivalent of this vision has two forms in *The Tempest*. The first is when Ferdinand and Miranda witness the epiphany of the goddesses, Ceres and Juno. It is described by Ferdinand as "a most majestic vision" (IV.i. 117), which makes "this place Paradise" (IV.i. 124). The central drama of the Eleusinian mysteries is recalled in the picture of Ceres wandering in search of her daughter on the sea-coast "sterile and rocky-hard" (IV.i. 69), and in the reference to the exclusion of Venus and her son from the rites (IV.i. 88—9). In the Eleusinian myth it was Venus who betrayed Proserpina to Dis

---

[32] As Prospero later explailns to him, "all thy vexations / Were but my trials of thy love" (IV.i. 5—6).

as she was gathering flowers in Sicily. Missing only from this evocation of the Eleusinian mysteries is Proserpina herself, until we realize that she is present in the person of Miranda, the returned Spring goddess whom Ceres celebrates in ll. 110—117 of this scene. It is she who will guarantee the perpetual Spring of the new Golden Age that had earlier been evoked by Gonzalo. Again we are reminded of the Eleusinian mysteries with their underlying concern for the fertility of the earth and the production of crops, above all cereals, the gift of Ceres to mankind. The Roman bishop, Hippolytus, recorded that the most solemn moment in the rites of Eleusis consisted in the silent display of an ear of corn.[33]

The majestic vision staged by Prospero for the young couple matches the culminating vision described by Plato in the *Symposium*:

The man who has been guided thus far in the mysteries of love, and who has directed his thoughts towards examples of beauty in due and orderly succession, will suddenly have revealed to him as he approaches the end of his initiation a beauty whose nature is marvellous indeed, the final goal, Socrates, of all his previous efforts.[34][5]

For Ferdinand the orderly succession of examples of beauty, each imperfect but each containing an element of full beauty, leads him finally to Miranda:

> Full many a lady
> I have ey'd with best regard, and many a time
> Th'harmony of their tongues hath into bondage
> Brought my too diligent ear: for several virtues
> Have I lik'd several women; never any
> With so full soul, but some defect in her
> Did quarrel with the noblest grace she ow'd,
> And put it to the foil: but you, O you,
> So perfect and so peerless, are created
> Of every creature's best
> (III.i. 39—48).

This speech, using the idiom of the courtly Platonism of the Renaissance, perfectly conveys the progressive stages in Plato's mystery-rites of love.

The second form in which Shakespeare stages the equivalent of the Platonic vision and the climactic moment in the Eleusinian mysteries is when

---

[33] For an account of the reconstructed rites of Eleusis, see Goblet D'Alviella, *The Mysteries of Eleusis* (Wellingborough: The Aquarian Press, 1981), Walter F. Otto, "The Meaning of The Eleusinian Mysteries" and Hugo Rahner, "The Christian Mystery and the Pagan Mysteries", both in *The Mysteries*, Bollingen Series 30, ed. Joseph Campbell, pp. 14—31 and pp. 337—401. Thomas Taylor's study, *A Dissertation on the Eleusinian and Bacchic Mysteries* (c. 1790), printed in *Thomas Taylor the Platonist: Selected Writings*, pp. 345—426, is still valuable.

[34] Plato, *The Symposium*, ed. W. Hamilton (Harmondsworth: Penguin Books, 1951), 211 A.

Miranda and Ferdinand are revealed to the astonished gaze of Alonso and his companions at the end of the play. It is the "wonder" that Prospero has promised them (V.i. 170), and having seen it they call it "a vision of the island (V.i. 176) and "A most high miracle" (V.i. 177). Colin Still is surely right in regarding these two visions of *The Tempest* as forms of greater and lesser initiation.

The Sleepers

The majestic vision witnessed by Miranda and Ferdinand ends abruptly as Prospero remembers the plot of the Three Drunkards against him. The elaborate, contrived vision dissolves and the spirits conjured up by Prospero vanish "to a strange, hollow, and confused noise" (IV.i. 137—8). They do not vanish "with" but "to" a discordant noise; it is possible that this stage-direction refers to discordant music, but is also conceivable that it is the sound made by changing scenery as it is cranked up or drawn noisily out of sight. The majestic vision ends in chaos, and the beautiful illusions of the Court masque with their sudden transformations, their clouds that move realistically across the stage, their "gorgeous palaces" and "solemn temples" are exposed as stage tricks. The illusion of the court masque holding an audience spell-bound becomes for Prospero an image of life itself:

> We are such stuff
> As dreams are made on; and our little life
> Is rounded with a sleep
> (IV.i. 156—159).

The word "rounded" in this speech has been variously interpreted as "surrounded", "rounded off", "completed" or "crowned". John Erskine Hankins has ingeniously suggested that Shakespeare was thinking of an idea found in Macrobius that the soul regains its original roundness after death after having been conical in shape like a raindrop during its descent into incarnation.[35] Attractive as this suggestion is, it is nevertheless contradicted by the overall pessimism of the speech. It might be possible to determine the intended meaning of "rounded" by considering the traditional use of the metaphor of life as a sleep or dream. In the *Republic* Plato says of the unenlightened human being that he is "sunk in sleep, and conversant with

---

[35] Hankins, *Backgrounds of Shakespeare's Thought*, p. 32.

the delusions of dreams; and that before he is aroused to a vigilant state, he will descend to Hades, and will be overwhelmed with a sleep perfectly profund.''[36] For the unenlightened person then, death is a passage from one dream-state to another. Similarly when Aeneas enters the Underworld he enters a kingdom of sleep and false dreams that is a copy of the living world of the average unawakened individual. As in T. S. Eliot's Virgilian poem, *The Hollow Men*, the two kingdoms of death closely resemble each other. The same view is expressed by Plotinus: ''to be plunged in matter is to descend into Hades, and there fall asleep.''[37] Ficino echoes the same idea when he states that men who have not been active in the pursuit of wisdom while alive, being ''only engaged in the delusion of dreams'', if they happen to die in this sleep, they ''would be afflicted with similar and still sharper visions in the future state . . . tormented with delusive semblances of reality.''[38] Returning to the words of Prospero cited above, they suggest that human beings are fashioned from the substance of dreams and that they live out a dream. When they die they enter a further dream-state, a state that rounds off as well as surrounds their previous one. It is this desolate prospect that gives Hamlet pause: to die, to sleep, perchance to dream,

> For in that sleep of death what dreams may come
> When we have shuffled off this mortal coil
> (III.i. 60—62)

Prospero is universalizing Hamlet's fears into a philosophy of futility. He too has become conscious of the shifting, deceptive nature of the reality that is revealed through the senses. It is a world of seeming, corresponding to the belief of the Platonic New Academicians that ''everything does not so much exist as seem to exist.''[39] In Virgil's words, Prospero has awakened to the fact that he too is emmeshed in ''umbrarum hic locus . . . somni noctisque soporae'' (*Aeneid*, VI. 283—4), this realm of shadows, sleep and drowsy night. It is an awakening that he finds deeply disturbing, just as it is for any human being who catches a glimpse of the unreality of so-called solid reality and finds that he is living in a ''house of empty dreams'' (*Aeneid*, VI, 283—4). And yet such an experience can also be seen as the precondition of full awakening. From this point onwards in the play, Prospero undergoes his own initiation and is led finally to an understanding of the true nature of the magical illusions he has been imposing on other human beings. He

---

[36] Plato, *Republic*, Bk. VII, cited in *Thomas Taylor the Platonist*, p. 349, n. 1.
[37] Plotinus, *Enneads*, I, 8, cited in *Thomas Taylor the Platonist*, p. 349.
[38] Ficino, *De immortalitate animae*, Bk. 18, cited in *Thomas Taylor the Platonist*, p. 350—1.
[39] See Michael Murrin, *The Allegorical Epic*, p. 37.

is approaching the state of the philosopher-kings in Plato's *Republic* (520) who once they become spiritually awake are enjoined to return to the dream kingdom of ordinary human affairs. Because they are awake they will easily recognize the shadowy nature of what the unwakened regard as reality. "Our state and yours will be really awake, and not merely dreaming like most societies today, with their shadowy battles and their struggles for political power, which they treat as some great prize." In *The Tempest* we see Prospero after all those years of study and withdrawal from public affairs attempting to intervene in the dream-like world of ordinary life with its empty shadowy ambitions. He tries to banish illusion by means of magical illusion, but finds that the dreamers are tenacious of their dreams.

Sleepy Language

From the point of view of the spiritually awake, Antonio and Sebastian are fast asleep, dreaming their dream of political power, but now transferred from Naples and Milan to be experienced more tantalisingly on this Tartarean isle. Awake in the ordinary sense of the word, they are nevertheless presented by Shakespeare as psychologically fast asleep. Antonio's strong imagination sees a crown descending on his companion's head, and the following dialogue ensues:

Seb.	What, art thou waking?
Ant.	Do you not hear me speak?
Seb.	I do; and surely

It is a sleepy language, and thou speak'st
Out of thy sleep. What is it thou didst say?
This is a strange repose, to be asleep
With eyes wide open; standing, speaking, moving,
And yet so fast asleep.

Ant.   Noble Sebastian,
Thou let'st thy fortune sleep — die, rather; wink'st
Whiles thou art waking.

Seb.   Thou dost snore most distinctly;
There's meaning in thy stores.
                     (II.i. 204—213).

Placed in the context of the Platonic metaphor of life as a dream state, this is the dialogue of dreamers, and Sebastian speaks wiselier than he knows when he half suspects that they are asleep. Neither of them realize that they are entertaining a dream of shadowy ambition in a purgative Tartarean realm where in the words of Ficino they will be "tormented with delusive semblances of reality". Their dreams become nightmares of frustration.

Their plot to assassinate Alonso and the others while sleeping is frustrated by Prospero's foresight. They are frustrated too like Tantalus as they step forward to eat the food that is temptingly spread before them. Finally they are deprived of movement and speech. The delusion from which they are suffering arises, as we shall now see, from a lethean forgetfulness of their true selves.

Platonic Forgetting and Remembering

For Plato human ignorance was a state of amnesia in which a human being had forgotten his divine origins. Between lives, he taught, the human being sees clearly or obscurely the eternal Ideas or Archetypes. To the extent that he has been immersed in the phenomenal world and led a selfish or criminal life, the soul of such an individual loses its wings, and as Plato says in the *Phaedrus* (246 E), after death is unable to rise to a contemplation of the eternal truths. The postmortem state of such individuals is determined by their spiritual state while alive. If they have been spiritually 'asleep' while alive, forgetful of their true spiritual natures, they will experience a similar state of sleep after death. The little lives of Alonso, Antonio and Sebastian in Italy based on a dream of ambition are rounded on the island with a sleep similar in nature to the one they had earlier lived out but now under conditions of purgative frustration. The soul, however, whose wings have been developed during a life of philosophic search and behaviour climbs higher after death and has a clearer vision of the Archetypes. Plato describes this vision in *Phaedrus* (250 B—C) in terms borrowed from the language of the Eleusinian mysteries:

steadfast and blissful were the spectacles on which we gazed in the moment of final revelation; pure was the light that shone around us, and pure were we, without taint of that prison-house which now we are encompassed withal, fast bound therein as an oyster in its shell.

As the soul which has enjoyed this vision next incarnates, it drinks symbolically of the cup of Lethe, and its memory of the vision is obscured, but, as in the case of Prospero, it is recoverable. The process of recovery is described by Landino in the following way:

The soul by gradually extricating itself from that forgetfulness (in which it has been sleeping as if oppressed by wine) becomes strong enough to use those twin wings of the soul.[40]

---

[40] Stahel, *Cristofero Landino's Allegorization of the Aeneid*, p. 207.

64

Prospero's "revels" speech marks the point in the play of his own remembering and awakening. As the firm contours of the hitherto familiar world dissolve, he experiences this awakening at first as deeply disturbing. He recognizes the illusory nature of the magical world he has created and beyond that of the so-called 'real' world. He now begins a process of liberating disillusion that is only completed when finally he abjures his rough magic. I have suggested that this liberation involves the recovery of the memory of our true nature. This is true not only of Prospero, but of other characters in the play.

The Tempest contains some thirty references to memory and forgetfulness and to the extent that this play was consciously written by Shakespeare as a drama of initiation, we would expect these references to have a Platonic significance. In order to understand the various allusions to forgetting and remembering allegorically, we would have to place them in the context of Plato's teachings about spiritual amnesia and anamnesia.

The whole of the second scene of Act I is in the nature of an exercise in memory in which Prospero tries to see how much Miranda remembers of her former life. When he tells her of his brother's treachery, she says that these things are "from my remembrance" (I.ii. 65), and when she has heard the whole of her father's memorial reconstruction of the past, she exclaims:

> I, not remembering how I cried out then,
> Will cry it o'er again
> (I.ii. 133—4)

But her memory is not entirely blank. When Prospero asks her if she can "remember / A time before we came unto this cell" (I.ii. 38—9), she answers to his surprise that she can. Prospero then asks:

> By what? by any other house or person?
> Of any thing the image tell me, that
> Hath kept with thy remembrance.
> (I.ii. 42—44)

And she answers:

> 'Tis far off,
> And rather like a dream than an assurance
> That my remembrance warrents.
> (I.ii. 44—6).

We might regard this as a simple testing of ordinary memory, were it not for the odd form of Prospero's second question: "By what? by any other house or person?". The preposition "by" is unexpected, and seems to mean "by what means have you remembered?". It is possible that Prospero is here referring to a memory system of the sort available in the sixteenth and seventeenth centuries. Among these systems, as Frances Yates has shown in her *The Art of Memory*, there was one type derived from Plato's teachings on memory. Basic to all the systems, was the arrangement of the facts to be remembered in various visual patterns. They could, for example, be placed in houses and associated with persons or symbols. Technically it was the *imagines* or images arranged in some imagined building that made it possible to remember the facts they were associated with.[41] But the purpose of the memory systems inspired by Plato was something more than a mere recollection of facts. By arranging information in a hierarchy of ever more inclusive sets, a means was provided whereby the mind could ascend from the phenomenal shadow world of complex facts to the relatively simple world of the divine Ideas or Archetypes. Used psychologically, such a memory system would enable an individual to recover the forgotten vision of ultimate reality and remember his own divine origins.

When we consider the long remembrance scene in *The Tempest* and Prospero's apparent references to the memory systems of the Renaissance in the context of Plato's teaching on *anamnesia*, we can see it as an allegorical account of Miranda's exile from her realm of origin which she dimly remembers as in a dream. The paradisial world represented by her early childhood is destroyed by the intrusion of sin in the persons of Alonso, Antonio and Sebastian, and she is forced into exile to await the moment of her return when a second Golden Age can be inaugurated. As we shall see in a later chapter, Miranda is related allegorically to the virgin Astraea of Virgil's *Fourth Eclogue* who went into exile at the end of the first Golden Age and was to return when the second Golden Age is established on earth. Her name also recalls the Wondrous Woman of Revelation 12 who is driven into exile to a place in the wilderness by the apocalyptic Man of Sin to await there the beginning of the Millennium.[42] Miranda's personal history, then, which is rehearsed in Act I, Scene ii, becomes an allegory of man's history, his loss of truth, his long search for it, and his final recovery of his forgotten divinity. Miranda is the bearer of this divinity in the play, living in exile on the island, beset by the three men of sin.

These three are suffering from Platonic amnesia. Antonio's crime is closely related by Shakespeare to an abuse of memory. He is one

---

[41] See Frances Yates, *The Art of Memory*, pp. 50 ff.

[42] As I shall suggest, it is this apocalyptic female wonder that may be referred to in the Rosicrucian *Confessio* (1615) in the phrase: *Miranda sextae aetatis.*

Who having into truth, by telling of it,
Made such a sinner of his memory,
To credit his own lie, he did believe
He was indeed the duke
(I.ii. 100—103)

The purpose of Prospero's initiatory ordeals is to awaken in them the memory of Antonio's crimes against him and those of the other two. Ariel tells them:

But remember—
For that's my business to you, — that you three
From Milan did supplant good Prospero
(III.iii. 68—70)

He tells them that humans forget but not the divine powers:

for which foul deed
The powers, delaying, not forgetting, have
Incens'd the seas and shores, yea, all the creatures,
Against your peace.
(III.iii. 72—75).

This purpose of reviving the painful memory of guilty actions in order finally to release them into true knowledge of themselves is reaffirmed by Gonzalo at the end of the play when he claims that "all of us" have found "ourselves / When no man was his own" (V.i. 213—3).

There are other thematic references to memory and forgetfulness in the play. Ariel has to "remember" Prospero of his promise to set him free (I.ii. 43), a promise that with his many preoccupations he seems inclined to forget. Prospero makes the accusation that Ariel "dost forget" (I.ii. 250—1) the torment inflicted on him by Sycorax. As we have seen, at a critical point in the play, it is Prospero who has "forgot that foul conspiracy" against his life (IV.i. 138). Antonio dismisses Gonzalo as "this thing of weak remembrance", who will be "as of little memory" when earthed (II.i. 227—8). At the end of the play, Prospero advises Alonso not to burden his "remembrance" with things that are now past (V.i. 199—200). All these various allusions to memory and forgetfulness give this theme a special prominence in *The Tempest*. I have suggested that their significance emerges when they are related to Plato's special doctrine of *anamnesia*, the recovery of memory as a redemptive technique. This metaphor of life as a forgetting is enriched by other Platonic metaphors that are to be found in *The Tempest*. One, life as a state of sleep, has already been discussed. Another, life as a state of drunkenness, remains to be examined.

Drunken Confusion

Describing the type of person who is deeply sunk in the material realm, Plato relates in the *Phaedo* (78 C) that such a person's soul "is dragged by the body towards objects, and itself wanders in a sort of dizzy, drunken confusion." In the same dialogue (69 B—C) we are told that those who instituted the mysteries have "hinted at the truth by declaring that all such as arrive in Hades uninitiated into the rites will lie in mud, while he that comes there purified and initiated shall dwell with the gods." In the *Republic* (363 D), the uninitiated are said to lie in mud and excrement. In his journey into the Underworld, Dionysius and his servant Xanthias in Aristophanes' *The Frogs* have to pass "Great Muck Marsh and the Eternal River of Dung" where various criminals are seen floundering, on their way to the meadows where they finally see bands of initiates celebrating the rites of Eleusis.

In *The Tempest* this state of drunken confusion is exemplified by the two Clowns and Caliban. Pickled throughout the play, they too succumb to the dream of power, and wandering "in a sort of dizzy drunken confusion", they attempt to carry out their plot against Prospero. They are easily distracted from their purpose, first by Ariel's invisible music and then by the garments hung out near Prospero's cell. Their fate, as Plato and Aristophanes suggested from their knowledge of the mystery rites, was to end up in mud and excrement, wallowing in Shakespeare's equivalent of "Great Muck Marsh and the Eternal River of Dung"; they end up

> I'th'filthy-mantled pool beyond your cell,
> There dancing up to th'chins, that the foul lake
> O'erstunk their feet.
> (IV.i. 182—4).

They emerge smelling "all horse-piss" (IV.i. 199). Like the Three Men of Sin, they too receive their appropriate punishment on this otherworld island.

It was their bungled plot to seize power on the island that led to the sudden termination of the masque of the goddesses and to Prospero's own rude awakening to the limitations of his power. The effect of their low plot is to seriously impair his own high drama of redemption. In Plato's phrase, "the mystery-rites of love" are threatened with profanation. There is a parallel to this situation that Shakespeare may have had in mind. The most notorious profanation of the Eleusinian mysteries in antiquity was perpetrated by Alcibiades and his companions. For miming the rites at a drunken party in a house in Athens, Alcibiades was banished and some of his companions were put to death. It may be this sacriligious incident that Plato hints at in the *Symposium*. In its first part Socrates concludes the discusison on the nature of love by recounting what Diotima has told him. She does so "in terms borrowed from the mysteries",[43] as for example, when she says:

So far, Socrates, I have dealt with love-mysteries into which even you could probably be initiated, but whether you could grasp the perfect revelation to which they lead the pilgrim if he does not stray from the right path, I do not know. (209 E)

As in the *Phaedrus*, we have in Diotima's instructions on the mysteries of love a form of verbal initiation couched in the language of mystery-rites such as those of Eleusis. No sooner has Socrates finished giving Diotima's account than there is a loud knocking at the door and Alcibiades with some companions makes a drunken entrance. What follows is in effect a profanation of all that Socrates has been saying. Alcibiades describes his physical passion for Socrates. His revelation becomes a parody of a mystery rite. He orders the servants and "any other vulgar or uninitiated person who may be present" to "shut their ears tight against what I am going to say" (218 D). As the night wears on, those who had earlier listened to the Socratic mysteries of love become drunk. By dawn only Socrates remains on his feet. The rest have succumbed to what Pico della Mirandola and Ficino called "a vulgar, sublunar excess" as distinct from spiritual inebriation which was "a sacred state of supernatural seizure".[44]

The effect of the intrusion of the drunken Alcibiades on Socrates' revelation of the nature of spiritual love is comparable to the effect of the Three Drunkards on Prospero's majestic vision. Just as Alcibiades was accused of parading in the borrowed robes of the Hierophant of Eleusis, so Trinculo and Stephano dress up as rulers of the island, and usurp the hierophantic role of Prospero. At the end of the play, Caliban, Stephano and Trinculo stagger on stage drunk, foul-smelling, scratched and bruised. Prospero turns to Alonso and the others and says:

> Mark but the badges of these men, my lords,
> Then say if they be true.
> (V.i. 267—8)

He then goes on to list their misdemeanours. The reference to the "badges" is obscure. Kermode notes that "it is not clear what Prospero meant the gentlemen to learn from observing the badges", and suggests that there may be an ironic reference to Antonio's usurpation, "but it is not easy to see how this could be acted."[45] There is the added problem that if he is referring to

---

[43] See Introd. to Plato, *The Symposium*, ed. W. Hamilton, p. 24.
[44] Cited by Wind, *Pagan Mysteries in the Renaissance*, p. 277.
[45] Kermode, Arden *Tempest*, note to V.i.67—8.

the badges worn by servants, these would have been concealed by the stolen apparel they are wearing.

If Prospero's island is in fact related to the classical Underworld, it is possible that these badges have a special character. In Plato's *Gorgias*, it is described how the soul of a dead person appears before Rhadamanthus who judges its moral state:

Having considered this and made a mark to indicate whether he regards him as curable or incurable, he despatches him to Tartarus, where he undergoes the appropriate treatment.''[46]

The nature of this marking is described at the end of the *Republic* (614). There we are told that the Judges of the Underworld fasten "the badge" of their judgment on the front of just souls, while they order "the unjust, who carried the badges of all they had done behind them" to take the left-hand path that led downwards. Here, it would seem, is the explanatory context that is needed to make sense of Prospero's words. He is referring to the "*sphragis*" or seal attached in front of or behind the souls of the dead to indicate their moral state. A similar use of the *sphragis*, in the form of the marking of the Cross on the brow, was used in Christian initiation. In Shakespeare's period this distinguishing seal was equated with a livery badge. In Hugh Latimer's *Sermon on the Livery of Christ* (1552), there is mention of a badge of love and of evil:

so our Saviour . . . would his Servants to be known by their liveries badge, which badge is love . . . But I think the devil hath a great many more servants than Christ hath; for there be a great many more in his livery than in Christ's livery.[47]

The badge referred to by Prospero is therefore a moral badge indicating that the three servants have been untrue to their masters. In a stage production, the symbolic nature of the badges they wear should be indicated in some way, perhaps by attaching tails to their stolen apparel.

In this chapter we have investigated the possibility that Shakespeare, as Colin Still first suggested, has written a ritual drama based on the knowledge available to him of the Eleusinian mysteries. We saw that in alchemy there has been a traditional association between ritual initiation and the performance of the alchemical *opus*. We also examined the influence of Virgil's *Aeneid*, particularly Book Six, on *The Tempest*, and saw that it was given an allegorical interpretation from at least the fourth century onwards. For

---

[46] Plato, *Gorgias*, ed. W. Hamilton (Harmondsworth: Penguin Books, 1960), 526.
[47] Cited in the *Viking Portable Renaissance Reader*, ed. J. B. Ross and M. M. Mclaughlin (Harmondsworth: The Viking Press, 1953), p. 734.

Servius, "to descend into the Underworld is the same as to celebrate the rites of Proserpina"; at the same time throughout his commentary he brings out Virgil's debt to Plato. Throughout the Middle Ages down to Landino, the interpretation of the *Aeneid* as an allegory of the Platonic search for wisdom remained standard, and it was suggested that it was the allegorized *Aeneid* of Landino that was familiar to Shakespeare and is echoed in *The Tempest*. Shakespeare could also have obtained information about the Eleusinian mysteries from the mythographic manuals of the period, above all from Gyraldus' *De deis gentium* which lists the principal sources of information about the Eleusinian mysteries. The scholarly works of Casaubon, Castellanus and Meursius were also mentioned as showing the continuing interest in the pagan mysteries during the early seventeenth century. Some of the works of Plato were then examined to bring out his use of the Eleusinian mysteries to describe the progress of the soul from a state of darkness to one of enlightenment, and it was suggested that this was a major source of Shakespeare's knowledge of the ancient mysteries and that Plato's influence pervades *The Tempest*.

There is nothing remarkable in this. As Edgar Wind has conclusively shown in his *Pagan Mysteries in the Renaissance*, the mysteries of the pagan world adapted to the psychology of Plato and his followers fascinated the Renaissance and powerfully influenced its thinkers, artists and writers. Shakespeare is an illustrious and late example of this influence. Before him and paving the way was the example of Spenser in the *Faerie Queene*. As Frank Kermode has suggested in his study of the Cave of Mammon episode in the Second Book:

The marrow of a Spenserian allegory is designed to be extracted by the same enlightened method as that of an Orphic mystery, an Egyptian hieroglyph, a Renaissance emblem, or indeed an ancient epic.[48]

In the same study (pp. 164 ff.) he suggests, as Upton had done in the eighteenth century, that Guyon is undergoing the tests of an initiation rite consciously modelled by Spenser on those of Eleusis. At the same time, as Kermode points out, "Guyon undergoes, like Aeneas in the allegorized *Aeneid*, a purgatorial experience" (p. 172). In addition to the Eleusinian and Virgilian parallels, Kermode also detects a dimension of Christian allegory, relating Guyon's initiatory trials and temptations to the temptations of Christ in the Wilderness. It is also possible, I believe, that Guyon's three-day spell in Mammon's Underworld realm corresponds to the three days in which

---

[48] Frank Kermode, "The Cave of Mammon" in *Stratford-Upon-Avon Studies, 2: Elizabethan Poetry*, ed. J. R. Brown and B. Harris (London: Edward Arnold, 1960), p. 155.

Christ traditionally harrowed Hell and to the three-day-long rite of adult in-itiation in the early Church. This too was regarded, as we shall see in the next chapter, as a descent into the watery realms of death followed by a resur-rection into a new life.

Chapter IV
The Tempest and Baptism

The third main image of human regeneration to be found in *The Tempest* is derived from the rite of Christian baptism. It might be objected that surely this play does not contain imagery drawn from alchemy, the pagan mysteries and Christian initiation as well. But, as we shall see, Christian baptism was closely linked with alchemy and pagan initiation in Shakespeare's day. It has already be shown that the alchemical process was often described in terms of an initiation into the pagan mysteries. It was also seen as a form of baptism. At the same time the adult baptism of the early Church was a subject of considerable interest and controversy in the Renaissance period, and its relation to the pagan mysteries was being discussed in England at the time *The Tempest* was being written and performed.

Alchemy and Baptism

As Carl Jung has pointed out, "the alchemists did not hesitate to call the transformation process a baptism", and it was for this reason that alchemical *aqua pontica* "behaves very much like the baptismal water of the Church."[1] Some examples will illustrate this. The *Hydrolithus Sophicus, seu Aquarium Sapientum*, published by J. A. Siebacher in 1619, is a description of the alchemical work in terms of Christian regeneration. Just as "the Chemical King is regenerated through water and the Spirit and achieves his perfection," so we achieve regeneration through baptism, "washing and purifying ourselves with the blood of Christ and becoming one body with Him . . . This regeneration of the human being, effected in holy baptism through the Holy Spirit, is none other than a certain inward, spiritual renewal of a fallen person."[2] The author gives this process of alchemical regeneration an alchemical significance. The process of regeneration takes place in "the furnace of tribulation" (*fornacem tribulationis*) and, made tolerable by the solace of the Holy Spirit, will continue "until the great

---

[1] Jung, *Mysterium Coniunctionis*, pp. 235—6.
[2] J. A. Siebacher, *Hydrolithus Sophicus, seu Aquarium Sapientum* (1619), p. 121; author's translation.

universal Sabbath and the Day of Peace of the seven thousandth year is achieved, when this spiritual recreation or *refrigerium* will cease in a single moment of change . . . and in its place a joy everlasting will appear."[3] Here the achievement of the *magnum opus* is equated with the final baptism of humanity and the entry into the Millennium or Golden Age. In this identification of alchemy and baptism, the alchemists were aided by the fact that traditionally Christian baptism involved a symbolic immersion in the salt sea. The waters of the baptismal font or bath was the sea of the world. *Mare saeculum est*, said St Augustine, the sea is the world subject to the devil. "By the depths of the sea is meant the seat of hell," wrote St Hilary.[4] When the candidate entered the baptismal bath it was in simulation of the three-day descent of Christ into Hell; the candidate also entered hell, died there and was reborn. A typological figure of baptism was the crossing of the Red Sea. "The Red Sea signifies baptism," said St Augustine.[5] This figure too was seized on by the alchemists:

And know that our Red Sea is more tincturing than all seas, and that the poison when it is cooked and becomes foul and discoloured, penetrates all bodies.[6]

The affinity found by alchemists between the stages of the alchemical work and the rite of baptism made it possible, I believe, for Shakespeare to combine both images at the beginning of *The Tempest*. The plunging of the castaways into the salt sea, the suffering of a "sea-change" in the depths and the effect of the brine on their clothes, are both alchemical and baptismal phenomena. When Ferdinand exclaims:

> Hell is empty,
> And all the devils are here.
> (I.ii. 214—5)

he implies that the raging sea has become a species of hell; in St Augustine's words on baptism: "The water leads him down, as if dying, into the grave; the Holy Spirit brings him up, as if rising again, into heaven."[7] This recalls the theme of descent into the waters of death found in alchemical descriptions of the stage of *mortificatio*. In the *Visio Arislei*, another King's Son is depicted as lying as a corpse at the bottom of the sea while those who tend him are exposed to every kind of terror.[8]

---

[3] Siebacher, p. 131.
[4] Jung, *Mysterium Coniunctionis*, p. 198.
[5] Jung, p. 199.
[6] Jung, p. 201, citing *Rosinus ad Euthiciam* in the collection *Artis Auriferae* (1593).
[7] Jung, p. 237.
[8] Jung, p. 292, referring to *Aenigmata ex visione Arislei* in *Artis Auriferae* (1593).

74

The theme of descent and ascent, death and rebirth, common to both alchemy and Christian baptism, is also found in the pagan mysteries. Those of Eleusis are believed to have included a reenactment of the descent of Proserpina, performed by the candidate, into the cave of the Ploutonion. The descent of Dionysus into the Underworld in *The Frogs* of Aristophanes is also closely associated with the rites of Eleusis,[9] and as we saw the descent of Aeneas in Book Six of the *Aeneid* was also equated by Servius with a celebration of the rites of Proserpina. Something of what happened at Eleusis is conveyed by Plutarch's description:

First labyrinthine turnings and arduous gropings, various unsuccessful and perilous passages in the darkness. Then, before the rite itself, all manners of terrors, shuddering and trembling, silence and terrified amazement. After this a wonderful light bursts forth, friendly landscapes and meadows receive us, voices and dances and the splendour of sacred songs are disclosed to us.[10]

The sequence, which is also followed in Book Six of the *Aeneid*, is initial labyrinthine wanderings, an experience of amazement and terror, followed by a vision of light. The same basic pattern is followed in *The Tempest*. There are the initial maze-like wanderings of the King's Party, followed by the experience of amazement and terror when Ariel appears as the Harpy at the end of Act III. Finally there is the culminating "vision" in Act V when Miranda and Ferdinand are revealed to the castaways.

This same initiatory pattern is also found in the elaborate ritual of initiation for adults that was developed during the early centuries of the Christian Church, and which was strongly influenced by the pagan rites of initiation, particularly those of Eleusis. This too began with a journey, typologically related to the journey of the Israelites through the Wilderness towards the Promised Land, lasting throughout the forty days of Lent. After the journey came the equivalent of Plutarch's "terrified amazement", the rite of baptism in which the Christian candidate entered Hell and underwent a symbolic death of the old Adam. The third stage, corresponding to the vision of light of the pagan mysteries, was marked by the entry of the new Christian into the church building to participate in the Feast of the Eucharist. He then became "a holy initiate", took part in the "truly sacred mysteries", and saw

---

[9] In *The Frogs* of Aristophanes, Dionysus, after passing Great Muck marsh and the Eternal Rivers of Dung where sinners wallow, comes to Elysium where he sees the Chorus of Initiates celebrating the rites of Persephone.

[10] Fragment of Plutarch in Stobaeus, *Anthologia*, IV, p. 107, cited in *The Mysteries*, Bollingen Series XX, p. 351.

the "pure light", as Clement of Alexandria wrote in language borrowed directly from the pagan mysteries.[12] These three stages correspond to what Dionysius the Areopagite, also echoing the language of the pagan mysteries, called *catharsis*, the stage of preparatory purgation, *muesis*, initiation by baptism, and *teleiosis* or *epoptia*, full participation in the mysteries of the Church.

Is it conceivable that Shakespeare could have referred to this ancient Christian rite in *The Tempest*? First of all, it can be pointed out that the matter of adult versus infant baptism had become a burning issue in the sixteenth century. It was above all the Anabaptists who from 1525 onwards had revived the practise of adult baptism as used in the early Church.[12] By the middle of the sixteenth century their ideas had been carried to England by the sect known as the Family of Love or Familists founded by Hendrik Niclaes.[13] After being banned by Elizabeth I in 1580, the Family of Love did not attract attention until the early years of James's reign. Thomas Middleton attacked them on stage in his *The Family of Love* (1608), and two years later Jonson satirized them in *The Alchemist* as the "the holy brethren of Amsterdam" (II.iv. 29—30) and as followers of "Harry Nicholas" (V.v. 117). The real "company of the separation" as Jonson calls them (IV.vii. 85) was the Second Church of the Separation founded by John Smyth.[14] Adult baptism was practised by this sect. In 1611 under the leadership of Thomas Helwys,[15] the Brethren returned to England and established the first Baptist Church at Pinners's Hall in London.[16]

In the year then that Shakespeare wrote *The Tempest* there had appeared in London the first Baptist Church openly advocating a return to the ancient rite of adult baptism. The same subject was also being discussed at a more learned level at James's Court during the same period.

As was mentioned in the previous chapter, the great classical scholar, Isaac Casaubon finally accepted in late 1610 the invitation of James I to settle in England after the assassination of Henry IV. He arrived in London in October, 1610, and was granted a pension by the King. In return Casaubon was to write a refutation of the official Catholic Church history written by

[11] Cited by Hugo Rahner in *The Mysteries*, p. 355.
[12] For a full account of this movement, see Claus-Peter Clasen, *Anabaptism: A Social History 1525—1618* (Ithaca: Cornell Univ. Press, 1972).
[13] A detailed study of the Family of Love in England has been made by Jean Dietz Moss in *"Godded with God": Henrik Niclaes and His Family of Love* (Philadelphia: The American Philosophical Society, 1981).
[14] See *D.N.B.*, under Smyth, John.
[15] See *D.N.B.*, under "Helwys, Thomas."
[16] See *D.N.B.*, under "Helwys, Thomas."

Baronius, and demonstrate that Protestantism was the true successor of the Christian Church before it had been corrupted by the papacy. As we learn from a letter written at this time, Casaubon had been collecting material for his refutation of Baronius for over a decade.[17] Throughout 1611, Casaubon became something of a favourite with James, and was in attendance "every Sunday, sometimes also on weekdays, and these were not audiences, but attendances prolonged for hours" (p. 304). He noted in his diary for September 19th, 1611: *gravia cum rege de rebus variis habui colloquia* (p. 304). These serious discussions with the King on a variety of topics in all probability included his forthcoming work on Church history. Kept busy by the King, Casaubon did not start work on his *Exercitationes de rebus sacris et ecclesiasticis* until January 1612, two and a half months after the first performance of *The Tempest*. By December 1612, sections of the work were in circulation (p. 374). In the same month, Casaubon's friend, Abraham Scultetus, chaplain to the Elector Palatine and in London for the royal wedding, told Casaubon that a plagiarist was about to print a version of his *Exercitationes*. The work of plagiarism was quickly suppressed. It seems that "Casaubon had talked unreservedly of the plan and topics of his book", and that it contents were well known (p. 375). The book was finally completed in April 1613, and printed in March, 1614. Exhausted by the effort, Casaubon died four months later.

The *Exercitationes*, over 800 pages long and with quotations from over 300 authors, was not an unqualified success. It lacked the vituperation customary in polemical works of the period. It is dry and scholarly. And yet it is quietly impressive. It is perhaps best remembered for the section in which Casaubon demonstrated that the Hermetic corpus so prized in the Renaissance for its high antiquity had in fact been compiled in the early Christian era. Mark Pattison, his biographer, has paid tribute to Casaubon's lasting contribution to the history of the Eucharist contained in the *Exercitationes* (p. 352). This work has another possible interest. Chapter 43 is devoted to a detailed comparison of the pagan mysteries and the rite of adult baptism as practised in the early Church. I would like to paraphrase this chapter so as to provide a glimpse of the sort of matters that James I delighted in discussing close to the time *The Tempest* was first presented at Court.

Casaubon begins this chapter by showing how the Church had borrowed the terminology of the pagan mysteries in order to describe its own rites. "It certainly ought to be known that when the first Christians called the

---

[17] Mark Pattison, *Isaac Casaubon* (1875), p. 402. The following page references in the text are to this work.

sacraments *mysteria, teletai* or *mystagogia*, they were borrowing these terms from the rites of the pagans that the Greeks called *mysteria* and the Latins *mysteria* or *initia*."[18] In borrowing these terms the Christians gave them a heightened significance and as in St Paul's case it made it easier to proselytize among the Greeks, but Casaubon wonders "whether this strategy, while useful at the time, was not afterwards harmful to truth . . . Certainly there were great men in the early Church who lamented the introduction of pagan rites into the Church", and he cites St Augustine and Tertullian in evidence (p. 545). He then goes on to document these borrowings from the pagan mysteries in more detail.

He mentions the pagan mysteries that existed in the ancient world: the rites of the Great Mother at Samothrace, of Hecate, of Ceres and Proserpina at Eleusis in Attica, of Bacchus, Mithras and Orpheus, and of Isis in Egypt. The rites are of two sorts, the greater and lesser, the lesser being preparations for participation in the greater mysteries. The goal or end of these rites was to restore the soul to the state it enjoyed before it descended into the body. He cites Olympiodorus' commentary on Plato's *Phaedo* concerning this goal, and suggests that it is none other than the state of perfection from which we fell in the old Adam and to which we are restored in the new Adam (p. 546). The goal of the pagan mysteries was to ensure that initiates after death would dwell with the gods, while non-initiates would wallow in filth and mud. Citing pagan authors, Casaubon states that originally the mysteries were instituted to improve human behaviour and correct men's lives. Participation in the mysteries was also said to confer certainty about a future life after death. He cites Cicero and Sophocles on this point. According to the Platonic philosophers, the goal of the mysteries was to make a man resemble God, even become God. Those who submitted to the discipline of the mysteries would be gradually purged of the pollutions of this life and the stain of sin, and passing through certain degrees of initiation at set intervals of time, they "would be led to the perception and knowledge of I know not what portentous secrets". He again cites Olympiodorus' commentary on Plato's *Phaedo*:

In the rites public purgations take place first; after these there follow others more secret; after these come the 'aggregationes'; then succeed the initiations; last of all are the *epoptia* (p. 547).

The *epoptia*, involving the faculty of sight, represented full participation in the rites, and there was nothing higher than the degree of *epopt*. According

---

[18] Isaac Casaubon, *Exercitationes de rebus sacris et ecclesiasticis* (1614), p. 544; author's translation and paraphrase here and in what follows. Page references in the text are to this work.

to Tertullian, a person taking part in the Eleusinian mysteries became an *epopt* within five years, and Casaubon suggests that the five degrees of initiation mentioned by Olympiodorus took place within this five-year period.

Casaubon goes on to trace resemblances between the pagan mysteries and Christian initiation. In some pagan rites water was used in a form of baptism. In others the symbols of bread and water were used, but not wine as in the Christian sacrament. Confession of sins was also required for admission to the pagan mysteries, as well as purity of motive, acts of self-denial, abstention from certain foods, and a vow to remain silent concerning the nature of the mysteries. Casaubon cites the story from Livy of the two uninitiated Athenian youths who were put to death for having sacriligiously entered the precincts of Eleusis with a crowd of mystae. He completes this section with the statement that he has discussed these features of the pagan mysteries "to the extent that they have some affinity with the sacred institutions of Christian religion" (p. 550).

The motive of the Church Fathers in adopting some of these features of the pagan mysteries was, according to Casaubon, "the more easily to lead minds corrupted by superstition back to the love of truth" (p. 550). It was for this reason that they called the Church rites *mysteria*. Baptism was time and again called a mystery by the Fathers, and so too was the Feast of the Eucharist. Similarly, the degrees of initiation in the pagan mysteries find their equivalent in the three degrees given by Dionysius the Areopagite in Christian initiation: *catharsis* or purgation, *muesis* or initiation, and *teleisosis* or *epoptia*, corresponding to full entry into the Church. To be a Christian epopt or full initiate amounted to becoming perfect through a knowledge of divine things and through an understanding of the sacraments, a perfection of the sort obtainable in this life, where we see through a glass darkly. "Therefore the *epoptia* of Christians should be considered a great felicity; not like those related by the lying Greeks . . . who believed the *epopts* to be the most blessed of men" (p. 550). Concerning the period of time it took to become a full initiate in the pagan mysteries, Casaubon finds certain parallels in Christianity. A shorter period than five years was required for those entering the Church for the first time, but even here stages of initiation were observed. There was an initial period of discipline. First there were the catechumens, then the *competentes* (those who had been baptized but did not fully participate in the sacraments), and finally the *fideles* who were fully initiated. The return of lapsed Christians to the Church took place in five stages as in pagan initiations and could extend to a period of ten years. It should be mentioned that Casaubon, here and throughout this chapter has adult baptism into the Church in mind, as the sources he cites make clear.

There were other similarities between the initiatory rite of adult baptism in the early Church and pagan initiation rites. "Just as those who were eventually to be created *epopts* after five years were taught to look forward with great desire to the time of the *epoptia*, or final ceremonies of initiation . . . so the catechumens were taught to seek communion with great longing" (p. 554). Until they were baptized the catechumens were not considered to be Christian, and could not take part in the liturgy of the Church. The formula of the pagan mysteries 'Procul este profani', (let the profane depart), was taken over by Christianity in the formula: 'omnes Catechumeni, foras discedite, omnes possessi, omnes non initiati' (let all catechumens, all possessed by evil spirits, all the uninitiated, depart). Similarly the silence observed by pagans concerning their mysteries was also strictly observed by Christians concerning theirs. This silence had to do with the arcana or secrets of the mysteries that were revealed to pagan and Christian initiates alike. Citing Cyril of Jerusalem, (whose *Catecheses* gives one of the fullest accounts of the early rite of adult baptism) Casaubon writes that the catechumens not yet qualified to know the sacred mysteries "hear a voice outside them", but after they have joined the faithful through baptism they are "taught inwardly" (p. 557).

Casaubon now embarks on a long discussion about the nature of the secrets that were guarded so closely in both the pagan and Christian mysteries. He quotes Dionysius the Areopagite on baptism: "Let us contemplate the sacred symbols of baptism one after the other; no-one who is not initiated can approach this spectacle" (p. 561). In his *Catechesis*, Chrysostomus remarks that the ceremonies of baptism "have a certain mystical meaning which should not be revealed in words" (p. 561). And yet such desirable reticence, Casaubon notes in one of his rare personal appearances, is no longer observed by certain modern theologians who consider themselves to be failing in their duty "if they do not expose certain profound secrets concerning divine wisdom before the lowest dregs of humanity. Thus it is common for questions concerning predestination, eternal damnation and other mysteries to be raised among the semi-literate and artisans sitting in their workshops" (p. 564). Casaubon proceeds to discuss the reasons for this silence, or for the obscurity of the language used by Dionysius the Areopagite when he speaks of the Christian mysteries. With this reference to the deliberate obfuscation of style of Dionysius, that favourite author of the Renaissance Platonists, Casaubon completes his survey of the relationship between the pagan mysteries and the rites of early Christianity. In the second of two brief appendices to the chapter, he shows that his friend, Scaliger, was correct in understanding the term *desiderata* to be a synonym for the pagan *epoptia* and for Christian initiation, and cites a passage from Tertullian on the Eleusinian mysteries in support.

Desiderata, therefore, meant "initiation into Christianity, that is, baptism". A little later Casaubon adds that baptism "was the principal initiation for Christians" (p. 568).

I have given this rather full summary of this chapter in Casaubon's *Exercitationes* to show the sort of scholarly interest that was being taken in both the pagan mysteries and Christian initiation at about the time *The Tempest* was produced at Court. It is not necessary to assume that Shakespeare, clad in the King's livery, had eavesdropped on the conversations that took place between James, Casaubon, his learned friend, Bishop Andrewes and other divines throughout 1611, and then went off to write a play on the theme of ritual initiation. At the same time, as the King's Servant bound to provide for the King's "Solace and pleasure when wee shall thincke good to see them duringe our pleasure", as the Licence to the King's Men of 1603 words it, Shakespeare seems to have taken care to reflect James's interests in at least some of the plays written after 1603. *Macbeth* clearly reflects James's obsessive interest in the supernatural, and as Arthur Melville Clark has suggested in his *Murder Under Trust: The Topical Macbeth*, may have been written at James's instigation. A similar striving to reflect James's particular interests has also been detected in *Measure for Measure*.[19] As I shall try and show, the final group of plays written by Shakespeare, *Cymbeline, The Winter's Tale, The Tempest* and *Henry VIII*, also reflect some of James's preoccupations of the time. The extent to which Shakespeare was a royal playwright, even *the* royal playwright, has not, I believe, been fully appreciated. The earliest known performances of *The Tempest* were both at Court, and it is reasonable to assume that it was written as royal entertainment. At the first performance James was present, and as I have been suggesting, there is much in the play that would have been of particular interest to him. When on November 1st, 1611, James saw *The Tempest* for the first time, after all his discussions with Casaubon, he should have had no difficulty in detecting the allusions to both the pagan mysteries and to the Christian mysteries of baptism with which they were so closely related. We have already seen how the opening scenes of the play can be interpreted both in terms of the pagan mysteries and of Christian initiation. Is there anything else in the play that specifically alludes to the rite of adult baptism?

One of the works consulted by Casaubon in preparing for the writing of the *Exercitationes* was the *Catecheses* of Cyril of Jerusalem, compiled in the 4th century A.D. A Latin edition of this work was published in 1560, and

---

[19] See Josephine Waters Bennett, *Measure for Measure as Royal Entertainment* (New York and London: Columbia Univ. Press, 1966).

reissued in 1564 and 1608. Casaubon's own copy, extensively annotated by him and used while writing the *Exercitationes*, remained in England and was consulted in 1703 by Thomas Milles in his authoritative edition of the *Catecheses*.[20] Cyril's work was compiled as instructions for adults wishing to be baptized into the Church, and is one of the fullest descriptions of this rite that has survived.

According to Cyril, the candidate for baptism enrolled his name at the church at the commencement of the forty days of Lent, and if found acceptable he then underwent a strenuous period of preparation which included seclusion from society, fasting, prayer and instruction. This period was compared typologically to the forty days spent by Christ in the Wilderness and the forty years spent by the Israelites wandering in the Wilderness before their entry into the Promised Land. During this period, the candidate or catechumen is under constant attack from the devil who tempts him to fall back into the old ways of sin and to succumb to doubt and despair. During this symbolic Journey through the Wilderness, the catechumen is to become mindful of the sinful Life he has led. This period of the catechumenate corresponds as we have suggested to the wanderings of the King's Party on the island up to the end of Act III. It is the stage of what Dionysius the Areopagite, echoing the language of the pagan mysteries, called Catharsis or purgation. Lost in the maze of the island, the castaways endure hunger and fatigue. In Alonso we witness the onset of despair. This despair is exacerbated on every occasion by Antonio and his willing tool, Sebastian, while Gonzalo does all in his power to keep the King's hope alive. We witness here a psychomachia with Gonzalo on one side and Antonio and Sebastian on the other, comparable to the struggle for the soul of the catechumen that takes place between the guiding priest and the devil during the forty days of Lent. As Dionysius relates it is the sponsor of the candidate for baptism "who acts as his guide and undertakes the supervision of his instruction in all that concerns his future life".[21] It is he who acts "as the unerring guide along the paths that God has traced out".[22] This, I would suggest, is Gonzalo's role in the play. He is Alonso's spiritual guide ever seeking to draw Alonso's attention to the positive signs in their experience on the island that their tribulations have a purpose. He draws attention to the change in the glosses of their clothes, to the parallels with what happened to Aeneas after

[20] See *Cyrille de Jerusalem: Catéchèses Mystagogiques*, ed. A. Piédagnel, pp. 41 ff.
[21] *Dionysius the Pseudo-Areopagite: The Ecclestiastical Hierarchy*, in *The Catholic University of America Studies in Sacred Theology*, Ser. 2, No. 83 (Washington, 1955), ed. Rev. T. L. Campbell, p. 29, n. 37.
[22] *Dionysius the Pseudo-Areopagite*, 2:5.

he had left Dido in Carthage. He points out how "advantageous to life" the island is, and "How lush and lusty the grass looks! How green!" (II.i. 48, 51), even as Antonio and Sebastian find it only barren and desert-like. In the same scene, he evokes a vision of a new Golden Age. Is it fanciful to suggest that Shakespeare may have known of the traditional interpretation of Psalm 23 as an allegory of baptism in all its stages? Cyril of Jerusalem interpreted the "green pastures" of this psalm as the evergreen words of the Scriptures, and as the place of greenness which is Paradise "from which we have fallen and to which Christ leads us and establishes us there . . . through the waters of peace, that is, baptism".[23] Expounding the words of verse 5, "Thou preparest a table before me in the presence of mine enemies", Cyril comments:

Before Thy coming, evil spirits prepared a table for men, foul and polluted and full of devilish influence.[24]

The table of verse 5 is contrasted with the table of the Eucharistic Feast to which the candidate is finally admitted after baptism. It is the same table of earthly temptation that is spread before the Three Men of Sin, associated by Shakespeare, as we have seen with the banquet spread before Tantalus in the Underworld. We find these Christian and pagan associations daringly united in Milton's rendering of the temptation of Christ in the Wilderness in *Paradise Regained* (ll. 401—3):

> With that
> Both Table and Provisions vanish'd quite
> With sound of Harpies wings, and Talons heard.

As we saw the temptations of Christ in the Wilderness was regarded traditionally as a type of baptism in all its stages.

All Gonzalo's attempts to "instruct" Alonso are frustrated by the King's own refusal to listen and by the incessant gibes of Antonio and Sebastian. At one point Sebastian remarks about Gonzalo's cryptic references to their new-dyed clothes: "No; he doth but mistake the truth totally" (II.i. 55). Who are we to believe: Gonzalo or his facetious adversaries? This question is central to an understanding of The Tempest. If Gonzalo is regarded as a somewhat foolish, old man, a kindly version of Polonius, who through his garrulity "certainly facilitates the work of the wicked",[25] by commit-

---

[23] *St Cyril of Jerusalem's Lectures on the Christian Sacraments*, ed. F. L. Cross (London, S.P.C.K., 1951), p. 69.
[24] *St Cyril of Jerusalem's Lectures*, p. 247.
[25] Arden *Tempest*, note to II.i. 78.

ting three errors of fact, then we accept the evaluation placed on him by Antonio and Sebastian: he "mistakes the truth totally". His cryptic remarks become no longer indications of a hidden significance of their experiences on the island, but clear signs of senility. Again, we ask, who is mistaking the truth totally? We have already explained one of Gonzalo's so-called slips. In the early seventeenth century the sites of Carthage and Tunis were believed to be the same, and even if Shakesepare had carried out archaeological digs in North Africa and found that they occupied different sites, it would not affect the allegorical significance of the equation of the two cities. His other mistake concerns his statement that in the Golden Age commonwealth of which he would be King, there would be "No sovereignty" (II.i. 152). In Saturn's Golden Age that Gonzalo would excel there is no enforcement of law. As Gonzalo explains such a king in such a realm would rule "by contraries", that is, by the negation of those conditions which in the ages succeding the Age of Gold made law necessary. The contradiction detected by Antonio and Sebastian becomes a paradox. In the Age of Saturn, the King was no King. As Ovid describes the Golden Age at the opening of the *Metamorphoses*, "sua sponte, sine lege, fidem rectumque colebant"— human beings practised good faith and justice, of their own accord, without laws. Concerning Gonzalo's third slip, he is guiltless, for he is not "wrong about the survival of Ferdinand".[26] He correctly tells the King that "he is, sure, i'th'island" (II.i. 320). It is Antonio and Sebastian who are wrong (II.i. 127, 231—3).

Gonzalo can only be seen as a foolish old man if we view him through the eyes of Antonio and Sebastian. If we see him as Prospero sees him, he appears in a different light. He is that "noble Neapolitan" who helped him when he and Miranda were driven into exile (I.ii. 161). In the final act of the play, he becomes for Prospero "Holy Gonzalo, honourable man" (V.i. 62) and he refers to him as

> O good Gonzalo,
> My true preserver, and a loyal sir
> To him thou follow'st
> (V.i. 68—70)

Such praise cannot be squared with a view of Gonzalo as simple-minded and as prating "amply and unnecessarily" (II.i. 259). It is called forth by Gonzalo's good offices both to Prospero and Alonso. In the case of Alonso, Gonzalo has acted as a spiritual mentor to him, comparable as I suggested to

---

[26] Arden *Tempest*, p. xxxviii.

the guide mentioned by Dionysius the Areopagite who leads the candidate for baptism "along the paths that God has traced out". This recalls the path through the Wilderness mentioned in *Isaiah*, 43:19: "I shall trace a way in the wilderness, a path in the arid waters". As Jean Daniélou has shown, these words were traditionally applied to the journey of the catechumen during Lent towards the experience of baptism.[27] They correspond to verse 5 of Psalm 23: "Even though I walk through the valley of the shadow of death".[28] In his commentary on Psalm 23, translated into English in 1571, Calvin paraphrased verse 5 in the following way: "God did but (as it were under a dark shadow . . . chalk out . . . the kingdome of his sonne".[29] In the final act of *The Tempest* Gonzalo prays that

> some heavenly power guide us
> Out of this fearful country
> (V.i. 105—6)

and when their wanderings come to an end with the revelation of Ferdinand and Miranda, he thanks the heavenly powers:

> Look down, you gods,
> And on this couple drop a blessed crown!
> For it is you that have chalk'd forth the way
> Which brought us hither.
> (V.i.201—204)

Shakespeare's use of the word 'chalk'd' with its chime of associations serves to remind us of the symbolic journey of the Israelites through the Wilderness towards the Promised Land and of the parallel journey of the catechumen during Lent towards the font of baptism.

It was a journey full of danger. In his *Catecheses*, Cyril of Jerusalem tells the catechumen:

Armed with these words, be alert. For our adversary the devil, as has just been said, roams as a lion, seeking someone to devour.[30]

Cyril is echoing the words in I Peter 5:8:

Awake! Be on the alert! Your enemy, like a roaring lion, prowls around looking for someone to devour.

---

[27] Jean Daniélou, *Bible et Liturgie* (Paris, 1951), p. 121.
[28] See Daniélou, *Bible et Liturgie*, Ch. II, pp. 240—258, for an account of the baptismal interpretation of Psalm 23.
[29] This example is cited in *N.E.D.* under "chalk." Two other examples are given from the seventeenth century: "Let your steps be sticht to wisdom's chalking", and "that way to eternal glory, which our Saviour hath chalked out."
[30] These words from I Peter 5:8—14 are cited by Cyril of Jerusalem in his *Catecheses* (ed. F. L. Cross), p. 53.

Typologically this satanic lion lurking to seize the unwary catechumen goes back to verses 11—13 of that psalm of tribulation, Psalm 22:

Be not far from me, for trouble is near; for there is none to help. Many bulls have compassed me: strong bulls of Bashan have beset me round. They gaped upon me with their mouths, as a ravining and a roaring lion.

This somewhat strange comparison of the bulls of Bashan to a ravening and roaring lion seems to have struck Shakespeare. If we regard Alonso as a catechumen undergoing the tests and preparations preceding baptism, the fact that he falls asleep in Act II, Scene i, indicates that he is spiritually in great danger. Antonio and Sebastian plot his death, but are forestalled by Ariel. Apparently echoing Cyril's words: 'Awake! Be on the alert!', Ariel sings:

Shake off slumber and be aware,
Awake, awake.
(II.i. 337—8)

and the sleepers awake to see Antonio and Sebastian standing over them with drawn weapons. In any baptismal allegory, they should represent the prowling satanic lion of Cyril and Peter, and the bulls of Bashan that resemble the lion of Psalm 22, and we would expect Shakespeare to indicate this. I believe he does so in the curious explanation that Sebastian and Antonio give for standing there with drawn weapons. Sebastian says:

Whiles we stood here securing your repose,
Even now, we heard a hollow burst of bellowing
Like bulls, or rather lions.
(II.i. 305—7)

and Antonio adds:

sure, it was the roar
Of a whole herd of lions.
(II.i. 310—331)

The "bulls, or rather lions", recall the bulls of Bashan that are likened to a ravening and roaring lion in Psalm 22, and that stand for the spiritual dangers that ever threaten the unvigilant catechumen. Sebastian but above all Antonio are the living representatives of these dangers.[31]

The journey of the catechumen culminated on the eve of Easter Sunday

[31] This allusion to Psalm 22 is also referred to by Kermode in the Arden *Tempest* in his note to II.i. 306—7. In a sixteenth-century allegorical interpretation of the legend of Jason and the Golden Fleece that will be mentioned in Ch. VII the roaring of the bulls of Colchis stands for the roaring of alchemical furnaces.

when he underwent the rite of baptism. Three times the candidate is immersed in the baptismal bath in emulation of the three days in which Christ harrowed hell. "By this action you are dead and you are reborn".[32] Cyril of Jerusalem speaks of the candidate entering the floods of Hades which are both a sepulchre and a mother.[33] In the waters of the baptismal bath there occurs the death of the old man "which is corrupt according to the deceitful lusts", and a birth of the new man sharing "the fashion of Christ's glory."[34] This death and rebirth was symbolized by the removal of the old clothes and the putting on of new white robes. Its symbolic significance is indicated by Cyril of Jerusalem: "thou must be continually robed in light; we mean not this, that thou must always wear white raiments; but with truly white and glistering and spiritual apparel, thou must be clothed withal."[35] We have already seen how Gonzalo's repeated cryptic references to the new-dyeing of their clothes can be given an alchemical interpretation. But because of the widespread use by alchemists of baptism as a symbol of transmutation, Gonzalo's references could also have a baptismal meaning. We saw that in the early ceremony of adult baptism the old clothes were discarded and new white robes put on after immersion. But Gonzalo speaks of the same clothes being cleansed after immersion in salt water. The precise source of this image is to be found in Revelation, 7:14:

These are they which came out of great tribulation, and have washed their robes, and made them white in the blood of the Lamb.

This passage is applied to baptism in the following passage from John Jewel's *A Treatise of the Sacraments* in the section "Of Baptism":

Through the power of God's working the water of the baptismal font is turned into blood. They that be washed in it receive the remission of their sins. Their robes are made clean in the blood of the Lamb.[36]

This exactly parallels Gonzalo's image of the washed clothes, and Ariel's reference to "the sustaining clothes" of the castaways that have "not a blemish, / but fresher than before." Immediately before this Ariel has just said of the castaways: "Not a hair perish'd," providing a further biblical context for the image of the new-dyed clothes. In Acts 27, Paul gives an account of his voyage to Rome during which "they were exceedingly tossed with a

---

[32] Daniélou, *Bible et Liturgie*, p. 62.
[33] Daniélou, p. 67.
[34] *Catecheses*, ed. F. L. Cross, pp. 59 and 63.
[35] *Catecheses*, p. 70.
[36] John Jewel, *A Treatise of the Sacraments* in *Works of John Jewel*, published by the Parker Society, 2 (18), 1106.

tempest", and "all hope that we should be saved was then taken away". But Paul assures those on board that there will be "no loss of any man's life among you". He tells them to "be of good cheer", but that they "must be cast upon a certain island". He comforts them by saying "there shall not an hair fall from the head of any of you". The Rheims Bible renders these last words: "there shal not an heare of the head perish of any of you."[37] The same allusion to Paul's escape from the tempest is present in Prospero's earlier assurance to Miranda:

> there is no soul—
> No, not so much perdition as a hair
> Betid to any creature in the vessel
> (I.ii. 29—31)

Just as the "two hundred threescore and sixteen souls" on Paul's ship are saved, so too are all the "fraughting souls" (I.ii. 13) aboard the King's ship. The contextual allusions in these passages tell us that they are aboard the traditional Christian "ship of baptism."[38]

We can pause a moment to consider the word "sustaining" in the phrase "sustaining garments." As Kermode notes, "editors have discussed at length the propriety of this epithet."[39] It has been pointed out that their billowing clothes would have hastened the death of the courtiers rather than helped them to safety. One commentator has suggested the emendation of "sustaining" to "sea-stained."[40] But if we treat *The Tempest* as a continuous allegory, the incongruity of the word "sustaining" invites us to seek a figurative meaning for it, just as we are invited to do by Gonzalo's words: 'Is not, sir, my doublet as fresh as the first day I wore it? I mean, in a sort" (II.i. 98—9). Similarly the clothes are "sustaining" in a figurative sense, or "in a sort". The clue to this figurative sense is provided by the allusion to Paul's shipwreck. The courtiers are "sustained" in the sense of being spiritually saved. Here, as throughout the play, the function of such textual incongruities is to impose a choice between the incongruous literal meaning and a congruous figurative one.

To return to Gonzalo's pointed references to the new-dyed clothes, they can be seen as an attempt to instruct Alonso in the hidden significance of

---

[37] This parallel is noted by Kermode in the Arden *Temepst*, note to I.ii. 217.

[38] For a discussion of the figure of "the mystical voyage of baptism", see Per Lundberg, *La Typologie baptismale* in *Acta Seminarii Neotestmentaci Upsaliensis*, ed. A. Fridrichson, X (Leipzig and Uppsala, 1942).

[39] Arden *Tempest*, note to I.ii. 218.

[40] See New Variorum *Tempest*, note to I.ii.256.

88

his experience on the purgatorial island. But the King does not listen, and so his descent into the cleansing baptismal floods of Hades continues, to culminate in a species of psychological death when he and his companions become distracted at the end of Act III. Their situation as they endure their induced madness throughout Act IV can be compared to that of the souls imprisoned in Hell waiting for Christ to release them during His Harrowing of Hell. Their state is sonorously captured in the words of the ancient Roman liturgy in a prayer for release:

O oriens, splendor lucis aeternae et sol iustitiae, veni ad illuminandos sedentes in tenebris et umbra mortis.
(O rising dawn, splendour of eternal light and sun of justice, come to those seeking illumination seated in the shadow and darkness of death).

Much of what has already been said about the alchemical *mortificatio* of the Three Men of Sin lends itself without difficulty to interpretation in terms of the Pauline teaching that baptism involves a death to sin and a death of the old Adam. Reminded of their sins, the Three Men of Sin enter into a death-like state of coma which lasts until they are finally released by Prospero. We have also examined this restoration to life in terms of alchemy, but the imagery of dawning light as Prospero describes the dissolving of the charm was as we saw universal in character and is found in alchemy, in the pagan mysteries and not least in Christianity. The splendour of eternal light and the sun of justice "scatters the darkness of the baptismal tomb". In Cyril of Jerusalem's words, the newly baptized are "led by the hand into the luminous and perfumed meadow of this paradise", words that evoke not only the brightly lit church that they now enter for the first time in their white robes and bearing torches, but also the analogous meadows of Elysium that Aeneas finally reaches and the plains of Rarium at Eleusis. The waters of the baptismal font into which the Paschal candle is plunged to symbolize the entry into the waters of the purgative and restorative Holy Spirit has achieved its work. Ariel has "flam'd amazement" on them; they have endured the wilderness of the island and suffered madness; finally they discover at the heart of the island a paradise.

Just as some rite of sacred marriage between Proserpina and her consort was witnessed during the rites of Eleusis, and just as the climax of the alchemical work was often signified by the marriage of the *sponsus* and *sponsa*, so too the rite of Christian baptism culminated in a marriage of the soul of the new Christian with Christ. Cyril of Jerusalem writes:

And wilt thou not then, when on the eve of consecrating thy soul to a heavenly spouse, let go carnal things that thou may take hold of things spiritual?[41]

---

[41] *St Cyril of Jerusalem's Lectures*, p. 44.

The torches borne by the catechumens as they enter the baptistery are called by Cyril "the torches of the bridal train,"[42] while the Feast of the Eucharist that followed was regarded as a marriage feast. In *The Tempest* the betrothal of Miranda and Ferdinand is conveyed in the imagery of alchemical union and of the sacred marriage of the pagan mysteries. But it also suggests the spiritual marriage that was the climax of the Christian rite of adult baptism.

In the symbolism of the early Church, the spiritual marriage of the individual through baptism was regarded as a foreshadowing of the final baptism of all humanity in the Last Days to be followed by the marriage feast of the Millennium.[43] In the same way, the betrothal of Miranda and Ferdinand can be understood in this wider millenial sense as an anticipation of the new dispensation to be established in Italy after their return, already foreshadowed in Gonzalo's description of the second Golden Age. As harbingers of a brave new world, Miranda and Ferdinand find their living counterparts in Elizabeth Stuart and Frederick the Elector Palatine. As we shall now see, they too were regarded as the harbingers of a new dispensation on earth.

---

[42] For a discussion of the marriage symbolism of baptism and its eschatological significance, see Daniélou, *Bible et Liturgie*, pp. 260—280.

Chapter V
Miranda Sextae Aetatis

From the time of the Church Fathers onwards the ritual of initiation at Easter was regarded as a foreshadowing of the baptism of humanity as a whole during the Last Days. The journey of the catechumen through the wilderness enacted in Lent was symbolic of the journey of mankind over the ages. The moment of baptism involving a death and a rebirth corresponded to the woes and tribulations of the Last Days, while the subsequent participation in the Feast of the Eucharist was an anticipation of the Millennium. Each individual act of Christian initiation therefore contained in small the long history of the race culminating in the final establishment of the New Jerusalem on earth. The same wider significance was also given by alchemists in the sixteenth and seventeenth centuries to each individual act of regeneration. Each alchemical experiment was a copy in miniature of a universal process, an idea found in Paracelsus and developed by his followers. "A Paracelsian . . . could speak in terms of a universal philosophy because Creation itself was for him a chemical process."[1] In his *A Dialogue Philosophicall* (1612), Thomas Tymme speaks of God creating the universe by "his Halchymicall Extraction, Separation, Sublimation, and Coniunction."[2] By analogy the final conjunction, worked out over long ages, corresponded to the inauguration of the Millennium on earth. "As the Creation was an alchemical process, so too the Last Judgement will be carried out in chemical fashion."[3] This alchemical purgation of mankind, the equivalent of the woes and tribulations of the Last Days, is referred to by the author of the *Aquarium Sapientum* as the "furnace of tribulation" that would continue "until the great Universal Sabbath and the Day of Peace of the seven thousandth year is achieved."[4]

To the extent that my claim that *The Tempest* is both a baptismal and alchemical allegory is correct, it becomes possible to interpret it by extension

---

[1] Debus, *The English Paracelsians*, p. 26.
[2] Debus, p. 88.
[3] Debus, p. 88.
[4] J. A. Siebacher, *Hydrolithus, sophicus, seu Aquarium sapientum* (1619) in *Musaeum Hermeticum* (1678), p. 131.

as an eschatological allegory depicting the final testing and purgation of mankind before the inauguration of the Millennium. The individual experiences of the characters in the play therefore become figurative of the apocalyptic experience of the whole human race. To make such an interpretation at least feasible, it is first of all necessary to establish the fact that history was almost exclusively seen as the working out of a divine apocalyptic drama in Shakespeare's period, and that there existed a widespread conviction that the final struggle against Antichrist was then taking place. To the best of my knowledge, Shakespeare's preoccupation with evil, with the nature of true kingship, with the vision of the just society, as found particularly in *The Tempest*, has never been adequately considered in relation to the apocalyptic hopes and forebodings that obsessed his contemporaries. This must be my excuse for drawing attention at some length to the findings of a number of scholars who have investigated this aspect of Shakespeare's age. They will provide the necessary context for a fuller understanding of *The Tempest*.

Millenarianism

Belief in the Last Days, in the struggle with Antichrist, and in the establishment of a Millennium is no longer widely held. Gone too is the habit of interpreting current affairs and the personalities involved in them in terms of the apocalyptic vision presented in the Revelation of St John. It was otherwise in the seventeenth century and in the centuries preceding. As Norman Cohn has amply demonstrated in his *In Pursuit of the Millennium*, an apocalyptic view of history survived with undiminished vigour down to the seventeenth century and even longer. In terrible and distorted form it reappears in Hitler's proclamation of the Third Reich of a Thousand Years, and in part it explains the fascination that Marx' vision of a stateless society based on economic equality continues to exert.

There are certain recurrent features in millenarianism. Immediately before the Second Coming, there would be a period of suffering and persecution inflicted on the faithful by Antichrist. Like the Woman of Revelation 12, with whom they identified themselves, the faithful would be driven into exile and would take refuge in the wilderness. Then the Monarch of the Last Days, the *dux evangeliorum* of the Sybilline prophecies, would emerge to do battle with Antichrist and prepare the way for the Return of Christ and the establishment of the Millennium. The defeat of Antichrist would be marked by the baptism of all humanity. A new age would dawn and the second Golden Age would be restored. Such in brief was the apocalyptic programme that underlay the outer events of human history. Century after century during the Middle Ages and on into the Renaissance, contemporary events were interpreted in terms of this programme, and the leading roles in it assigned to living rulers. As they died, new potentates took over their roles.

In the development of European millenarianism, a powerful and lasting influence was exerted by Joachim of Fiore (1145—1202), and a word must be said about this important figure. Central to his prophetic teachings, based on an elaborate numerological concordance of the Old and New Testaments, was the idea that the Divine Plan manifested in history in three major, overlapping spiritual eras called *status*, each corresponding in sequence to the three Persons of the Trinity, the Father, the Son and the Holy Ghost. According to Joachim, the third *status* of the Holy Spirit had just been inaugurated by St Benedict. In addition to this Trinitarian scheme, Joachim also had a septenary division of history in which the end of the sixth age coincided with the beginning of the third *status* when the Millennium would commence. The sixth age therefore was the brief period of the reign of Antichrist on earth. As we shall see at a later point in this chapter, we have here a clue to the meaning of a Latin phrase that occurs in the Rosicrucian pamphlet, the *Confessio* of 1615: *Miranda sextae aetatis*, and possibly of the name Miranda in *The Tempest*. During the *sexta aetas* or sixth age, Joachim taught, there would appear what he called the *viri spirituales*, a new order of spiritual men who working under the direct influence of the Holy Spirit would prepare for the coming millenial third *status*. Their coming would be heralded by certain heavenly phenomena corresponding to the two luminaries of Genesis 1:6 or to the bright stars of the Sybilline prophecies. It is possible that the Rosicrucians of the early seventeenth century regarded themselves as the prophesied *viri spirituales* of Joachim, emerging in 1604, when Kepler's two new stars appeared in the heavens, to build their House of the Holy Spirit. It was the *viri spirituales* who in the sixth age would bring the Church through the desert and across the Jordan into the Promised Land.[5] It is impossible here to trace the enormous influence exerted by Joachim's prophecies down to at least the seventeenth century. For this the reader is referred to Marjorie Reeves' fascinating and scholarly account in her *Influence of Prophecy* and in her *Joachim of Fiore*.[6] Here I shall concentrate on the influence of Joachim in England, and give a survey of the apocalyptic tradition in Protestant Britain down to the time that *The Tempest* was written.

[5] See Marjorie Reeves, *Joachim of Fiore and the Prophetic Future* (New York and London: Harper and Row, 1976), p. 29.
[6] Marjorie Reeves, *The Influence of Prophecy in the Later Middle Ages* (Oxford: Oxford Univ. Press, 1969). This authoritative study of the ideas and influence of Joachim of Fiore forms the basis of the more popular presentation in her *Joachim of Fiore and the Prophetic Future*.

Millenarianism in England

The history of apocalyptic thought in England has been traced by a number of scholars, and the following survey is based on their work.[7] The earliest and most important of the Protestant interpreters of the Book of Revelation was John Bale. His *The Image of bothe Churches* (1545) adopts Joachim's scheme of seven ages from the death of Christ to the end of the world, corresponding to the seven seals of Revelation. Babylon and Antichrist would be overthrown in the seventh age, and this he regarded as the purpose of the Reformation of his own times. Antichrist was, of course, identified by Bale with the Roman Church. He made use of these apocalyptic ideas in his *A Comedy concerning Three laws* (1531), where the three laws are those of nature, bondage and grace operating in sequence during the three *status* or seven ages from Adam to the end of the world.

Coming to the period when Shakespeare was active as a writer, there is an increasing tendency in Britain to interpret Revelation in terms of her role as the place of refuge for the persecuted true Church during the final period of woe and tribulation. Such an interpretation was sanctioned at the highest level. In 1588 James VI of Scotland wrote *A Fruitfull Meditation* on Revelation 20:7—10, relating these verses to such contemporary events as the defeat of the Spanish Armada. It was, as we shall see, this work of James that was being read by the followers of Elizabeth Stuart and Frederick the Elector Palatine when they entered Prague in 1619 to inaugurate, so they believed, the Millennium. Another significant interpreter of Revelation was the Scottish mathematician and alchemist, John Napier, whose *A Plaine Discovery of the Whole Revelation of Saint John* was published in 1593 with a dedication to James VI, and again in 1611, the year when *The Tempest* was acted at Court. Here too we find an echo of the Joachite scheme of three ages each with seven periods, but now given exact dates. The second age, according to Napier, extended from 71 A.D. to 1541 when the seventh seal was opened resulting in the Reformation. The third age would culminate in 1688 with the return of Christ. Napier's purpose in interpreting history as the working out of the prophecies contained in Revelation was practical. As he wrote in his dedication to James, he wished "to incourage and inanimate Princes, to be ready against that greate day of the Lords revenge".[8] He called on

---

[7] In addition to the works of Marjorie Reeves, I have also consulted Katherine R. Firth, *The Apocalyptic Tradition in Reformation Britain* (Oxford: Oxford Univ. Press, 1978), and Christopher Hill, *Antichrist in Seventeenth-Century England* (Oxford: Oxford Univ. Press, 1971).

[8] Cited Firth, p. 134.

94

James and other princes "without pitie, ruth, and mercie to procede with all possible extremitie against that devilish seat of Rome to the utter extirpation thereof."[9] It was the secular rulers, acting either as the agents of God or of Antichrist, depending on one's religious viewpoint, who would be the principal actors in the apocalyptic drama then taking place. In England the role of leading the forces of Light against the Antichrist was assigned first to Elizabeth I and then to James I. James's two eldest children, Prince Henry and Princess Elizabeth were also assigned apocalyptic roles.

Representative of apocalyptic works being written in England close to the time of the first performance of *The Tempest* is Thomas Brightman's *A Revelation of Revelation*, first published in Latin at Frankfurt in 1609 and subsequently in English in several editions. In this influential work Brightman interprets the Seven Vials of Revelation in terms of contemporary history. The Fourth Vial corresponds to the author's present:

this boiling heate of the Sunne is nowe every daye to be loked for, that is, some more cleare opening of the Scriptures, whereby the man of sinne may be more, vehemently scorched.[10]

The boiling heat of the sun may be a reference to the widely discussed entry in 1584 into the astronomical and astrological Fiery Trigon.[11] The 'man of sinne' was equated with the Antichrist in the exegetical literature of the period, and as we shall see, it is possible that the phrase "three men of sin" used of Alonso, Antonio and Sebastian in *The Tempest* (III.iii. 53), may derive from this apocalyptic title. It is the Man of Sin or Antichrist who persecutes the true Church, identified by Brightman with the persecuted Woman in the Wilderness of Revelation 12:6. He calls this period of persecution "this storme of Antichrist", which when it has blown over will be followed by "gawdy dayes". Then in the seventh age there shall be "indeed that golden age and highest tip of holy felicity and happinesse, which mortall men may expect or think of in this earthly and base habitation."[12] The vintage harvest will be reaped in "our owne Realme of England".[13] Brightman suggests that the Golden Age will be inaugurated by a worthy prince, corresponding to the Son of Man seated upon a cloud of Revelation 14:14. This worthy prince, he hints, might well be a German reforming ruler. It is likely

---

[9] Cited Firth, p. 138.
[10] Cited Firth, p. 170.
[11] The Fiery Trigon is the pattern of three constellations in which conjunctions of Saturn and Jupiter successively occurred every nineteen years from 1584 onwards. See below, p. 97, for a further discussion of the astrological significance of the Fiery Trigon.
[12] Cited Marjorie Reeves, *Joachim of Fiore and the Prophetic Future*, p. 156.
[13] Reeves, *Joachim of Fiore*, p. 156.

that Brightman is here thinking of the Elector Palatine, the head of the Protestant Evangelical Union, who from 1610 onwards was Frederick V and who
in 1613 became the husband of Elizabeth Stuart. The scenario conjured up
by Brightman—the storm of the Last Days raised by the Man of Sin or Antichrist against the Wondrous Woman of Revelation 12, her flight to a
remote wilderness and her rescue by the Man on a White Horse in the form
of a German Protestant prince, followed by a new Golden Age—recalls the
basic dramatic situation of *The Tempest* with its focus on a young woman
significantly named Miranda, driven into exile on a remote island by three
men of sin and about to be rescued by a young prince, and with its evocations
of a second Golden Age and a brave new world.

We have seen how from Bale down to Brightman there is an increasing
tendency to assign to Britain and its rulers a special role in the drama of the
Last Days. As Katherine Firth remarks, "by the end of the first decade of
the seventeenth century, the apocalyptic tradition has not only been fully ab-
sorbed in British Protestantism, but had also become the subject of quite
sophisticated study".[14] This learned study not only took the form we have
just examined of applying the Book of Revelation to past, contemporary and
future events, but also involved the interpretation of signs in the heavens that
were believed to portend apocalyptic events. Since the whole action of *The
Tempest* takes place under the influence of an auspicious star, it is worth
seeing how Shakespeare's contemporaries regarded such influences on
human affairs. Such heavenly phenomena as the appearance of new stars
(in 1572 and 1604), eclipses (for example in 1598 and 1605), and planetary
conjunctions, particularly that or Jupiter and Saturn (in 1584 and 1603), ex-
cited an almost obssessive interest and were always interpreted (often with
a blend of foreboding and exultation) as signs of impending changes in
human affairs. It was universally believed that history as an eschatological
process was synchronized with the movements of the heavenly bodies. We
saw that Joachim of Fiore had prophesied that the transition from the second
to the third age and the appearance of the *viri spirituales* would be heralded
by two bright stars in the heavens. This corresponded to the commencement
of the limited period of persecution during the Last Days, and was also indicated by the appearance of "a great wonder in heaven", the Woman of
Revelation 12.

The *nova* or new star that shone brightly in the constellation Cassiopeia
from 1572 to 1574 was observed throughout Europe, and was widely interpreted as a sign announcing the Second Coming. Both John Dee and Tycho

---

[14] Firth, *The Apocalyptic Tradition*, p. 179.

Brahe wrote tracts on it, explaining its astronomical and astrological significance.[15] Another heavenly event of far-reaching significance and the subject of much speculation occurred some ten years later. This was a conjunction of Saturn and Jupiter in the first of a new triplicity of constellations each associated with the element of fire, known as the Fiery Trigon. The transition into a new trigon occurred every 200 or 240 years, and the return into the Fiery Trigon marked the beginning of a new great cycle. "It was an epoch-making event, looked upon as portending the arrival of a new phase of history, the prophetic fulfillment of religious innovation, great political mutations."[16] This new cycle began with the conjunction of Saturn and Jupiter early in 1584, and was continued in the second conjunction of these planets late in 1603. This conjunction of 1603 was witnessed by Robert Fludd, the English supporter of the Rosicrucians and Paracelsan physician, and is described by him in his *Tractatus Apologeticus* (1617). There he specifically relates this conjunction and the appearance of Kepler's *novae* to the renewed activity of the Rosicrucians.[17] This connection between the major conjunction in a constellation of the Fiery Trigon in late 1603 and Kepler's new stars of 1602 and 1604 and the emergence of the Rosicrucians is confirmed in the writings of the Rosicrucians themselves. The *Fama Fraternitatis* of 1614 refers to the Fiery Trigon in the following passage:

verily we must confess that the world in those days was already big with these great commotions, labouring to be delivered of them; and did bring forth painful, worthy men, who brake with all force through Darkness and Barbarism, and left us who succeeded to follow them: and assuredly they have been the uppermost point in *Trygono igneo*, whose flame now should be more and more brighter, and shall undoubtedly give to the World the last light.[18]

As an example of one who has paved the way for their own emergence under the influence of the Fiery Trigon, the *Fama* goes on to mention Paracelsus. The emergence of the Rosicrucians was ordained to take place, the *Fama* tells us, 120 years after the death of their founder, Christian Rosenkreutz, in 1484, that is, in 1604, when the second of Kepler's two stars was discovered blazing in the heavens. The *Confessio*, the second of the two principal Rosicrucian pamphlets, published in 1615, mentions both of the new stars as "certain Messengers" sent to testify to God's will.[19] An engraving in

---

[15] By a measurement of the parallax of the nova of 1572, John Dee showed in his *Parallaticae commentationis praxeosque* (1573) that the new star was in the heavenly sphere, hitherto thought to be unchanging.

[16] Margaret E. Aston, "The Fiery Trigon Conjunction: An Elizabethan Astrological Prediction," in *Isis*, 61 (1970), 159—187.

[17] Robert Fludd, *Tractatus Apologeticus* (1617), Part I, Ch. 5, pp. 70—71.

[18] *Fama Fraternitatis* (1614), printed in *A Christian Rosenkreutz Anthology*, p. 167.

[19] *Confessio Fraternitatis* (1615), in *A Christian Rosenkreutz Anthology*, p. 186.

Theophilus Schweighardt's *Speculum Sophicum Rhodo-Stauroticum* (1618), shows these two stars in their appropriate constellations pouring down their influence on the Invisible College of the Rosicrucians. There is a fervent millenarian note in these Rosicrucian pamphlets, and it is clear that they regarded the great conjunction of 1603 and Kepler's stars of 1602 and 1604 as heavenly signs that the period of the Last Days and of preparation for the Millennium had commenced. As Frances Yates has suggested their millenarian movement became closely connected with Frederick, the Elector Palatine, and his wife Elizabeth Stuart.[20]

We have so far given a brief account of the apocalyptic tradition in Britain during the sixteenth and early seventeenth centuries, showing how Britain's role in the drama of the Last Days becomes increasingly central. We have also seen how the major acts in this drama were seen as determined by certain astronomical events. It was these events in the heavens that provided the cue for the leaders in the countries involved in the final struggle to assume their roles. They were instructed in the parts they were to act not only by the theologians and exegetes of the period pondering on the meaning of Revelation, but equally importantly by the poets. Frances Yates has traced the literary cult built up around Elizabeth I in her *Astraea: The Imperial Theme in the Sixteenth Century*. The Astraea referred to in the title is the goddess of justice who fled the earth at the end of the first Golden Age and would, as Virgil's *Fourth Eclogue* prophesied, return at the commencement of the second Golden Age:

> Magnus ab integro saeculorum nascitur ordo.
> Iam redit et virgo, redeunt Saturnia regna.
> (The great line of the centuries begins anew.
> Now the Virgin returns, the reign of Saturn returns.)

These famous lines, applied to Elizabeth, make her the inaugurator of a new Golden Age in the British Isles. As Frances Yates also shows, Elizabeth was equated with other mythological virgins, and even took over some of the attributes of the Virgin Mary.[21]

This royal myth, with suitable changes, was projected onto James I by the propagandists and writers of his reign. For a fascinating study of the iconography of the Stuart cult the reader is referred to Graham Parry's *The*

---

[20] Frances Yates has explored the connections between this royal couple and the Rosicrucian movement in her *The Rosicrucian Enlightenment*.

[21] Frances Yates, *Astraea: The Imperial Theme in the Sixteenth Century* (Harmondsworth: Peregrine Books, 1977), pp. 78—9.

Golden Age Restor'd: The Culture of the Stuart Court, 1603—42.[22] Here
again, as Graham Parry brings out, the central theme of the royal promotion
was James as a male Astraea, inaugurating a new Golden Age. With his
motto *Beati Pacifici*, he was presented as a new Solomon both in learning
and in his striving to establish an age of millenial peace. But with his dread
of physical violence, James was not cut out for the role of the intrepid Man
on a White Horse, and the panegyrists found it hard to present him as a
fearless military leader against the forces of Antichrist. This role fell to his
more pugnacious son, Prince Henry. With the establishment of his own court
in 1605, Henry emerged as the leader of the militant, Protestant faction at
Court, with his vast and hazy plans of leading an army into Germany to do
battle with the Hapsburg foe. In the eyes of his contemporaries, it was young
Henry rather than the timid King who would lead the crusade against Antichrist.[23] His sudden death in the autumn of 1612 left his apocalyptic role
vacant, and his natural successor was his young friend, Frederick the Elector
Palatine, head of the Protestant Union and suitor to Elizabeth Stuart.

Before turning to a consideration of *The Tempest* in the light of these
millenarian expectations of the period, I would like first to mention two
curious documents that were received at the Court of James I within weeks
of the first performance of *The Tempest*. They raise the whole question of
whether millenarian, Rosicrucian ideas had reached James's Court at this
early date, and this in its turn has a bearing on the claim that has been made
that *The Tempest* is virtually a Rosicrucian document.

Two Royal Christmas-Cards

The documents are in the form of two large scrolls sent to James I and his
son Prince Henry in the winter of 1611 as Christmas greetings from Michael
Maier, royal physician and secretary to the Holy Roman Emperor, Rudolf
II, author of a number of excellent alchemical allegories and subsequent to
1611 closely associated with the Rosicrucians. As we have already seen,
Maier was a friend of Sir William Paddy, one of James royal physicians,
of Francis Anthony, the inventor of the potable gold elixir, and probably
of Robert Fludd, another defender of the Rosicrucians. We have also suggested that the spiritual alchemy that has been traced in *The Tempest* was

---

[22] Graham Parry, *The Golden Age Restor'd: The Culture of the Stuart Court, 1603—42*
(Manchester: Manchester Univ. Press, 1981).
[23] See Parry, *The Golden Age Restor'd*, pp. 82—89.

of the sort that these English Paracelsians would have understood and commended. Maier certainly would have appreciated it. It should be mentioned that at the time Maier sent his Christmas greetings to James and Henry, his master, Rudolf II, was being dispossessed of his powers by his brother, Matthias, for gross neglect of government and addiction to occult studies including magic and alchemy. Rudolf was negotiating with James, the young Elector Palatine and possibly Prince Henry, for their support in reinstating him. It was against this background that *The Tempest* was first performed on November 1, 1611, and that Maier sent his Christmas cards to the King of Britain and his son.

The first document, addressed to James, was discovered in the Edinburgh Public Records Office by Mr Adam Mclean, who has given a description of it in his *The Hermetic Journal*.[24] Through his kindness, I have been able to examine photocopies of this document. It contains an opening dedication to James, a number of Latin poems, and a musical fugue and canon. Its most arresting feature is an eight-petalled rose in the centre of the scroll made up of letters executed in red and gold ink. Surrounding this rose of letters is a circle composed of eight phrases describing the qualities Maier wishes James to possess. The eight lines of gold letters running from the centre of the rose to the circumference, dividing the petals, have been interpreted by Adam Mclean as forming a cross, but I think this is doubtful. These eight lines are described elsewhere on the scroll as *interstitia foliorum Rosae*. Read in sequence the letters of these eight lines produce the following sentence:

VIVE IACOBE DIU REX MAGNE BRITANNICE SALVE TEGMINE QUO VERE SIT ROSA LAETA SUO

This can be translated: "Long live James, King of Great Britain, hail, may the Rose be joyful under thy protection." Given Maier's later connections with the Rosicrucians, it is natural to assume, as does Mr Mclean, that Maier is inviting James to take the Order of the Rosy Cross under his protection. The Rose also figures in the following poem by Maier to James I:

Regum a rege, Deo Rex omnia fausta capessat.
Anglia ab Angelica sit bene tecta manu.
Advolitent laeto bis quattuor optima sceptro.
Rosa nec erucis sit ROSA, nec Boreae.
Copia Amaltheae vigeat fructu ubere cornu.
Tristis Eris regnis exulet adsit Eros.
Aura bifrontis redeantut ut secula Iani.
Qui Deus est et homo quod det Ihesus amen.

---

[24] Adam Mclean, "A Rosicrucian Manuscript of Michael Maier," in *The Hermetic Journal*, 5 (1979), 1—7.

I have translated this poem as follows:

Through God, the King of Kings, may the King obtain all good fortune.
May England be well guarded by the angelic hand.
May twice-four blessings speed to his joyous sceptre.
May the ROSE not be gnawed by the canker or the North Wind.
May the bounty of Amalthea flourish with the fruit of the copious horn.
May gloomy Eris be banished from the Kingdom, let Eros appear,
That the Golden Age of the double-faced Janus may return.
May Jesus grant all this, who is both God and man. Amen.

Here again the Rose is invoked in connection with the establishment of a new Golden Age, but no hint is given as to its precise significance. Nevertheless in view of the close association of the Rose with the millenarianism of the Rosicrucians and Maier's subsequent connection with them, it seems to me likely that it is this millenarian Rose of the Protestant Fraternity of the Rosy Cross that Maier wishes James to take under his protection. Associated with Amalthea's horn of plenty, with the reign of Eros and the establishment of the Golden Age of Janus,[25] the Rose seems to symbolize a new millenarian dispensation to be established in the land of roses and of the Royal Rose, with James as its inaugurator and protector.

The second document, sent by Michael Maier to Prince Henry, was located by the present writer in the manuscript collections of the British Library.[26] It closely resembles the Edinburgh document in general style, lavish size (it is two feet long and one and a half feet wide), in its use of red and gold lettering and in similarities of phrasing in the dedication. It confirms the authenticity of the Edinburgh document. It is dedicated to Prince Henry, and like the greetings to King James it celebrates both Christmas and "the coming New Year of good omen, 1612" (*noviq' ineuntis 1612 anni auspicium*). It contains complimentary verses to Henry, anagrams on his title, "Henricus Walliae Princeps", and a number of rebuses. In one of two long Latin poems Maier introduces the theme of the Golden Age by recalling that the Saturnalia of ancient Rome, like the Christmas he is celebrating, marked a brief return to the conditions of the Golden Age. In the centre of the scroll corresponding to the position of the Rose in the Edinburgh document there is a poem in red and gold lettering in the form of a pyramid. The

---

[25] James might well have recognized this allusion to the double-faced Janus, for on his official entry into London in 1604 he was shown a ceremonial arch designed by Ben Jonson displaying the figure of Janus with the inscription: *Redeunt Saturnia Regna*. See Parry, *The Golden Age Restor'd*, p. 18.

[26] B.M. Royal MSS. 14 B xvi.

first and last letters of the horizontal lines of inscription that fill the pyramid and form its outline are executed in gold lettering. Read in sequence these letters make up the following inscription:

ALTA PETENS VIRTUS ET SANGUIS REGIUS IN TE SIC / HENRICE MICANT UT SINT OMNIA CERTA PIIR / AMIDEM QUOD LAUDIS OPUS TUA FACTA REQUIRANT OLIM / CUM FIRMATA VIRUM TE FECERIT AETAS

This can be translated:

> The lofty virtue and royal blood in you, O Henry,
> so shine forth that they are certain portents.
> Your deeds require a pyramid as a work of praise
> Now that your majority has made you a man.

There is nothing in this document of a Rosicrucian character.

It is difficult to assess the significance of these two documents sent by Maier to James I and Prince Henry close to the time of the first performance of *The Tempest*. If we could be sure that the reference to the *rosa* pointed to the Rosicrucians, it would be highly significant. Given the situation of his master, Rudolf II, which will be more fully described in the next chapter, it seems more likely that Maier is trying to win the sort of support from James for Rudolf that was being planned by his son, Prince Henry, and his future son-in-law, Frederick of the Palatine. These plans involved offering protection to the Protestant Evangelical Union and as a pledge of it agreeing to the marriage of Elizabeth Stuart to the Elector Palatine. It is not impossible that Maier's Rose stands for the Union itself. Frances Yates has suggested that the rose design with a cross in the centre found in Simon Studion's apocalyptic work, *Naometria* (1604), might refer to "some kind of alliance of Protestant sympathizers, formed to counteract the Catholic League."[27] Studion twice mentions a Protestant union, the *Confederatio Militiae Evangelicae* as having been formed in 1586.[28] In direct line of descent from this alliance with its Joachite inspiration was the Protestant Evangelical Union of 1608.[29] Frederick V, its head from 1610 onwards, was subsequently identified by his opponents with the millenarian programme of the

---

[27] Yates, *The Rosicrucian Enlightenment*, p. 35.

[28] The existence of the Confederatio of 1586 has been doubted (see McIntosh, *The Rosy Cross Unveiled*, p. 40), but surely the Confederatio is identical with the alliance of Protestant powers that Ségur-Pardaillon set out to negotiate on behalf of Henry IV in 1583. This alliance was inspired by the Joachite ideas of Brocardo who believed that Joachim's Third Status was imminent. See Reeves, *Joachim of Fiore*, pp. 144—8.

[29] See Yates, *The Rosicrucian Enlightenment*, pp. 33—6.

Rosicrucians. It is therefore possible that the Rose and Cross combined had both a politico-religious significance and an esoteric one at this time.[30] We should not exclude the possibility that Maier's Rose represents the exoteric and esoteric aspects of Protestant millenarianism. Bearing this possibility in mind, we can now consider the claim that *The Tempest* is "almost a Rosicrucian manifesto."[31]

Miranda Sextae Aetatis

It should be stated at the outset that there is no direct evidence linking *The Tempest* with what has been called the Rosicrucian movement. Whatever parallels can be found between the two can be explained by the fact that they share a common background in the speculative millenarian Protestantism of the early seventeenth century. The spiritual alchemy that has been traced in the play and which is present in Rosicrucian publications derives from the writings of Paracelsan alchemists and physicians. The fervent millenarian note that is heard in the Rosicrucians pamphlets, the *Fama* and the *Confessio*, and which I believe is present in *The Tempest*, can also be traced to a common source in the widespread millenarianism of the period. But this explanation of resemblances between certain features of *The Tempest* and Rosicrucianism in terms of a shared background does not exclude the possibility of direct contact even if this cannot be proved. It is a fact, as Frances Yates has demonstrated in her *The Rosicrucian Enlightenment*, that the young couple who witnessed a performance of the play at their wedding in 1612—13 were specifically associated with the Rosicrucians. A satirical print attacking Frederick and Elizabeth after their defeat at the Battle of the White Mountain in 1619 clearly describes the millenarian role in which they had been cast:

> The round wooden ball represents the world
> To which the Bohemians married the Palatine,
> They expected to teach the world,
> And to reform all schools, churches and law courts,
> And to bring everything to the state
> In which Adam found it,
> And even to my state, Saturn's,
> And this was called the golden time.
> To that end the high society of the Rosicrucians
> Wish to turn all the mountains into gold for their own good.[32]

[30] See Yates, p. 57.
[31] Yates, *The Occult Philosophy in the Elizabethan Age* (London: Routledge and Kegan Paul, 1979), p. 171.
[32] Cited Yates, *The Rosicrucian Enlightenment*, p. 57.

It is my own belief that Frederick and Elizabeth had been cast in the roles of harbingers of the Golden Age from 1610 onwards when negotiations for their marriage were started, and that *The Tempest* was expressly written in 1611 to celebrate their betrothal which was expected to take place in the spring or summer of that year. For reasons that will be explained in the next chapter, the betrothal and wedding were postponed for some two years. *The Tempest*, then, following this interpretation, is in part a dramatization of the millenarian hopes already being focussed on the Elector Palatine and Elizabeth Stuart. It is impossible to say how far these hopes also included a specific Rosicrucian element. Michael Maier's two Christmas cards to James and Henry provide the only possible evidence that Rosicrucian ideas had reached the Stuart court at this early date, but unfortunately, as we have seen, this evidence is ambiguous. The only other indication that *The Tempest* might have had a direct Rosicrucian inspiration is to be found in a single word in the text. But even here this single point of contact can be explained in terms of a common background.

The word is the name of the heroine of the play, Miranda. The meaning of her name is clearly revealed by Ferdinand. Even before Miranda has disclosed her name, Ferdinand addresses her as "O you wonder" (I.ii. 429). Later he exclaims: "Admir'd Miranda! Indeed the top of admiration" (III.i. 37—8). For him she is "peerless" and "perfect", "the goddess on whom these airs attend", a "maid" and "virgin" who combines the best qualities of all the women he has previously known. Miranda, therefore, as her Latin name suggests, is a female wonder and a source of admiration. In disclosing her name to Ferdinand, Miranda has broken a promise to her father:

> O my father,
> I have broke your hest to say so
> (III.i. 36—7).

Her name should have been kept secret, suggesting that it possesses some value or some significance which Prospero does not wish her to divulge. Let us ask what this maidenly wonder named Miranda would have suggested to at least some among the audience that watched *The Tempest* in 1611 and 1612—13, assuming that the name contained a more recondite meaning.

In the *Confessio Fraternitatis* printed at Cassel in 1615 an offer is made to the learned of Europe to reveal certain "mysteries and secrets" that have hitherto been held back. The nature of these mysteries and secrets is hinted at in a phrase that occurs in the following passage which is translated direct from the Latin of the 1615 edition:

104

Nor is it strange that our lofty, unexpected willingness overwhelms many with a conflict of thought, to whom as yet the wonders of the sixth age are as yet unknown.[33]

Thomas Vaughan's translation of the same passage, made in 1652 runs as follows:

For it is to be taught and believed, that this our unhoped willing offer wil raise many and divers thoughts in men, unto whom (as yet) be unknown *Miranda sextae aetatis.*[34]

The original Latin makes it clear that the phrase left in Latin by Vaughan means "the wonders of the sixth age".

The phrase "Miranda sextae aetatis" clearly alludes to that Sixth Age referred to by Joachim of Fiore which was both the time of the Last Days of woe and tribulation as well as the prelude to the Seventh Age when the Millennium would be established. Taking the word *miranda* to mean wonders, these are the various portents noted by the apocalyptic writers of the period announcing imminent profound changes in human affairs: the expansion of human learning, the discovery of printing, the voyages of discovery and the conversion of pagans being carried out in distant lands. As Marjorie Reeves has shown, these phenomena were interpreted by Catholic and Protestants alike as fulfillments of the apocalyptic prophecies.[35] These wonders occurring during the tribulations of the Last Days were for those who could correctly interpret them a source of hope. However dire the onslaughts of Antichrist, these portents were a guarantee that shortly the new age would dawn. As we shall see, the "impossible matter" pointed out by Gonzalo to the King and ridiculed by Antonio and Sebastian performs the same function as the apocalyptic portents detected during the Last Days. The common "hint of woe" is counterbalanced by "the miracle" of their preservation, and Gonzalo advises Alonso to "weigh / Our sorrow with our comfort". (II.i. 1—9).

The wonderful portents of the Sixth Age also included the emergence of a new order of spiritual men, Joachim's *viri spirituales*, who under the direct guidance of the Holy Spirit and closely associated with the Virgin Mary

---

[33] The Latin of the 1615 ed. of the *Confessio* runs: *Neq enim absurdum est pleriqu' altam inexpectatum facilitatem cogitationum conflictu obrui, quibus nondum sextae aetatis miranda innotuerunt.*

[34] In the lightly corrected version of Vaughan's translation of 1652 given by Frances Yates in *The Rosicrucian Enlightenment*, pp. 238 ff., the phrase in Vaughan's text, *Miranda sextae aetatis*, is incorrectly rendered *Miranda sexta aetatis*. I am grateful to Miss Molly Bennett of the Bodleian Library for checking this detail in Vaughan's translation of the *Confessio*.

[35] See Chs. IV to VI in Reeves, *Joachim of Fiore*.

would prepare the way for the Second Coming. For Joachim this new spiritual order had been started by St Benedict, and the monastic order that he established was symbolized by Mary as a young woman.[36] The young Virgin was identified in exegetical and prophetic literature with the young woman of Revelation 12 whose wondrous appearance in the heavens would announce the commencement of the final struggle with Antichrist and the imminence of the Millennium:

And there appeared a great wonder in heaven, a woman clothed with the sun, and the moon under her feet, and upon her head a crown of twelve stars.[37]

This Wondrous Woman gives birth to a male child, the Christ of the Second Coming, who is snatched up to heaven. The Woman, pursued by the Dragon or Antichrist, then "fled into the wilderness, where she hath a place prepared of God, that they should feed her there a thousand two hundred and threescore days" (Revelation 12:6). During the period of her exile in the wilderness Antichrist reigns on earth persecuting the faithful and misleading the masses by means of the False Prophet. Finally the Antichrist and his followers are defeated by the apocalyptic Man on the White Horse, and the marriage of the Woman of the Wilderness announces the inauguration of the Millennium. Such in brief was the scenario of the Last Days and the beginning of the Millennium to be derived from the Book of Revelation.

The same scenario is to be discerned in the basic plot of *The Tempest*. There too a young woman is driven into exile by Men of Sin, and compelled to take refuge in a remote spot until the time for her return to the world is fulfilled. Her name, Miranda, is, I believe, intentionally evocative of the woman of Revelation 12, the "great wonder", and is related to the *Miranda sextae aetatis* of the Rosicrucian *Confessio*.[38]

---

[36] See L. Tondelli, *Il Libro delle Figure dell'Abate Giachino da Fiore* (Turin: Societa Editrice Internazionale, 1940), I, 96, n. 1, citing Joachim of Fiore, *Tractatus in quattuor Evangelia*: "Maria, aetate iuvencula, designat monasticam illam religionem, scilicet quam sanctus instituit Benedictus."

[37] This is the translation given in the King James Version (1611).

[38] Space does not permit me to show just how significant the Woman of Revelation 12 was in the apocalyptic thought of the period, but the following indications can be mentioned. As scholars have recognized, Book One of the *Faerie Queene* draws heavily on Revelation, and it has been noted in particular that Una is modelled on the Woman in the Wilderness of Revelation 12 (see Josephine Waters Bennett, *The Evolution of the 'Faerie Queene'* (Chicago: Chicago Univ. Press, 1942), p. 109). This is yet another sign of the close affinity between the allegorical worlds of the *Faerie Queene* and *The Tempest*. The same apocalyptic woman appears in another famous allegory, *Christianopolis*, published by Johan Valentin Andreae in 1620. The utopian community on a distant island to which the reader is invited to sail is called "The Woman in the Wilderness."

Miranda

If we see Miranda in this way, as the harbinger of a new dispensation in human society, it ought to be possible to interpret other features in *The Tempest* in terms of the drama of the Last Days. For example the island to which she and her father are exiled ought to resemble in some way the place in the wilderness "prepared of God" to which the Woman of Revelation 12 flees followed by the Antichrist or the biblical Man of Sin. The island of *The Tempest* certainly has some puzzling features, and these seem to recall the idea of a paradisial community established in some remote wilderness. The island is described paradoxically as both desert-like and inhospitable to life and as lush and fertile. Here Gonzalo would establish his second Golden Age. Hidden from sight until the very end of the play is Miranda, while around her move the significantly named "three men of sin". Her exile to the island, like that of the Woman in the Wilderness, is divinely ordained. She and her father have been "blessedly holp hither" (I.ii. 63). All that happens to them has been arranged by "Providence divine" (I.ii. 159). It is the gods above, as Gonzalo says, who have chalked forth the ways on the long journey through the wilderness and who will place a crown on Miranda and Ferdinand as they prepare to return to establish a brave new world, a second Age of Gold.

But to be able to do this, the final purgation of mankind must take place, and it is this that Prospero has taken upon himself to carry out by magical means. All his efforts are concentrated on the three men who have driven him and his daughter into exile.

It is above all Antonio who plays the role of Antichrist in the play. He is the arch deceiver, ever twisting words and meanings in order to thwart Gonzalo's effort to comfort the King. The same verbal cunning traps his follower, Sebastian, into plotting the death of Alonso and the others. Just as his close literary relative, Iago, is associated with the devil when Othello at the end of the play looks down at his feet to see if they are cloven, so Antonio's kinship with the Devil is subtly suggested in *The Tempest*. As Christopher Hill has suggested, the phrase "three men of sin" may be a deliberate echo by Shakespeare of the Biblical "Man of Sin" in 2 Thessalonians 2:3—4, equated in the Geneva Bible and by Calvin with Antichrist.[39] Of the three men of sin in *The Tempest* it is Antonio who remains quite unmoved and unchanged by his experiences on the island. With the appearance of Miranda he lapses into almost total silence. There is no contrition, no

---

[39] Hill, *Antichrist in Seventeenth-Century England*, pp. 3—4, and Appendix III, p. 185.

acknowledgement of guilt. If I am correct in identifying him with the Biblical Man of Sin, this would help in solving a minor crux of the play. In the final scene of the play, Sebastian says of Prospero: "The devil speaks in him" and Prospero answers:

> No.
> For you most wicked sir, whom to call brother
> Would even infect my mouth, I do forgive
> Thy rankest fault
> (V.i. 129—132).

The punctuation in the Folio is:

> No:
> For you (most wicked Sir . . .

Commentators have either emended the word "No" to "now", proposed that it be eliminated or interpreted it to mean that "No, I will tell no tales" or "No, I am no devil". I suggest that Prospero hears Sebastian's remark, denies that he is the devil, and in the pause that follows turns to his brother and gazes at him, implying "no, the devil is not in *me*, but rather in this person". There is one final reference to Antonio. In the Epilogue Prospero speaks of having "pardon'd the deceiver" (l. 9). Again, like Iago, Antonio's outstanding characteristic is deceit. His role in the play is to deceive the other castaways as to the significance of their tribulations, to induce despair and doubt, and to awaken ambition and treachery in Sebastian. He can be compared to Archimago in the *Faerie Queene*, "the Architect of cancred guile" (II.i.i.). Like him, Antonio uses the magic of words to mislead. He is the black magician of the play, and like Archimago he resembles the "false prophet" of Revelation 19:20 who deceives the people into worshipping Antichrist.[40] In *The Tempest* the black magic practised by Antonio is temporarily defeated by the higher magic of his brother, Prospero.

This Thing of Darkness

The defeat of Antonio's satanic plot is paralleled in the play by the defeat of the plot of the Three Drunkards to kill Prospero and seize power on the island. The two clowns, Stephano and Trinculo, are aping their masters, and in the new social hierarchy they create Caliban becomes their slave. He

---

[40] See Norhnberg, *The Analogy of the Faerie Queene*, p. 128, for a discussion of Archimago as the arch magus and deceiver.

mistakes Stephano for a god, and proceeds to worship him. Caliban too is deceived by false appearances. How should this be interpreted in terms of apocalyptic allegory?

Caliban is in many ways Shakespeare's most extraordinary creation. It is true that he can be regarded as a representative of the natives of the New World described by Montaigne in his essay on Cannibals. There, something of the aboriginal innocence of the first Golden Age had, it was believed, been preserved. The discovery of the New World by Columbus was taken as a sign that the baptism of the whole world and the coming of the Millennium were both imminent, and it has been suggested that Columbus saw himself as a "Joachite Messiah" preparing the world for a new dispensation.[41] The Fransciscan missionaries active in the New World regarded the natives as "a *Gens Angelicum*, reborn in the innocence of Adam before the Fall, amongst whom the terrestrial paradise could be recreated. They would be ruled paternally by the friars and preserved from the contamination of grasping Europeans."[42] Caliban can be likened to these survivors of prelapsarian humanity, even if he has undergone some contamination from grasping Europeans, but this does not fully explain his character. There is nobility in it, but there is also something monstrous. As Frank Kermode has suggested he also has affinities with "the uncivilized inhabitants of the Indies, with the wild or savage man of Europe."[43] He is repeatedly described in the play as a monster, slow and shambling, of "vile race" (I.ii. 360), incapable of speech until taught by Miranda, in shape an abortion, and as

> A devil, a born devil, on whose nature
> Nurture can never stick; on whom my pains,
> Humanely taken, all, all lost, quite lost;
> And as with age his body uglier grows,
> So his mind cankers.
> (IV.i. 188—192).

Here there is no hint of an original innocence corrupted by contact with civilization; he is corrupt from the beginning. Caliban's basic bestiality is suggested too by the descriptive phrases of the two clowns. In appearance he is fish-like but with the arms and legs of a human. Trinculo calls him a "puppy-headed monster" (II.ii. 154). We are given the impression of some monstrous hybrid washed up from the sea, more akin to the hybrids of

---

[41] Reeves, *Joachim of Fiore*, pp. 128—9.
[42] Reeves, p. 130. I am grateful for Dr Reeves for pointing out to me that the Fransiscans of the sixteenth and seventeenth centuries used the Woman in the Wilderness as the symbol of their missionary endeavours in the New World.
[43] Arden *Tempest*, pp. xxxviii—xxxix.

mythology than to any savage encountered by the voyagers of the time. And yet this monster can learn language, is responsive in his own way to the beauty of Miranda, and is capable of worshipping Stephano as though he were a god. He takes deep delight in the invisible music of the island, and in dreams has visions of the clouds opening to shower riches upon him. How are we to reconcile these monstrous and these human traits? The clue I believe lies in the nature of his parents. He is the son of a witch, Sycorax, and of the devil.

Alongside the orthodox tradition that Adam was created by God in his own image, there existed in the sixteenth century a tradition that can be traced back to the Gnostics that the first man was demonic in origin. This tradition was mediated in part by the *Corpus Hermeticum*, translated into Latin by Ficino in 1463. The seventeen editions printed in the sixteenth century include the widely influential *Pimander* which has been described as "a prime document of independant pagan Gnosticism."[44] It was also mediated through the writings of the alchemists of the Renaissance who "saw themselves as Gnostic saviours whose job was to redeem base matter."[45] Central to this tradition is the idea that the divine spark is imprisoned in matter which is thought of as evil. The creation of man is "an imitation, illicit and blundering, of the divine lower powers."[46] The creation of Adam and Eve is described as "involving copulation between the male and female demons."[47] One Manichaean Gnostic text describes this process as follows:

And from the impurity of the he-demons and from the filth of the she-demons, the evil mother of all demons formed this body, and she herself entered into it. Then from the five light-elements, Ormuzd's armour, she formed the good Soul and fettered it in the body. She made it as if half blind and deaf, unconscious and confused, so that at first it might not know its origin and kinship.[48]

According to Gnosticism, the physical universe, the Kingdom of Darkness, and physical man were created by a lower deity, known variously as the Demiurge, Jehovah or Samael. Imprisoned in matter, the soul forgot its divine origins, and as in Platonism this state of imprisonment was likened to a state of sleep, of drunkeness or of numbness.[49]

---

[44] Hans Jonas, *The Gnostic Religion* (Boston: Beacon Press, 1958), p. 41.

[45] Allison Coudert, *Alchemy: The Philosopher's Stone* (London: Wildwood House Ltd., 1980), p. 104. See Jung, *Mysterium Coniunctionis*, p. 264, where the importance of gnosticism for alchemy is discussed. Christopher McIntosh in *The Rosy Cross Unveiled*, p. 18, also draws attention to the Gnostic character of the Rosicrucian movement.

[46] Jonas, *The Gnostic Religion*, p. 202.

[47] Jonas, p. 277.

[48] Jonas, facing p. 340.

[49] Jonas, pp. 68—74.

These Gnostic ideas on the origin of man, so congenial to the alchemists, appear in a Gnostic work, the *Kore Kosmou,* or *Virgin of the World,* published in Latin translation in 1591 and 1593, where the decision of the upper gods to cleanse the lower world of Ignorance is described. As Frances Yates has shown, this Gnostic work was probably used by Giordano Bruno in his *Spaccio della besta trionfonte* (1584) where he describes the expulsion of the Triumphant Beast from the world of men.[50] At much the same time as Bruno's *Spaccio* appeared in England, Edmund Spenser was writing the *Faerie Queene.* Book Six is devoted to the attempt of Calidore to rid the world of a similar monster, the Blatant Beast. I would suggest that Caliban is in line of descent from these literary Beasts of the sixteenth century, and through them from the Gnostic Adam. As such he represents man in his primordial beginnings, close to the animal world and yet possessing by virtue of the imprisoned soul the potentiality for growth. In Jan Kott's apt words: "Prospero wanted to perform on the island the history of the world to serve as a warning to the ship-wrecked, and to the audience . . . Caliban's history is a chapter from the history of mankind."[51] Because of the close affinity of *The Tempest* to the *Faerie Queene,* I think that Caliban's nature can most easily be understood by comparing him to Spenser's Blatant Beast. In the following section I shall use Norhnberg's invaluable discussion in "The Beast Enlarged" in his *The Analogy of the Faerie Queene* (pp. 688—697).

The Blatant Beast is described by Spenser as a "dog" or "curre" given to Envy and Detraction. Like Cerberus it has three heads, and their significance is described in the *Metamorphoses Moraliter,* attributed to Thomas Waley, as follows:

Cerberus is a detractor: because he is known to have three heads and three barking dogs to emit three kinds of evil detraction; moreover by evil words he is used to alarming the whole world with strife and contention.[52]

Caliban also uses language to detract:

> You taught me language; and my profit on't
> Is, I know how to curse
> (I.ii. 365—6).[53]

[50] See Frances Yates, *Giordano Bruno and the Hermetic Tradition* (Chicago: Chicago Univ. Press, 1964; Vintage Books, 1969), pp. 215—217.
[51] Jan Kott, *Shakespeare Our Contemporary* (London: Methuen,1 967), pp. 271 and 272.
[52] Norhnberg, *The Analogy of the Faerie Queene,* p. 694.
[53] At II.ii. 3—4 Caliban says that despite the fact that the spirits can hear him, "yet I needs must curse", indicating a compulsion to curse that is beyond his control.

Caliban is also the fomenter of strife and contention between people. He sets Stephano against Trinculo, and both of them against Prospero. He incites them to rebellion, and here again Caliban resembles the Blatant Beast. As the many-headed monster, the Beast stands for the mob riotously subverting the established order of society in its search for a "liberty" (VI.xii. 36) which is in effect licence. Thus the Beast in the *Faerie Queene* exemplifies that *evaganti frena licentia* of Horace's *Fourth Ode*, that mad vagrant license which the reign of Augustus will bring to an end. Similarly Caliban sets out in league with the two Clowns to overthrow established authority in the name of liberty. Caliban leads the way crying "Freedom, high-day! high-day! freedom! freedom, high-day", while Stephano sings "Thought is free" to the wrong tune (II.ii. 186—7, III.ii. 121—2).

It has been pointed out that among the many ancestors of Spenser's Blatant Beast is the Great Beast of Plato's Republic.[54] Plato compares the sophists with their popular ideas to a large, powerful beast with its varying moods and wants. The Beast is composite like the Chimaera, Scylla or Cerberus, and resembles the lower nature of a human being with its mixture of good and bad traits. It is for this reason that the soul must be strengthened so as to assume responsibility for the many-headed beast and "tame his wildness."[55] By analogy the just ruler must take on the responsibility for civilizing the masses over whom he rules. Here again Plato's Great Beast is the many-headed mob or the unruly personality that requires the discipline of the wise ruler or of the soul to bring it to order. This defines Prospero's final relation to Caliban. With a struggle, he again reassumes responsibility for "this thing of darkness". His temporary forgetfulness of it immediately led to rebellion and an outbreak of demagogic licence.

The Beast of *The Republic* has close affinities with another Platonic beast, the hermaphroditic creature described by Aristophanes in the *Symposium*. Combining the two sexes in one body, it was circular in form with four limbs and two heads. Because of their overweening pride and great strength, the aboriginal race of Hermaphrodites staged a rebellion against the gods. After their defeat, Jove decreed that they should be split in half to form the two separate sexes. Here again we find an association between some monstrous forerunner of the human race and rebellion. The kinship of Plato's Hermaphrodite and the hermaphroditic Adam of rabbinical tradition was noted in the Renaissance.[56] It might well be asked at this point what possible con-

---

[54] See Richard Neuse, "Book Six as conclusion to the *Faerie Queene*", in *Critical Essays on Spenser from E.L.H.* (Baltimore: Johns Hopkin Press, 1970), pp. 228—9.

[55] Plato, *Republic*, ed. Cornford, pp. 309—310.

[56] Norhnberg, *The Analogy of the Faerie Queene*, p. 600, and n. 458.

nection there could be between this four-legged monster of Plato and Caliban.

In Act II, Scene ii of *The Tempest* the audience is treated to a highly comical episode. Stephano, drunk, staggers on stage and is confronted by a monster: "This is some monster of the isle with four legs", he mutters. It also has two heads:

Four legs and two voices, a most delicate monster! His forward voice, now, is to speak well of his friend; his backward voice is to utter foul speeches and detract.
(II.ii. 91—94).

The monster that Stephano stumbles on is, I suggest, a compound of Plato's Beast in the *Republic* and the four-legged Hermaphrodite of the *Symposium*. Concerning the great Beast Plato tells us that it has a mixture of tame and wild heads symbolizing the mixture of truth and lies that makes sophistry so dangerous. This is echoed in this scene by the reference to the voice that speaks well of a friend and the other that detracts. Here then we find Shakespeare perfectly balancing delight with instruction in an emblematic scene on the stage. The four-legged monster with two heads seen by the fuddled Stephano prepares us, even as we chuckle, for the act of rebellion that follows. It is a repetition of the primal rebellion. What is enacted before the audience as the three Drunks plot to seize power is archetypal in character. Some act of rebellion preserved in myth as having been perpetrated by some monstrous predecessor of the human race continues to reverberate throughout history. For a brief moment this monstrous ancestor takes form on a Jacobean stage as two men creep under a gabardine, and then it dissolves into the play's present as they act out their little plot. This is the art of allegory at its highest.

Caliban emerges as earthy Primordial Man, the rabbinical Adam fashioned out of red clay, a creature of darkness formed by demonic powers, given to rebellion and discontent, and yet haunted by intimations of something higher. His lineage stretches back to the remote past, but he lives on into the present as the gullible mob, easily swayed by the sophistic oratory of an Anthony. In his pursuit of liberty, Caliban ends up exchanging one master for another, just as Plato predicted that demagogy would collapse into tyranny. He mistakes Stephano for a god and worships him. In this he resembles the many people described in Revelation who would be misled in the Last Days by the "false prophet". This is the second Beast who "deceiveth them that dwell on the face of the earth" into worshipping Antichrist, and who sets the mark of Antichrist on them (Rev. 13:16—17).In the Last Days many will fall away, and "many false prophets will arise and lead many astray" (Matthew 24:9ff.) Caliban is among the many who are led astray and follow false gods. There is no need to doubt his anger or his sincerity at the end of the play:

> I'll be wise hereafter,
> And seek for grace. What a thrice-double ass
> Was I, to take this drunkard for a god,
> And worship this dull fool!
> (V.i. 294—7)

In the apocalyptic scheme of the play, the Three Drunks stand for the lowest stages of human development. Stephano and Trinculo stand for the average person of Shakespeare's age, vigorous, crude, easily misled or distracted by appearances as with the clothes hung out on the line. Caliban is primitive man, full of rancour and malice, and yet capable of worship and of dreaming. All three of them ape the act of usurpation of their superiors.

I have left Prospero's role in the apocalyptic allegory till last. It is he who is staging the whole apocalyptic scenario. As has often been said of him, he plays the part of God in relation to the mortals in his power. He is invisible to them and in the judgment scene of III.iii he watches the proceedings from "on the top" like some Olympian god. And yet in certain respects he is far from god-like. Unlike the powers above, "delaying, not forgetting", he forgets. He is not very successful in his attempt to change human nature. Alonso is most changed, Sebastian somewhat, but Antonio although defeated remains irremediably himself. If Caliban's change of heart is sincere at the end of the play, as I believe it is, then we are forced to admit that Prospero is guilty of a serious error of judgement. He has described Caliban as one

> on whose nature
> Nature can never stick; on whom my pains,
> Humanely taken, all, all lost, quite lost;
> And as with age his body uglier grows,
> So his mind cankers
> (IV.i. 187—192).

Here dismissed as beyond redemption, Caliban's final words about seeking grace prove Prospero quite wrong. But it is not alone Prospero's forgetfulness or lapse of judgement or his limited success in changing the Three Men of Sin that betrays his human fallibility. There is also the fact that he finally regards the very magic he has been practising as inadequate and abjures it as "rough". This makes it impossible to regard him as allegorically representing God or Providence in the play.

There seems to be only one way that Prospero's role in *The Tempest* can be given an apocalyptic interpretation in line with the rest of the interpretation offered in this chapter, and that is to regard him as the type of the human being who is playing God, even usurping his role. He has arrogated to himself the right to carry out by means of magic an apocalyptic purgation of society, and there is a definite element of Faustian presumption in this project. But he is a Faustus with a difference. He is inspired by a noble dream, the dream of a restored Golden Age to be ushered in by Miranda, and for a while he believes that he has the right to manipulate the human beings in his power into love or into repentence. He is in fact compelling his former enemies to undergo the rigours of initiation and subjecting them to alchemical purgation as though he were God. The abandoned title of John Fowles' *The Magus*, which is based on *The Tempest*, was "The Godgame"; it would have been a suitable subtitle for *The Tempest* too.

I shall return to the subject of the sort of magic that Prospero practises and finally abjures in the seventh chapter of this study. Our immediate task is to try and show that the apocalyptic theme that has been traced in *The Tempest* not only reflects the general apocalyptic mood of the times but also the specific apocalyptic situation that had arisen in Europe in 1611 when *The Tempest* was first produced.

Chapter VI
The Hermetic Monarch: The Political Allegory of *The Tempest*

Two performances of *The Tempest* are known to have taken place during Shakespeare's lifetime, one on November 1st, 1611, at Whitehall in the presence of the King, and the other some time during the wedding festivities in honour of Elizabeth and Frederick held early in 1613. It has been widely assumed, in line with the suggestion of Dover Wilson in his Cambridge edition of the play, that *The Tempest* was radically rewritten after its first performance at Court in order to make it suitable for the wedding celebrations a little over a year later. This of course carries the implication that in its original form the play had no connection with the wedding, the most sumptuous of James's reign. Dover Wilson's case for an extensive rewriting of *The Tempest* has been challenged by Frank Kermode in his Arden edition of the play, and he makes out a strong argument in my view for regarding the Folio text as substantially the same as the play performed in 1611.[1] Where the betrothal masque in the play is concerned, the majority of scholars regard it as an addition made to the play for the royal betrothal or wedding. The primary reason for this view is that no betrothal or wedding is known to have been celebrated at Court in November, 1611. Kermode who believes that the masque is "an integral part of the play" explains it by relating it to similar masques in various Blackfriars plays of the period introduced purely as entertainment.[2] Here again there is the implied assumption that *The Tempest* was not especially written to celebrate the wedding of Elizabeth and Frederick.

In the last Chapter, I tried to show that *The Tempest* is a millenarian allegory that reflects the apocalyptic mood of the times in which it was written. I also suggested that specifically the play is connected with the millenarian roles that from about the middle of 1610 onwards Elizabeth Stuart and Frederick V of the Palatine were being expected to play in European affairs. If this is true, it follows that Shakespeare wrote *The Tempest*

---

[1] Kermode, Introd. to Arden *Tempest*, pp. xvii ff.
[2] Kermode, p. xxiii.

with this couple in mind and in anticipation of their betrothal or marriage. Critical opinion, as we have just seen, is against this view, and is generally agreed that the principal dramatist of James's Court took an old play and refurbished it, perhaps hastily, as a homage to the young couple. For various reasons I believe this opinion is mistaken. The fact that no betrothal or wedding took place at Court in November, 1611, does not necessarily exclude the possibility that *The Tempest* was written in expectation of a wedding that was to have taken place then but was for some reason cancelled. This was indeed the case with the marriage of Elizabeth and Frederick.

The possibility of a marriage between them was first raised in 1610. In May of that year, the assassination of Henry IV of France deprived the Protestant Evangelical Union led by Frederick IV of the Palatine of its principal protector. In July of the same year the Catholic League was formed to pose a further threat to the Protestant Union. To counter this, Frederick IV sought to enlist the support and protection of James 1. Negotiations were started in the summer of 1610 "both for an alliance between England and the Union, and for a marriage between Frederick V [heir to Frederick IV] and James's daughter, Elizabeth."[3] In September Frederick IV died, and he was succeeded by his fifteen-year-old son as Frederick V, who automatically became head of the Protestant Union. His projected marriage to Elizabeth now assumed considerable political importance. It would strengthen the Union in a struggle against the forces of the Counter Reformation interpreted, as we have seen, in apocalyptic terms as the forces of Antichrist.

We can follow the protracted negotiations for the marriage through the reports of the Venetian ambassador at James's Court and other contemporary accounts. On September 2nd, 1610, he reported that "their majesties are inclined to no one so much as to the Prince Palatine who is thought to be a youth of remarkable qualities,"[4] and in the same month he wrote that it was the ambition of Frederick IV to have his son marry Elizabeth. His son had the backing of all the German Protestant princes, and James I "leans more to the Count Palatine," while Anne, his Catholic wife, favoured a Spanish alliance.[5] Thus, by the end of 1610, a division of opinion had arisen at Court about the marriage of Elizabeth that was to last down to the time of her actual wedding with Frederick two years later. The Catholic op-

---

[3] Geoffrey Parker, *Europe in Crisis, 1598—1648* (London: Fontana Paperbacks, 1979), p. 85.
[4] *Calendar of State Papers, Venetian, 1610—13* (London: H.M. Stationary Office, 1905), p. 41.
[5] *Calendar of State Papers, Venetian*, p. 111.

117

position to Frederick was led by Queen Anne. His most fervent supporter was Prince Henry. James wavered between the extremes. According to one chronicler of the period, Francis Osborne, it was young Prince Henry who "gave the first incouragement to the Prince Elector to attempt his sister, desiring more to head an Army into Germany than he durst make shew of."[6] Osborne tells us that Henry was "saluted by the Puritans as one prefigured in the *Apocalypse* for Rome's destruction."[7] Here we catch a glimpse of the tendency of the period to view politics apocalyptically and to cast its leading figures in apocalyptic roles. For Henry and his followers in England, the marriage of Elizabeth and Frederick, the leading of an army into Germany, and the defeat of Antichrist were of a piece.

The negotiations for the marriage continue into 1611. On February 24th, the Venetian ambassador reported that the Palatine, "having changed his mind about coming in person," was instead sending an envoy to negotiate for the hand of Elizabeth.[8] In March he speaks "of the great support for the Palatine who will be coming himself in a few months." The King is "greatly inclined to the match," and both the French and the Scots are urging Frederick's suit. On April 21st he reports that the eldest son of the Duke of Neuberg is expected in England to "ask for the Princess in the Palatine's name."[10] On July 7th he announces that the Elector Palatine is coming in person.[11] The same news was relayed by Dudley Carleton to a correspondent on July 15th: "the Palatine of the Rhine is coming."[12]

From the beginning of 1611, then, down to mid-July, the period when Shakespeare may have been writing *The Tempest*, there was a constant expectation in England that the Elector Palatine or a representative would arrive to claim the hand of Elizabeth. It was, I suggest, in anticipation of this event that Shakespeare wrote *The Tempest*, complete with its betrothal masque. For reasons that will be explained later the Elector Palatine did not come. Nevertheless Shakespeare's new play was presented at Court on November 1st, 1611 as the opening play of the Christmas festivities. We must ask why a play written to celebrate a specific betrothal was acted even although the expected betrothal was postponed. The answer lies in the intense

---

[6] Francis Osborne, *Traditional Memoirs on the Reign of King James* in *Works* (1673), p. 542.

[7] Osborne, p. 529.

[8] *Calendar of State Papers, Venetian*, p. 181.

[9] Ibid., p. 202.

[10] Ibid., p. 204.

[11] Ibid., p. 207.

[12] *Calendar of State Papers, Domestic, 1611—1618*, p. 59.

interest being taken in the first royal match of James's reign, and in the hopes of the majority that it would be a Protestant match. As we saw the Court was divided into two factions. A play like *The Tempest* with its young royal couple and also celebrating a betrothal would have been highly topical in the autumn of 1611. It is this topicality that explains why it was performed in advance of the event it was written to celebrate.

Evidence of the widespread interest being taken in the betrothal and marriage of Elizabeth is provided by a number of other plays written before November, 1611, and I would like to discuss these briefly because they show that *The Tempest* was not alone in alluding to this subject of national importance. The first is Beaumont and Fletcher's *Philaster*, first mentioned in John Davies of Hereford's *Scourge of Folly* which was entered for publication on October 8, 1610.[13] Although completed by the end of 1610, this play was not produced until the winter of 1612—13 during the wedding festivities of Elizabeth and Frederick when it was given two performances. Graham Parry has suggested that it was popular because of its topicality. Its plot "expressed the sense of dangers averted and emphasizes the exceptional good fortune of Elizabeth in finding against the odds a husband to whom she was affectionately drawn, and who was a firm anti-Spanish figure".[14] Parry also suggests that the anti-Spanish tone of the play reflects popular opposition to James's occasional plans of marrying off his children to a Catholic prince. It is equally possible that it reflects the opposition to the pro-Catholic faction at Court led by Queen Anne and which from late 1610 onwards was pressing for a Catholic match. I am suggesting that *Philaster*, like *The Tempest*, was written perhaps at the end of 1610 in support of the match between Elizabeth and Frederick then thought to be imminent. It retained rather than gained topicality when it was finally produced at court in 1612—13.

References to the question of the marriage of the royal children have been detected in another play that is often associated with *Philaster*. This is Shakespeare's *Cymbeline*. Normally dated to 1609—10 on the basis of what J. M. Nosworthy, the editor of the Arden edition of the play, has called "a pitifully slight body of external evidence",[15] the only solid piece of evidence points to a performance of the play some time between May 15th and September 12th, 1611, when Simon Forman recorded in his diary his impressions of *Cymbeline*.[16] The play was therefore performed at a time when Frederick

---

[13] See Andrew Gurr, Introd. to Revels Plays ed. of *Philaster* (Manchester: Manchester Univ. Press, 1969), p. xxvi.

[14] Parry, *The Golden Age Restor'd*, p. 100.

[15] Nosworthy, Introd. to Arden *Cymbeline* (London: Methuen, 1955), p. xv.

[16] See Chambers, *Willilam Shakespeare*, II, 337.

was constantly expected to arrive to claim Elizabeth as his bride despite the opposition to the match of the Catholic faction at Court. The play's connections with the royal family have been noted by commentators.[17] Graham Parry has pointed out that the cedar imagery used of Cymbeline links him with James, while the reference to birds and especially the Phoenix links Imogen with Princess Elizabeth.[18] It can be added that the name Posthumous Leonatus would have recalled Frederick V as the surviving son of the old Lion of the Palatinate, Frederick IV, and that the Queen's opposition to the marriage of Imogen and Posthumous on account of his inferior rank exactly corresponds to Queen Anne's objection that the Palatine was unworthy of a daughter of the King of Britain. As we have seen, the basic situation of *Cymbeline* as produced in the late Spring or Summer of 1611 accurately reflects the tensions at Court concerning the marriage of Elizabeth. There is no need to argue, as Frances Yates has done, that *Cymbeline* was adapted in readiness for the wedding festivities of 1612—13 in order to glorify King James and his children, and then cancelled because the death of Prince Henry destroyed the balance of the play.[19] No large-scale adaptation would have been necessary since in its original conception *Cymbeline* in 1611 was already concerned with the hoped-for marriage of Elizabeth and Frederick.

The third play in which references to the royal match have been detected is also by Shakespeare. This is *The Winter's Tale* seen at the Globe by Simon Forman on April 20th, 1611. It was performed at Court on November 5th, four days after the first performance of *The Tempest* and again during the wedding festivities of 1612—13. Graham Parry writes of this last performance that the play "must have taken on fresh significance when played before Elizabeth and Frederick, as it could be made to mirror their courtship and express the hopes for a brilliant future now vested in this couple after the recent death of Prince Henry, who could be poignantly identified with the precocious young Mamilius, the heir to Leontes' throne who dies so suddenly in the play."[20] Here again Parry's suggestion that *The Winter's Tale* took on "fresh significance" at its second performance at Court is not strictly true; it rather *retained* the significance it had had during its performances at the Globe and at Court in 1611. Like *Philaster* and *Cymbeline* and, I sug-

---

[17] For a survey of criticism linking *Cymbeline* to the contemporary cult of the Stuarts, see F. David Hoeniger, "Shakespeare's Romances Since 1958: A Retrospect," in *Shakespeare Survey*, 29 (1976), 3—4.

[18] Parry, *The Golden Age Restor'd*, pp. 103, 105.

[19] Yates, *Shakespeare's Last Plays* (London: Routledge and Kegan Paul, 1975), pp. 41—99.

[20] Parry, *The Golden Age Restor'd*, p. 102.

gest, *The Tempest, The Winter's Tale* reflects the mood of intense expectation in England in 1611 that Elizabeth would marry her Protestant Prince. In each of these plays the successful marriages or betrothals with which they end anticipate the real-life event by over a year, although, as we have already seen, when they were written the betrothal and marriage seemed imminent. In the case of *The Winter's Tale*, the death of Prince Henry in November, 1612, may be reflected, as Parry suggests, in the sudden death of Mamilius in the play. It is just possible that a similar revision occasioned by the death of Henry would explain Ferdinand's reference to Antonio's "brave son" (I.ii. 441), who otherwise makes no appearance in *The Tempest*.

If my suggestion is accepted that *The Tempest* as originally written in 1611 was intended as a celebration of the forthcoming betrothal of the royal couple, its second performance was in the nature of a revival, put on perhaps for the sake of the Elector Palatine who had not yet seen it. The play he saw was not hastily adapted by Shakespeare for the occasion, but was virtually the same play as had been performed about a year previously. For many of those present it was not new, and even, as we shall see a little out of date where topicality is concerned. But there may have been a brand new play specially written for the occasion of the wedding by Shakespeare, one that was apparently eagerly awaited. This is his final play, *Henry VIII*. As R. A. Foakes has pointed out, "the play may have had a more specific connection with the triumphs of the wedding [of Elizabeth and Frederick], in its pageantry, and its celebration of peace, its processions, perhaps reflecting the progress of Princess Elizabeth to the bridal ceremony."[21] The wedding revived memories of the days of the old Elizabeth, now returned in the form of her young namesake, and the identification of the two Elizabeths was common at the time of the wedding. The prophecy of peace and prosperity made by Cranmer over the cradle of the infant Elizabeth I is equally applicable, as Foakes suggests, to both James and to Elizabeth Stuart. There is no record of *Henry VIII* having been performed at Court during the wedding festivities of 1612—13, but Foakes makes the interesting suggestion that it may have been this play that is referred to in a contemporary account of the wedding:

Much expectation was made of a stage play to be acted in the Great Hall by the King's players, where many hundred of people stood attending the same; but it lapsed contrarie, for greater pleasures were preparing.[22]

---

[21] R. A. Foakes, Introd. to Arden *Henry VIII*, p. xxx.
[22] Foakes, Introd. to Arden *Henry VIII*, p. xxx, citing *The Magnificent Marriage of the Two Great Princes* (1613), from Chambers, *William Shakespeare*, II, 342.

We have seen that three plays by Shakespeare, *Cymbeline, The Winter's Tale* and *Henry VIII* appear to contain topical references to the betrothal or wedding of the Elector Palatine and Elizabeth. Two of them were performed in 1611. This argues a considerable interest on the part of Shakespeare in this young couple, and this strengthens my contention that *The Tempest* too celebrates them in the persons of Ferdinand and Miranda.

I suggested a little earlier that in some respects *The Tempest* seen during the winter of 1612—13 was already a little out-of-date, and I shall now try and explain this in terms of the major crisis that developed in Europe during 1611, reaching a climax in November when *The Tempest* was put on at Court. It was this crisis that prevented the Elector Palatine from coming to England to claim Elizabeth as his bride. I shall first of all describe this crisis in broad outline, and then focus on the person who was at the centre of it, the hermetic Holy Roman Emperor, Rudolf II, in process of being deposed by his brother Matthias. I shall suggest that in November, 1611, the figure of Prospero in *The Tempest*, deprived of power by his own brother, would have irresistably reminded the audience of Rudolf II.

The Hermetic Monarch

The European crisis that erupted in Europe in 1611 had to do with a struggle for control of the Holy Roman Empire, traditionally ruled by a Catholic Hapsburg chosen by the electoral princes of Germany. In 1611 the Holy Roman Emperor, Rudolf II, was well on the way to being deposed by his brother Matthias, and in an attempt to regain power, Rudolf was appealing to James and to the Protestant Evangelical Union for support. It is probable that Prince Henry's plans of leading an army into Germany was aimed at the reinstatement of Rudolf. It is clear also that by the end of 1611 an agreement had been reached between James and Rudolf to prevent Matthias succeeding as Holy Roman Emperor, and to elect in his stead James's brother-in-law, the King of Denmark.[23]

The plans for the deposition of Rudolf II and his replacement by his brother Matthias go back to 1606 when it was agreed by the Hapsburg dynasty that Rudolf should be removed for gross neglect of government caused by his addiction to occult studies. In June, 1608, Rudolf was compelled to surrender the crowns of Austria, Hungary and Moravia to Matthias, leaving Rudolf only with the imperial crown and the crown of

[23] *Calendar of State Papers, Venetian,* pp. 426, 434, 443.

122

Bohemia. With the object of wresting even these from Rudolf, Matthias entered Prague at the head of a Catholic army in March, 1611. Rudolf fled to his palace, the Hradschin, where along with his artists, alchemists and astrologers, he was to remain a virtual prisoner until his death on January 20th, 1612. In April, 1611, Matthias was declared King of Bohemia and was crowned on May 23rd. It now only remained for him to obtain the imperial crown. Rudolf, always ambiguous in his relations with Rome, now turned to the Protestants of Europe for support. To arrange this support a Diet made up of the Protestant princes of the Evangelical Union was convened at Rothenberg in September. It was attendance at this Diet as head of the Union that prevented the Elector Palatine from coming to England to win Elizabeth. On October 28th (four days before the performance of *The Tempest* at Court) envoys were sent from the Diet to England asking James I to take the Union under his protection, support the reinstatement of Rudolf by mililtary intervention, and agree to the marriage of the Elector Palatine and Elizabeth. At the same time Rudolf was negotiating with the Protestants for military support. He offered to make the Elector Palatine's chief adviser, Christian of Anhalt, a member of his secret council, and to marry the Elector's widowed mother.[24] James, as we saw, responded favourably to the appeals from the Protestant Diet and from Rudolf. Early in November, it was announced that the King had finally agreed to the marriage of his daughter to the Elector Palatine "who by the best-affected is here wished for in good devotion".[25] The European crisis, then, on November 1st, 1611, when James I and his courtiers sat down to watch *The Tempest*, centred on a monarch all but deposed by his brother for having neglected his duties as a ruler and for devoting himself to hermetic studies, and who was appealing to be released from his imprisonment in the Hradschin by the Protestant forces of Europe led by the Elector Palatine and his hoped-for-bride, Elizabeth Stuart. Even if Shakespeare had not intended his audience to think of the hermetic Emperor when they saw Prospero, I believe that James and many in the audience on that occasion would inevitably have done so. But for reasons that will now be given I believe that Shakespeare in his portrait of the magician-ruler did intend his audience to think of the best known living example of such a ruler in Europe at that time, Rudolf II.

That Shakespeare was aware of Rudolf and could allude to the rapproche-

---

[24] Philippe Erlanger, *L'Empereur Insolite: Rodolphe II de Habsbourg, 1552—1612* (Paris: Albin Michel, 1971), p. 250.
[25] Sir Ralph Windwood, *Memorials*, III, 301, cited by Nichols, *The Progresses of King James the First* (1828), II, 432.

ment between the Emperor and James that goes back to 1610 when James dedicated his *Premonition to all most Mighty Monarchs of Christendom* to Rudolf may be indicated by a passage in *Cymbeline*. It will be remembered that this play was performed at the Globe some time after May 15th, 1611. In the 5th Act of the play the soothsayer interprets the riddle of the vision of Jupiter and concludes in this way:

> For the Roman eagle,
> From south to west on wing soaring aloft,
> Lessen'd herself and in the beams o'th'sun
> So vanish'd; which foreshadow'd our princely eagle,
> Th'imperial Caesar, should again unite
> His favour with the radiant Cymbeline,
> Which shines here in the west.
> (V.vi. 471—477).

Cymbeline speaking in the accents of the King of Peace, James himself, replies:

> Publish we this peace
> To all our subjects. Set we forward: let
> A Roman, and a British ensign wave
> Friendly together
> (V.v. 479—482).

I believe that these words spoken in the early summer of 1611, and which are part of the "pseudo-history" of the play,[26] refer unambiguously to the rapprochement of James and the Imperial Caesar, Rudolf. We have already seen how the imagery used of Cymbeline and Imogen associates them with James and Elizabeth, and that the name Posthumus Leonatus recalls Frederick V, the son of the Lion of the Palatine. If these identifications are correct, the "imperial Caesar" can only refer to Rudolf. Let us now consider the resemblances of Rudolf II to Prospero in *The Tempest*.

In the long speech in which Prospero explains how he and Miranda came to be on the island, he tells her that he was "prime duke" of Milan, the first among the Italian signories,

> being so reputed
> In dignity, and for the Liberal Arts
> Without a parallel; those being all my study,
> The government I cast upon my brother,
> And to my state grew stranger, being transported
> And rapt in secret studies.
> (I.ii. 72—77).

---

[26] See J. M. Nosworthy, Introd. to Arden *Cymbeline*, p. xix.

Here Prospero is revealed as a bookworm rather than a man of action, happier in the library rather than in the council-chamber. He is famed for his cultivation of the liberal arts, but also for "secret studies" that cause him to neglect his duties as a ruler. He goes on:

> I, thus neglecting worldly ends, all dedicated
> To closeness and bettering of my mind
> With that which, but by being so retir'd,
> O'erpriz'd all popular rate, in my false brother
> Awak'd an evil nature
> (I.ii. 89—93)

This important statement indicates clearly Prospero's recognition that his own neglect of government caused by immersion in esoteric studies aroused a latent evil in his brother. The balance between activity and withdrawn self-betterment has been lost. In Europe in 1611 the consequences of preferring secret studies to practical government were vividly exemplified by the case of Rudolf II.

Visitors to Prague during the first decade of the seventeenth century were struck by the Emperor's inaccessibility and the extreme difficulty of conducting any business with him. A member of a Tuscan embassy reported in 1609 the long delays that preceded an audience with Rudolf. After praising his exceptional knowledge of things, he adds that Rudolf has, however, ruined everything "by taking up the study of art and nature, with such an extreme lack of moderation that he has deserted the affairs of state for alchemists' laboratories, painters' studios, and the workshops of clockmakers. Indeed he has given over his entire palace to such things and is using all his revenue to further them. This has estranged him completely from common humanity".[27] These observations of the Tuscan envoy sound almost like a paraphrase of Prospero's own words cited above. He continues: "Disturbed in his mind by some ailment of melancholy, he has begun to love solitude and shut himself off in his palace as if behind the bars of a prison" (p. 45).

Rudolf's "closeness" like Prospero's was caused by the nature of his studies. In the Proposition drawn up by the Hapsburg Archdukes in 1606 giving the reasons for deposing Rudolf the character of these studies is revealed:

His majesty is interested only in wizards, alchymists, kabbalists and the like, sparing no expense to find all kinds of treasure, learn secrets and use scandalous ways of harming his enemies (p. 196).

---

[27] R. J. W. Evans, *Rudolf II and His World* (Oxford: Oxford Univ. Press, 1973), p. 45. This major study of Rudolf and of the hermetic culture of Rudolfine Prague forms the basis of this account of Rudolf. The following page references in the text are to this work.

Locked up for long periods inside the Hradschin in Prague, Rudolf devoted himself to building up a private, magical world of his own that only a few privileged visitors were allowed to glimpse. Part of it was composed of his celebrated art collection, one of the largest ever known with some three thousand paintings and eighteen thousand engravings. It included works of Cranach, Titian, Corregio, Brueghel and above all Dürer for whose works Rudolf had a special passion. In his Cabinet of Arts and Marvels were kept some of his most prized items: skeletons of rare animals, the rod that once belonged to Moses, a grain of the earth from which God created Adam, some iron nails from Noah's Ark, rare stones and gems, marbles whose grains and coloration by happenstance formed a picture of the devil or a whole city. In the gardens around the Hradschin the Emperor gathered a "profusion of strange plants and creatures" (p. 178). Rudolf visited his various collections regularly, using them, as R. J. W. Evans has suggested, for private contemplation in an attempt to find in the Baroque confusion of their detail an underlying unity. Like Prospero, Rudolf was without parallel for the liberal arts, and the Rudolfine Kunstkammer was "widely regarded as one of the miracles of the age" (p. 178).

No less famous was Rudolf's library. In the Proposition of 1606 describing his incapacity as a ruler, it is stated that "he also has a whole library of magic books" (p. 196). Like his other collections, Rudolf's library was hermetic in character, containing works on astrology, magic, cabalism, numerology and millenarian prophecy. The works of Paracelsus and his followers, many of them patronized by Rudolf, were well represented. Lull, Roger Bacon, Agrippa and other occultists found a place in the library, as did the works of Plato and the Neoplatonists. Contemporaries were "struck by the large number of mystical, Hermetic, and secret books" (p. 126). One of the most notorious of these was the medieval *Picatrix*, a treatise on necromancy, which Rudolf is said to have used to place a curse on his brother, Matthias, during 1611. Symptomatic of Rudolf's obsessive interest in "secret studies" was his desperate attempt to obtain the chest that had belonged to the Paracelsan physician, Oswald Croll, in the belief that it contained "strange and wondrous things—evidently occult literature" (p. 142). It will be remembered that Croll was the author of the influential *Basilica Chymica* (1609) and of the *Tractatus de Signaturis Internis Rerum* (1608) which I suggested earlier may have been known to Shakespeare when he wrote *The Tempest*. It should also be pointed out that Croll was the agent in Prague of Christian of Anhalt, principal adviser to the Elector Palatine.

In *The Tempest* special emphasis is placed on Prospero's library in Milan. He bitterly complains to Miranda of his brother's gibe that "my library /

Was dukedom large enough" (I.ii. 109—10). When they are banished from Milan, Gonzalo

> Knowing I lov'd my books, he furnish'd me
> From mine own library with volumes that
> I prize above my dukedom.
> (I.ii. 166—168).

The nature of these books is indicated by Caliban:

> there thou mayst brain him,
> Having first seized his books . . .
> Remember
> First to possess his books; for without them
> He's but a sot, as I am, nor hath not
> One spirit to command . . .
> Burn but his books
> (III.ii. 85—93).

It is clear that these books would in many cases be identical in type with those on the shelves of Rudolf's library. They are the magical works necessary to Prospero for carrying out the magical act of transmutation on the island. With them he is able to control spirits, raise a tempest and suspend the normal workings of nature for his own purposes.

In addition to his collection of magical works, Prospero also

> has brave utensils, — for so he calls them —
> Which, when he has a house, he'll deck withal.
> (III.ii. 94—95)

These utensils must have been among the "necessaries" provided by Gonzalo along with the books of magic when Prospero was exiled from Milan. As I have suggested these "utensils" are not culinary pots and pans, but the equipment needed by an alchemist to perform the Work. Among the utensils would have been pelicans, alembics, curcurbits, pans and ladles, bellows, the standard equipment in other words of the many alchemical laboratories existing in Europe in the early seventeenth century.[28] Prospero's cave, like that of Kelpius in the community of the Woman of the Wilderness in the New World, housed an alchemical workshop and a library of the requisite works. Outside it were stacked the thousands of logs necessary to keep the fires going.

---

[28] An idea of the sort of utensils used by Prospero is conveyed in the following description of Rudolf's alchemical laboratory in the Hradschin: "On wooden pins, driven into crevices of the stone walls at convenient intervals, hung utensils identical in shape with those used in culinary operations." See Henry Carrington Bolton, *The Follies of Science at the Court of Rudolf II, 1576—1612* (Milwaukee: Pharmaceutical Review Publishing Co., 1904), pp. 132—4.

We may imagine that the alchemical laboratory in Milan from which Gonzalo hastily took the most essential utensils was not unlike the best equipped alchemical laboratory in Europe of the time, that of Rudolf in Prague. Throughout his long reign, hundreds of alchemists, including both charlatans and genuine seekers, were attracted to Prague by Rudolf. In 1584, John Dee and his assistant, Edward Kelley, gave a demonstration of the alchemical Art to the Emperor, and it is this event that is referred to in Jonson's *The Alchemist*: Mammon speaks of Subtle, the alchemist and Paracelsan physician, as

> A man, the Emperor
> Has courted above Kelly: sent his medals
> And chains, t'invite him.
> (IV.i. 89—91).

The Emperor's laboratories were housed in a building close to the Hradschin, and contained three large furnaces, one for smelting ores, one a large *Bain-marie* or water-bath used for maintaining steady low temperatures, and a furnace used in distillation. Rudolf took a personal interest in the experiments carried out there under the direction of Tadesius Hajek, one of the Emperor's Paracelsan physicians. A painting by Vacslar Brozik shows Rudolf and a party of courtiers watching a demonstration of an alchemical transmutation. An old man with a long white beard is explaining to an inscrutable Rudolf the long-sought secret, while others examine a piece of metal. A fire blazes in the background. In the foreground we see a litter of alchemical "utensils", and scattered over the table are the sheets of the alchemical book describing how the projection is to be achieved.[29] It was a scene that Rudolf had often witnessed, hence perhaps his impassive expression. By the end of his life he had been fooled too often to be easily impressed.

Rudolf's patronage of alchemists extended to the many Paracelsan doctors active in Bohemia. These included such figures as Heinrich Khunrath, Nicholas Barnaud,[30] Martin Ruland, author of the Paracelsan *Lexicon Alchemiae* (1612), Oswald Croll, and not least, Michael Maier.[31] It was

---

[29] This painting, now in the Fischer Collection, Pittsburgh, is reproduced in Neil Powell, *Alchemy: The Ancient Science* (London: Aldus Books, 1976), p. 90.

[30] Nicholas Barnaud relates in his *Commentariolum in aenigmaticum* (1597), pp. 10—11, how he witnessed an alchemical projection in the presence of Hajek, chief alchemist to Rudolf.

[31] Another prominent Paracelsan physician in Prague was Christopher Guarinoneus, known after a spectacular cure of the Pope in 1600 as Doctor Elixirabilils. The members of the medical academy he founded in Prague and named after Rudolf II included Maier, Croll, Boethius and Martin Ruland, all Paracelsan physicians; see H. C. Bolton, *The Follies of Science*, p. 97, 109.

128

through Maier, as we have seen, that contact was established between the influential Paracelsan physicians of Prague and those of London, and this contact can now be dated to late 1611 when Maier sent his two Christmas-greetings to James I and Prince Henry.

The millenarian note in these two curious documents is an indication of the deep interest of Rudolf in millenarianism especially during the first decade of the seventeenth century. Kepler's work *De Stella Nova* ((1606) is dedicated to Rudolf, and deals with the astrological and chiliastic significance of the two *novae* that appeared in 1602 and 1604, and which were named after Kepler. It was these same stars that the Rosicrucians associated with the discovery of the tomb of Christian Rosenkreutz and with a new phase in the work of the Rosicrucians, work cryptically related by them to *Miranda sextae aetatis*. It cannot yet be proved, but it seems likely that until the death of Rudolf in 1612 Prague was one of the major centres of the apocalyptic movement that is later associated with the Rosicrucians. The foundation of a "society of peace" by Rudolf in 1610 with regalia made in his own workshops can be seen as one expression of the growing desire for millenarian peace in Europe. R. J. W. Evans has linked Rudolf's project with "the notion dear to Comenius of a 'peaceful centre', a *Centrum Securitatis*, and a Paradise of the Heart which would follow after and resolve the Labyrinth of the World."[32] This notion of a labyrinthine search for a centre of peace, reflected in *The Tempest* as the maze-like search for the paradisial centre of the island where Miranda waits, arises from a major preoccupation of this unsettled period:

The idea of the 'labyrinth' was a prevalent one at the time, and others viewed it, like Comenius, in eschatological terms, with connotations of pilgrimage and alienation. Rudolf's obsession with prophecy and chiliastic beliefs was a survival from the years round 1600 . . . and the vision of an inner paradise, a centre of security, finds close parallels in the symbolism of alchemy and the religious mystics.[33]

Like the long line of Holy Roman Emperors who were his ancestors, Rudolf too was the inevitable centre of an apocalyptic cult. His motto, *Adsit*, (may he appear), was interpreted to mean that with his appearance the Antichrist would be defeated; like James of Britain he was represented as a second Augustus, establishing imperial peace and restoring the Golden Age.[34] His motto, *Adsit*, was also expanded into the words *Auxilium Domini Sit Iniquis Terror*—may the aid of God be a terror to evil-doers.

---

[32] Evans, *Rudolf II*, pp. 81—2.
[33] Evans, p. 277.

Once again we are compelled to make a difficult mental adjustment to understand how politics was conceived of in this period. In Prague in 1611, just as in London, the political struggle for power in Europe was seen as a struggle between good and evil. Rudolf's appeal for help to the Elector Palatine, the Palatine's wooing of Elizabeth, Maier's two Christmas greetings to James and Henry, young Henry's plans of leading an army into Germany, were regarded as moves in a final apocalyptic showdown which would be succeeded by the longed-for Peace of a Thousand Years. For Protestants in 1611, the unwilling leaders of this final confrontation were two figures who bore a remarkable resemblance to each other, Rudolf II and James I.

Both longed for peace and dreaded war. In Maier's greetings to James he states that the thing most worthy of a great king is to govern in peace and not harass his kingdom with war and strife.[35] The same words would have pleased Rudolf II. R. J. W. Evans has drawn attention to this and other similarities between the two rulers. Both prided themselves on their extensive learning, and were flatteringly praised for it. They shared an almost obsessive interest in the world of the supernatural.[36] Both rejected the extremes of Protestantism and Catholicism, and sought a middle way between them, hoping thereby to bring peace to Europe and avoid the violence that each of them personally feared. In character both monarchs were secretive and disliked public appearances. "Their private life was abnormal, dictated by brusque and unaccountable changes of temper, characterized by sexual irregularity and artifically created favourites who reflected only their masters' moods."[37] R. J. W. Evans neatly compares them by saying; "If James was the wisest fool in Christendom, then Rudolf was perhaps the wisest madman." It is therefore not strange that the two monarchs were eventually drawn to each other. We saw that in 1609 James dedicated his defence of national sovereignty against the Papacy to Rudolf, probably aware of the Emperor's deep distrust of Rome. Rudolf reciprocated by sending James a celestial globe and a clock in the same year.[38] As Matthias stripped his brother more and more of effective power, Rudolf began turning

---

[34] See Erlanger, *L'Empereur Insolite*, pp. 111, 128.

[35] The words, *magnique res precis Ac Digna rege est gestire pace Nec instari Eius regna Bello aut Rixa*, are inscribed in one of the petals of the central Rose.

[36] They differ radically, however, in their attitude to the realm of magic. Unlike Rudolf, James regarded all forms of magic as satanic, even, as we shall see, when practised for good ends.

[37] Evans, *Rudolf II*, p. 81.

[38] Evans, p. 81, n. 1.

to the Protestants for support, and this included appeals to James. As we saw, the rapprochement between James and Rudolf is probably referred to at the end of *Cymbeline*.

I have suggested that the audience present at the first performance of *The Tempest* would inevitably have found striking resemblances between Prospero and Rudolf. I have argued that it was Shakespeare's intention that they should do so, just as the young couple in the play who would return to take over from Prospero were intended to recall the similar role of Frederick and Elizabeth in relation to the aged Rudolf in Prague. I believe that this would have been perfectly clear to the audience watching *The Tempest* in November 1611. At the same time, it would be a mistake to regard this play as a palpable political allegory such as Middleton's anti-Spanich, *The Chess-Game*, simply to be translated into its topical equivalent. The relationship of the main characters in *The Tempest* to living individuals such as Rudolf or Elizabeth and Frederick is something more than mere identification. The world of *The Tempest* is an idealization of the real world in and around 1611, not a realistic copy. It presents a vision of what was happening then but distanced by art in order to clarify the issues involved. Here and there incidents and characters coincide with contemporary events and living persons, just as Spenser's Fairyland and the fictive charcters that inhabit it shiftingly suggest Elizabeth's England and its leading personalities. The vision of *The Tempest* is related to the real world of 1611 in the same way that a vivid compelling dream remembered after sleep mirrors a person's waking life. Such a dream is both topical and archetypal, and throws light on the current situation of that individual by relating it to perennial or universal myths of human behaviour.

The Royal Wedding

With the death of Rudolf II in January, 1612, *The Tempest* lost some of its topicality. During the interregnum following his death, the Elector Palatine automatically took over the administration of the Empire,[39] and it is clear that among the militant Protestants led by Prince Henry there was hope that Frederick V would "attain the Emperiall Diadem."[40] The pressure on James to declare officially his support for Frederick as husband to Elizabeth was mounting, and in May, 1612, he agreed to the marriage, "subject to the

[39] *Calendar of State Papers, Venetian*, p. 539.
[40] Osborne, *Traditional Memoirs*, p. 541.

Princess' pleasure, who wishes first to see the Palatine and be wooed a while."[41] The Elector Palatine finally landed in England in October. The sudden death of Henry early in November caused a further postponement of the betrothal and wedding. On December 27th the betrothal ceremony took place, and on St Valentine's Day, February 14th, the long-awaited wedding took place. It was preceded and followed by the most spectacular and costly festivities so far in James's reign. I would like to look at these festivities from the point of view of the image of Elizabeth and Frederick that was projected in them. As we shall see, it is identical in themes and iconography to the image of the royal couple in *The Tempest*.

For Londoners the kenyote of the royal celebrations was publicly sounded in the two elaborate shows staged on the Thames opposite Whitehall on the days immediately preceding the wedding. On February 11th huge crowds witnessed an allegorical fireworks display, and two days later on the eve of the wedding a mock sea-battle depicting the capture of Algiers. It is significant that "Prince Henry had [had] a hand in contriving the fireworks and the river battle."[42] Both can be interpreted as allegorical renderings of the militant Protestant policies that he and the Palsgrave had entertained at this time. The fireworks display carried out on pontoons floating on the Thames told the story of how Lady Lucida is imprisoned in a castle by the magic arts of Mango, a "black-sould, hell-commanding magitian."[43] St George arrives to rescue her. On the bridge leading to the forty-foot-high tower where the Magician lives, St George with a burning feather in his helmet, a blazing lance and a fiery sword defeats first a flame-throwing Dragon and then a Giant. He finally captures Mango and releases the distressed damsel, Lucida. The theme of this fireworks display, as Graham Parry points out, is "close to that of Book I of the *Faerie Queene*, where English-Protestant St George defeats the Papal magician Archimago, routs the giant Orgoglio or pride, and destroys the great Dragon who represents the devil and all his works, to secure the release and companionship of Una or Truth."[44] The Palsgrave had been installed as a Knight of the Order of the Garter and of St George only a few days before, and it is clear that the fireworks display deals with the role Frederick was expected to play as a new St George in the

[41] *Calendar of State Papers, Venetian*, p. 539.
[42] Parry, *The Golden Age Restor'd*, p. 4.
[43] This account is based on the description of John Taylor the Water-Poet, printed in Nichols, *The Progresses of King James*, 2, 530 ff. An m.s. in the British Library, B.M. Royal 17. C. xxxv, contains some interesting coloured illustrations of the main episodes in the fireworks display.
[44] Parry, *The Golden Age Restor'd*, pp. 96—7.

struggle against Rome and the Antichrist. The evocation of Book I of the *Faerie Queene* is especially interesting. As we saw, in this Book Spenser combines the theme of St George with that of the apocalyptic Rider of the Book of Revelation rescuing the Woman in the Wilderness from the persecution of Antichrist. I have suggested that the same apocalyptic theme is found in *The Tempest*, with Miranda as the Wonderful Woman of Revelation 12 also in exile on the wilderness of the island and about to be released by Ferdinand. Iconographically, therefore, Spenser's Una and the Red Crosse Knight, the Lucida and St George of the firework display, and Shakespeare's Miranda and Ferdinand are equivalent.

The second public show also has a bearing on *The Tempest* which has not, to my knowledge, been commented on. This was the spectacular sea-battle between British warships and the galleys of the Turks that took place on the Thames between Whitehall and Lambeth on the afternoon of February 13th, "with the drums, trumpets, flutes and guns filling the ayre with repercussive acclamations" until finally the defeated Turkish commander of the castle on the Lambeth side of the river had been presented to the King and the Palsgrave at Whitehall steps.[45] The name of the castle displayed on a placard was Argier, the contemporary spelling of the name Algiers. Argier is also mentioned in *The Tempest* as the place from which Caliban's mother, Sycorax, was expelled, "For mischiefs manifold, and sorceries terrible" (I.ii. 264). She was expelled rather than executed "for one thing she did". What connection, if any, is there between this somewhat cryptic reference to Argier in *The Tempest* and the enactment of a sea-battle at Argier on the Thames in connection with the marriage of Elizabeth and Ferdinand?

The answer I believe lies in a suggestion first made by Charles Lamb that Shakespeare was referring to the celebrated attempt by the Holy Roman Emperor, Charles V, to defeat the Turkish pirates stationed in Algiers during an expedition there in 1541. The attempt failed according to an account that Lamb discovered in *The Accurate Description of Africa* by John Ogilby (1670) because a "witch of the town" used her powers to raise a violent tempest that scattered the Emperor's fleet and sunk many of his ships, forcing him to raise the siege.[46] This expedition like the earlier one of 1532 when Charles V captured Tunis was regarded by contemporaries as an apocalyptic event fulfilling the prophecies of the Book of Daniel and of Joachim of Fiore and preparing for a new Golden Age.[47] The dream of

---

[45] A vivid account of the sea-battle is given in John Taylor, *Heaven's Blessing and Earth's Joy* (1613), printed in Nichols, *The Progresses*, II, 529 ff.

[46] See the New Variorum *Tempest*, p. 60, where Lamb's suggestion is given in full.

[47] Reeves, *Joachim of Fiore*, p. 113.

defeating the successors of Barbarossa in North Africa with its inevitable apocalyptic overtones lived on into the seventeenth century, and was entertained by James 1.[48] The sea-battle on the Thames on February 13th, 1613, therefore, was a call to renew the crusade against the Turks begun by Charles V in the early part of the sixteenth century, and in particular to clear Algiers of its pirates who remained a threat to British ships throughout James's reign. In the case of Shakespeare's cryptic reference to Argier in *The Tempest*, it would seem that Lamb is right in relating it to Charles V's expedition to Algiers of 1541. The basic story of the play for which no source has yet been found may be derived from some account of the Emperor's attempts to pacify Tunis and Algiers. The unpopular marriage of Alonso's daughter, Claribel, to the African King of Tunis, is never fully explained in the play, but historically the time for such a dynastic union between Naples and Tunis would have been in the years following the capture of Tunis in 1532 when a native dynasty sympathetic to Christians was established there.

The militant themes of the two water-shows inspired by Prince Henry, and directed at Rome and at the Turk, the two representatives of Antichrist in the Protestant apocalyptic tradition, express the mood in which the wedding of Elizabeth and Frederick was celebrated.[49] The same mood, less militant but equally imbued with millenarian expectations, is found in the poetry and masques written to mark the event. Typical of the poetry of the period is the *Epithalamium* written by John Donne for the wedding. There is one passage in it that gives further evidence of the fact that Elizabeth was not only associated with the Phoenix (like Imogen in *Cymbeline*), but also with the heavenly wonder of Revelation 12:1:

> Up then faire Phoenix Bride, frustrate the Sunne,
>   Thyself from thy affection
>   Takes warmth enough, and from thine eye
> All lesser birdes will take their Jollitie.
>   Up, up, faire Bride, and call,
> Thy starres, from out their severall boxes, take
> Thy Rubies, Pearles, and Diamonds forth, and make
>   Thy selfe a constellation, of them All,
>   And by their blazing, signifie,

---

[48] Throughout James' reign the Barbary pirates operating from the ports of North Africa were a constant threat to British shipping. In 1621 James despeatched an expedition to subdue the pirates of Algiers.

[49] Thomas Campion refers in his *Songs of Mourning*, written after Henry's death and dedicated to the Elector Palatine, to the Prince's backing of voyages of exploration and to his plans of defeating "Christian-hating Thrace", that is, Turkey, had he lived. See Parry, *The Golden Age Restor'd*, pp. 89—91.

134

That a great Princess falls, but doth not die;
Bee thou a new starre, that to us portends
Ends of much wonder; and be Thou those ends.[50]

It is known that Donne was particularly interested in the new stars named after Kepler that appeared in 1602 and 1604, and which, as we have seen, were closely associated with the emergence of the Rosicrucian order.[51] Here Elizabeth Stuart is not only compared to a new star, but to a new star that portends "Ends of much wonder". She is called upon to be those ends herself. Given the millenial hopes evoked by this marriage, it is impossible to avoid the impression that once again the figure of the Wondrous Woman of Revelation 12 is being evoked in relation to Elizabeth Stuart. She is the wonder in the heavens, the "new starre", whose appearance announces a new dispensation. As Graham Parry remarks, "in the context of 1613, those 'ends of much wonder' must have been political, referring to men's expectation of the powerful new political and religious union that was created by this marriage".[52] Donne hyperbolically proclaims that it will bring a new age into being: "May all men date Records, from this thy Valentine."

A more direct evocation of the dawning Golden Age is found in the first of the Court Masques performed on the night of the wedding, *The Lord's Masque* devised by Thomas Campion, with elaborate stage scenery and devices arranged by Inigo Jones. The first part of this masque depicts the creation of the first human beings by Prometheus from stars moving "in an exceeding strange and delightful manner".[53] As we learn later in the masque, these first human beings belong to the original Golden Age:

Turn, turn, and honour now the life these figures bear;
Lo, how heav'nly natures far above all art appear!
Let their aspects revive in you the fire that shin'd so late,
Still mount and still retain your heavenly state.
Gods were with dance and with music serv'd of old,
Those happy days deriv'd their glorious style from gold;
This pair, by Hymen join'd, grace you with measures then,
Since they are both divine and you are more than men.
(ll. 389—396)

[50] John Donne, "Epithalamium, Or marriage Song on the Lady Elizabeth, and Count Palatine being married on St Valentine's Day," lines 29—40.
[51] See C. M. Coffin, *John Donne and the New Philosophy*, Diss. in *Studies in English and Comparative Literature*, No. 126 (Columbia: Columbia Univ. Press,1937), pp. 126 ff.
[52] Parry, *The Golden Age Restor'd*, pp. 105—6.
[53] Campion, *The Lords' Masque*, lines 173—4, in *A Book of Masques: In Honour of Allardyce Nicoll* (Cambridge: Cambridge Univ. Press, 1967), p. 110.

These words are addressed to the masquers, lords and ladies of the court, commanding them to dance before Elizabeth and Frederick as though they were gods living in the Golden Age. By gazing on their features, they will revive in themselves the fire of the stars, for Elizabeth and Frederick are divine. At one point in the masque the gods join the mortals, as Frederick and Elizabeth are drawn into the dance of the masquers. Towards the end of the masque the Sybil delivers a prophecy in Latin: with their marriage the strength of Britain is joined to that of Germany; one mind, one faith, one worship of God and simple love unite both nations; from Elizabeth will issue kings and emperors. Again the marriage is given a European significance and a prophetic character by silently substituting Germany for the much smaller Palatinate over which Frederick ruled. Was this in allusion to the hopes entertained by Prince Henry and even by James himself that his son-in-law would be more than a mere Palsgrave, perhaps even Emperor?

On the night following the performance of Campion's *Lords' Masque, The Masque of the Middle Temple and Lincoln's Inn* by George Chapman was presented. Inspired by the current interest in the Virginia plantation in which Prince Henry had had a financial stake, this feeble masque has the Princes of Virginia come to England to celebrate the wedding. Governed by the Briton Phoebus, Britain had become the home of Fortune and its bright sky

> (Enlightened with a Christian piety)
> Is never subject to black error's night.

In the conversion of the pagan Indians from worshippers of the sun to worshippers of James which occurs in the masque, Chapman refers optimistically to Britain's millenarian role as the spreader of Christianity to the parts of the world now being opened up by the voyagers. As Hugh Broughton wrote in his *A Revelation of the Holy Apocalypse* in 1610: "Now God driveth us to both Indias, not for Pepper and Tobacho: but in time to show his name."[54] By contrast Shakespeare in *The Tempest* demonstrates the difficulties of carrying out this idealistic mission, both in Prospero's attempts to educate Caliban and change his nature and in the corrupting effect of Stephano and Trinculo on him. Such pessimism is absent from Chapman's masque. The conversion of the pagan Indians, as in the apocalyptic literature of the period, is a sure indication that the Golden Age

---

[54] Hugh Broughton, *A Revelation of the Holy Apocalypse* (1610), p. 141, cited by Reeves, *Joachim of Fiore*, p. 156. Broughton and his ideas are ridiculed, as we have learnt to expect, by Jonson in *The Alchemist*, II.iii. 238, and throughout IV.v.

is imminent. Guaranteeing it are the Bride and Bridegroom who are praised
by Chapman as the twins, Love and Beauty, born in the Golden Age:

> "Mine" and "thine" were then unusde,
> All things common, nought abusde,
>   Freely Earth her frutage bearing.
> Nought then was car'd for that could fade,
> And thus the Golden Worlde was made.
>
> Now may the blessings of the golden age
> Swimme in these nuptials, e'en to holy rage,
> A hymn to Sleep prefer and all the ioyes
> That in his empire slumbers ever flow
> In these, and theirs in springs as endlesse growe.[55]

On two nights running, Elizabeth and Frederick, have been eulogized as
harbingers of the Golden Age, and it is perhaps for this reason that in the
third masque the accent is placed on their role as establishers of a universal
peace.

    This masque, *The Masque of The Inner Temple and Gray's Inn*, written
by Francis Beaumont in cooperation with Francis Bacon, was to have been
performed on February 16th, but because the King was exhausted from a
series of late nights, it was postponed until the following Saturday. The central device of this masque is a competition between Mercury and Iris to celebrate the marriage of the Rhine and the Thames, ending with Mercury
ordering the Olympic games to be renewed in honour of these "wish'd nuptials". The peace established throughout Greece at the time of the Olympic
games is, it is hinted, being established throughout the world by Jove's
representative on earth, James, and by the marriage of Elizabeth and
Frederick. It is the same millennial peace that is prophesied by Cranmer at
the end of *Henry VIII* (V.v. 39—47). As we saw, it has been suggested that
it was this new play that was to have been performed by the King's Men on
the same day as Beaumont's masque, possibly just before it, and which was
cancelled because of the large crowds that had gathered to see the masque
and perhaps because of the King's exhaustion after all the late-night revel-
ling.

    From this brief account of the main items in the wedding celebrations, we
can sense the immense enthusiasm that this match inspired in the nation. In
the poems, tracts, sermons and in the public spectacles and court entertainments produced to celebrate it there is a powerful sense of expectation

---

[55] Cited by Nichols, *The Progresses of King James*, II, 583—4.

and a hope that "Ends of much wonder" are imminent. In Frederick, wearing the insignia of the Order of the Garter, a new St George had appeared to rescue a maiden in distress, a Lucida, a Una, the Woman in the Wilderness. The Turk was to be defeated and the New World planted in preparation for the universal peace of the Millennium. The old Elizabeth had returned in the person of her sixteen-year-old namesake to reestablish the Golden Age. These were the themes of the celebrations, and they are identical with the themes that we have found in *The Tempest*. When this play received its second recorded performance some time during the wedding festivities, perhaps close to the day of the betrothal on December 27th, 1612, its relevance to the marriage of Elizabeth and Frederick would have been patent. In his own way and with a greater range of reference than his fellow-writers, Shakespeare also celebrates this marriage. As I have suggested, the relevance of *The Tempest* to the marriage was not accidentally acquired in the winter of 1612—13, but was integral to the play even in 1611. The nuptials, as Francis Beaumont pointed out in his masque, were "long-wish'd".[56] During the time between mid-1610 when the match was first proposed and the actual wedding early in 1613, the millenarian roles that Frederick and Elizabeth were to play were being defined for them. After their sumptuous marriage, they returned to Heidelberg to act out these roles in earnest.

Their subsequent career from 1613 to 1620 has been traced by Frances Yates in her *The Rosicrucian Enlightenment*, where she brings out its strong millenarian character and its links with the programme of the Rosicrucians. In 1619 they accepted the invitation of the Bohemians to become King and Queen of Bohemia, and for one brief winter they lived in Rudolf's old capital of Prague. It seemed as if the dream of a brave new world were coming true. A contemporary print shows Elizabeth and Frederick leading the Israelites through the wilderness and into the Promised Land.[57] A letter sent out of Prague at this time mentions that the followers of the Winter King and Queen of Bohemia were reading the apocalyptic *Exposition . . . of the xx chap. Revelation* written by James I.[58] Babylon was falling and the New Jerusalem was being established on earth. Another print celebrating the coronation of Elizabeth and Frederick carries the same millenariam

---

[56] Beaumont, *The Masque of the Inner Temple*, 1. 113, in *A Book of Masques*, p. 135.
[57] Reproduced in Yates, *The Rosicrucian Enlightenment*, plate 18 d.
[58] This letter is summarized in *Sir Henry Wotton: Life and Letters*, ed. L. Pearsall Smith (Oxford: Clarendon Press, 1907), I, 173. The *Exposition* referred to is *A Fruitful Meditation containing a Plaine and easie exposition . . . of the VII, VIII, IX, X verses of the 20 Chapter of the Revelation*, written by James as King of Scotland in 1588.

message. The royal couple are shown beneath a divine sun. To the right, a blazing city, covered by black smoke, is being destroyed by lightning. Devils hover over it, and monks are seen fleeing. To the left of them a sun is shown rising over a tranquil city.[59] In subject matter and layout this print is based on Botticelli's *Crucifixion* of 1502. Like his *Nativity* of 1500 which has been called "one of the greatest documents of Joachimist thought", the *Crucifixion* is also strongly influenced by the ideas of Joachim of Fiore and is apocalyptic in character.[60] Using probably a print of Botticelli's painting, the designer of the 1619 coronation print has transferred the apocalyptic message to Elizabeth and Frederick, made Prague the New Jerusalem and retained Rome as a symbol of the Fall of Babylon. After one brief millenial winter, the dream was shattered. James refused to come to the aid of his daughter and son-in-law. The imperial Catholic armies gathered, and in November, 1620 the army of Frederick and Elizabeth was defeated at the Battle of the White Mountain. They were driven into exile, and the protracted horrors of the Thirty Years' War commenced. Yet again the strength of the Antichrist had been underestimated.

The dream that was shattered at the Battle of the White Mountain was the dream of a regenerated world. We have seen in this chapter something of the nature of this potent dream, deriving ultimately from the prophecies of the Book of Revelation and in part from the myth of the returning Golden Age. The fascination of this millenarian dream, enriched by the thought of Joachim of Fiore, seems to have intensified around the year 1600. We have traced its influence in the thinking of the Paracelsan alchemists of the period and in the related movement of the Rosicrucians. For Protestants this dream became embodied in the persons of Elizabeth Stuart and Frederick the Elector Palatine, and as I have suggested their millenarian roles were being defined from 1610 onwards. In this process of what might be called mythic investment, the poets and dramatists of the time played an important part, and among them we must include Shakespeare.

I have also tried to show in this chapter that the various images of regeneration investigated earlier and regarded as central to *The Tempest* found topical expression in the European crisis of 1611. In that year, the political drama of regeneration was focused in the hermetic Holy Roman Emperor, Rudolf II, locked in the Hradschin with its library of magical books and its

[59] Reproduced in Yates, *The Rosicrucian Enlightenment*, plate 8.
[60] See Donald Weinstein, *Savanarola and Florence: Prophecy and Patriotism in the Renaissance* (Princeton: Princeton Univ. Press, 1970), pp. 336—8, for an apocalyptic interpretation of Botticelli's *Crucifixion*.

well-equipped alchemical workshops, all but deposed by his brother, Matthias. It was focused too in Prince Henry and his friend the Elector Palatine with their plans of leading an army in support of Rudolf. But it was above all in young Elizabeth Stuart, Donne's new star promising ends of much wonder, that the dream of regeneration found its most vivid embodiment. It is she who is celebrated in *The Tempest* as Miranda, a name which evokes the Wonder of Revelation 12 that announces the final struggle against the Man of Sin and the imminence of the Millennium and which is echoed in the Rosicrucian phrase *Miranda sextae aetatis.* By her association with the Woman of Revelation 12, Shakespeare's Miranda becomes kin to Spenser's Una and to the Lucida of the fireworks spectacle. The play seen by James and his courtiers on November 1st, 1611 and which was performed again at Court about a year later was therefore intensely topical. It dealt with the crucial events and issues of the day.

Among the issues taken up in *The Tempest* there was none more crucial than the question of the means to be employed to realize the dream of regeneration. We have seen that during Rudolf's long reign, Prague had become the hermetic capital of Europe and the centre of the new Paracelsan magic with its blend of medical alchemy, goetic magic and millenarianism. It was in Prague, in the circles that Rudolf encouraged and patronized, that the dream of an alchemically purged and magically regenerated world was nurtured.[61] Through the hermetic Emperor's secretary and physician, Michael Maier, these ideas had reached London by late 1611. In *The Tempest* Shakespeare considers this dream and the magico-alchemical means by which certain of his contemporaries believed it could be achieved. At the end of the play he pronounces judgment on the magical means employed by Prospero and by implication on those advocated by the visionaries of London and Prague. It is a negative judgement that profoundly affects our response to the whole play.

---

[61] Some idea of how widespread this movement was is provided by the commonplace book of Joachim Meursius, Rosicrucian and "travelling theosophist", preserved in the town library of Lübech. Among those mentioned there are Robert Fludd, Johann Arndt, the German theologian and friend of Johann Valentin Andreae, Jakob Böehme the mystic, Michael Maier, Joachim Jungius Paracelsan physician and friend of the educationalist Comenius, Andreae himself perhaps the key figure in the whole movement, and Henry Nollius another Paracelsan physician. See Sten Lindroth, *Paracelsism i Sverige till 1600-talets mitt* in *Lychnos-Bibliotek* 7 (Uppsala: Almquist and Wiksell International 1943), p. 172. Lindroth's important study of Paracelsism still, unfortunately, remains untranslated.

Chapter VII
Rough Magic

In the fifth act of *The Tempest*, just as Prospero's project is about to be completed, he makes a long speech invoking the spirits by whose aid he has performed the magical operation. Towards the end of this speech he abruptly announces:

> But this rough magic
> I here abjure.
> (V.i. 57—8)

An audience unprepared for this rejection of what has just been described as "my so potent Art", or perhaps misled by the previous echoes from the speech of Medea in Ovid's *Metamorphoses* where similar spirits are invoked for use rather than rejection, would also be puzzled by Prospero's dismissive, almost contemptuous tone of voice. The powers that he has acquired after years of study are now seen as no more than rough magic. They are "abjured" a word suggesting a solemn, ritual rejection of something reprehensible. This abjuration also involves all that has been achieved by means of this rough magic. The whole project of regeneration, expressed in the lofty terms of reconciliation and harmony, millennial peace and apocalyptic wonders is called in question by these unexpected words of Prospero.

No interpretation of the play in images of regeneration can be complete if these harsh words of abjuration are not taken into account. I propose therefore in this final chapter to limit myself to a consideration of these few, crucial words and of the speech in which they occur, and shall attempt to define Prospero's final attitude to the Art which he has been practising. I shall give first of all the views of other critics on this speech of abjuration, then my own interpretation, and finally I shall see to what extent the view of the play as a whole presented in the previous chapters is modified by this interpretation.

It is a commonplace of *Tempest* criticism to say that Prospero practises white magic while Sycorax practises black magic. Hallett Smith, for example, states that:

Prospero's magic is white magic, not black; he would be regarded by a Jacobean audience in much the same way as a modern audience views a scientist.[1]

---

[1] Hallett Smith, "*The Tempest* as a Kaleidoscope," in *Twentieth Century Interpretations of The Tempest*, p. 5.

The suggestion is that a Jacobean audience would have found Prospero's raising of a tempest, his use of spirits, his power of inducing sleep or temporary insanity in other human beings, just as acceptable as we would a scientist on stage carrying out an experiment with, say, a hologram. We might not understand, but we would not object. It is implied among other things that James I would have had no objections to Prospero's magical practises. The same implication is present in the remark of Northrop Frye that "Prospero is a tempest-raiser like the witches in *Macbeth*, though morally at the opposite pole; he is a white magician".[2] It is assumed that in the matter of raising a tempest, it is the motive and not the act that determines whether or not it is white magic, and that a Jacobean audience would have observed this distinction.

Even if it is granted that in contrast to Sycorax, Prospero is a white magician, we are still faced with the problem of why Prospero should finally reject it as "rough magic". If it was white and beneficial, why abjure it? Patrick Grant has suggested one answer: Prospero "learns a practical magic, distinct from the evil magic of Sycorax, which at last he puts off, presumably having acquired the wisdom to do without it".[3] Later in the same article he writes:

Shakespeare is not saying, however, that Prospero is an evil magician when he conjures Ariel and raises a storm. Plainly the evil belongs to Sycorax. What Shakespeare does say is that Prospero's Neo-Platonic magic is good essentially because it enables Prospero to understand enough to forgive his enemies.[4]

Prospero, it seems, practises magic in order to learn how to forgive. Once he has learnt forgiveness, he abandons it. Using the same argument, it could also be said that Prospero practises magic on his former enemies *until* he learns to forgive them; he abjures his magic *because* he has finally learnt how to forgive. Frank Kermode gives a similar explanation to Grant's of Prospero's purpose in practising magic:

When Prospero achieves this necessary control over himself and nature he achieves his ends (reflected in the restoration of harmony at the human and political levels) and has no more need of the instrument, "rough magic".[5]

Again, we can wonder why a magic that has brought about such positive results both individually and socially should be rejected in the end as "rough". The restoration and harmony is in any case by no means complete.

---

[2] Northrop Frye, Introd. to Penguin edition of *The Tempest*, p. 20.
[3] Patrick Grant, "The Magic of Charity: A Background to Prospero," in *Review of English Studies*, 27 (1976), 9.
[4] Grant, p. 9.
[5] Kermode, Introd. to Arden *Tempest*, p. xlviii.

Could it be that it is not so much that Prospero has no more need of the instrument of "rough magic" as that such an instrument is finally seen to be not only inadequate but culpable?

The assumption that Prospero was a white magician carries with it the belief that James I before whom the play was acted on November 1st, 1611, would have endorsed Prospero's magical practises. Patrick Grant speaks of James "being pleased to see himself in Prospero".[6] Kermode writes that "the personal requirements of mage and prince are the same", and, "like James I", Prospero possesses these requirements.[7] A similar view is found in C. J. Sisson's article, "The Magic of Prospero".[8] In Prospero, he writes, we see "the learned and philosophical ruler, working justice, righting wrongs, defeating rebellion, in his own right as the Vicar of God in his own country, a visible Providence—a conception that would be grateful to the learned and philosophical King James the First".[9] To this identification of James I and Prospero there is a major objection. First of all, James as a ruler did not work justice, right wrongs or defeat rebellions by means of magic and the use of spirits. As we saw in the last chapter, this was true of Rudolf II. He attempted to rule by magic to the exclusion of all the normal means. For James such methods were anathema. There is every reason to believe that James, the author of the authoritative handbook on demonology as far as his subjects were concerned, would not have approved of Prospero's magic and would have welcomed his final abjuration of it. I shall return to this in a moment. There is an aspect of Prospero's abjuration of his magical art that must first be mentioned.

As is well recognized, his abjuration speech at the beginning of Act V is modelled on the speech of invocation delivered by Medea in Book VII of Ovid's *Metamorphoses*, and it is now accepted that Shakespeare used both the original Latin as well as Golding's translation of this passage. During the sixteenth and seventeenth centuries Medea was regarded primarily as a witch, closely related to the witch Circe.[10] It is the same passage from Ovid that Middleton gives to Hecate in his *The Witch*.[11] Sycorax in *The Tempest* is also in part modelled on Ovid's Medea, and like her, Sycorax is able "to control the moon" (V.i. 270).[12] Why does Shakespeare associate both

---

[6] Grant, p. 1.
[7] Kermode, Introd. to Arden *Tempest*, p. xlix.
[8] In *Shakespeare Survey*, 11 (1958), 70—77.
[9] C. J. Sisson, "The Magic of Prospero", in *Shakespeare Survey*, 11 (1958), p. 76.
[10] See Norhnberg, *The Analogy of the Faerie Queene*, pp. 509—510, n. 193.
[11] Kermode points this out in App. D in the Arden *Tempest*, p. 150.
[12] See Kermode's note on V.i. 270, in the Arden *Tempest*, and Introd., p. cl.

Sycorax and Prospero with Ovid's Medea? Does this not raise the suspicion that the magic of Sycorax and Prospero is not as sharply contrasted as is usually claimed? Aware of this unsavoury link between the "white" and "black" magicians of the play, Kermode claims that "only those elements which are consistent with 'white magic' are taken over for Prospero".[13] The use of spirits to raise tempests and resurrect the dead are therefore to be regarded as white magic, while controlling the moon belongs to the realm of black magic. In Kermode's view, the allusions to Ovid in Prospero's speech serve to bring out the purity of Prospero's magic:

I do not think that there is any reason to doubt that Shakespeare's audience was quite capable of the degree of discrimination required to perceive that there were two opposed kinds of magic in *The Tempest*, and that their opposition provided an important structural tension. Those who knew Ovid would have the additional knowledge that the action of these was epitomised in the imitation of his Medea passage.[14]

Again, it is hard to see why those with a knowledge of Ovid should not have drawn the opposite conclusion that Prospero's magic was not dissimilar from that of Sycorax. This possibility has been noted by C. J. Sisson:

There are disconcerting phrases, indeed, in Prospero's invocation in V.i. which seem inconsistent with the general picture of his white magic and import an an element of what he himself calls 'rough magic', the violence and chaos of black art. It is difficult to reconcile ourselves, for example, to his claim to have opened graves and to have resurrected the dead . . . The invocation in fact conflicts with his conception of Prospero as a white magician.[15]

Having made this admission, Sisson goes on to deny that it was intended: Shakespeare has been "unwary in his borrowing from Ovid, and has read too much of Ovid into Prospero's speech."[16] Once again we meet with this almost compulsive desire to protect Prospero from any suspicion that his magic is other than purely white. To avoid this suspicion, Sisson resorts to the explanation that Shakespeare was not aware of the implications of echoing the Medea passage in Prospero's speech of abjuration. He was nodding. I shall assume however in what follows that it is not Shakespeare who is nodding, and that the association of Prospero's "rough magic" with Medea's was deliberate.

Enough has been said to show that the general consensus of critical opinion is that Prospero practises white magic throughout the play, and that a

[13] Kermode, App. D, in the Arden *Tempest*, p. 149.
[14] Kermode, App. D in the Arden *Tempest*, p. 150.
[15] Sisson, "The Magic of Prospero", in *Shakespeare Survey*, 11 (1958), 76.
[16] Sisson, p. 76.

Jacobean audience would have found nothing in it to object to. I have suggested that this view raises a number of difficulties. First of all, there is the difficulty contained in Prospero's use of the words "abjure" and "rough magic", which, as I shall argue, suggest a powerful rejection of the magic he has been practising. Secondly, it is by no means certain that a Jacobean audience or James I would have regarded Prospero's magic as favourably as modern critics of *The Tempest* tend to do. Finally, there is the specific difficulty of accounting for the allusions in Prospero's speech of abjuration to the magic of Medea. Let us examine these difficulties one by one, beginning with Prospero's words of abjuration:

> But this rough magic
> I here abjure.

The word "rough" carried much the same meaning in Shakespeare's day as it does now: imprecise, lacking exact detail, crude or approximate. It also carried the meaning, then as now, of "violent, marked by violence, or harsh treatment of others".[17] Related to this last meaning is one now obsolete but current in the seventeenth and eighteenth centuries: "of remedies, medicines, etc., violent in effect; strong, remedial", as in one example from 1705: "His purgative Medicines are generally very rough and strong".[18] We can therefore interpret the phrase "rough magic" as crude magic, violent in its effects and comparable to a medical purge. This purgative magic can be compared to the violent workings of Paracelsan medicine. In his *Disputationes de Medica Nova Paracelsi* (1572—3) Thomas Erastus speaks of the "hurt and danger of mynerall medicines".[19] Thomas Moffett, an English defender of the new Paracelsan medicine, mentions in his *De Jure et Praestantia Chemicorum Medicamentorum* (1584) the common charge that

chemical remedies are by far the most dangerous, and that various illnesses have been carried to excessive violence in applying them.[20]

John Cotta, physician and writer on witchcraft, speaks in his *Short Discourse of the Unobserved Dangers of severall sorts of Ignorant and Unconsiderate Practisers of Physicke in England* of a patient who was seized by convulsions after taking some of Paracelsus' "ladanum pills".[21] Attention was frequently drawn to the dangers to patients of taking unprepared

---

[17] See *N.E.D.* under "rough", 5.
[18] See *N.E.D.* under "rough", 8.
[19] Debus, *The English Paracelsians*, p. 63.
[20] Debus, p. 72.
[21] Debus, p. 79.

antimony, a favourite Paracelsan remedy.[22] The same dangers, needless to say, attended medication by arsenic and mercury, the latter first used by Paracelsus as a cure for syphilis. Like Prospero's magic, such medicine could indeed be "rough".

The word "abjure" means much the same as in Shakespeare's day: "to renounce on oath; to retract, recant, or abnegate".[23] In the sixteenth and seventeenth centuries the word was also associated with the ritual renunciation of a heresy.[24] The word "abjure" therefore cannot be interpreted as meaning that Prospero simply gives up magic, or stops using it because the magical operation has been completed. It implies a solemn renunication of practises now seen as reprehensible. He abjures his potent magical art as a heresy was abjured. His abjuration is immediately followed by the decision to perform the rite of breaking his staff and burning his book of magic. It is my view that this change of heart, this tardy recognition that what he had hitherto regarded as white magic was deeply tainted, would have met with the approval of most of those in the original audiences of *The Tempest*, not least of James I. To understand such approval of Prospero's abjuration, we have to make a crucial but neglected distinction between the way Renaissance practitioners of theurgic magic regarded themselves and the way they were regarded by the majority of their contemporaries, learned and unlearned alike.

As a result of the researches contained in such works as D. P. Walker's *Spiritual and Demonic Magic from Ficino to Campanella*, Frances Yates' *Giordano Bruno and the Hermetic Tradition* and *The Occult Philosophy in the Elizabethan Age*, and Peter J. French's *John Dee: The World of an Elizabethan Mage*, a new and somewhat startling light has been cast on Renaissance interest in magical practices.[25] Stemming from Ficino and inspired by the magical treatises in the Hermetic Corpus as well as by the magical Platonism of the Alexandrian School, there arose a powerful resurgence of belief that spiritual entities could be contacted, controlled and used for lawful purposes. In the eyes of its practitioners such magic was white, and was sharply distinguished by them from black magic with its use of spirits for evil ends. The difference lay in the motive. It is from this point

---

[22] See Nicholl, *The Chemical Theatre*, p. 72.

[23] See *N.E.D.* under "abjure", 1.

[24] For examples of this usage, see *N.E.D.* under "abjure", 1a, and under "abjuration", 1.

[25] D. P. Walker, *Spiritual and Demonic Magic from Ficino to Campanella* in *Studies of the Warburg Institute*, Vol. 22 (London: Warburg Institute, 1958); Frances Yates, *Giordano Bruno and the Hermetic Tradition* and *The Occult Philosophy in the Elizabethan Age*; Peter J. French, *John Dee: The World of an Elizabethan Magus* (London: Routledge and Kegan Paul, 1972).

of view that modern critics of *The Tempest* have spoken of Prospero as a white magician in line of decent from such practitioners as Trithemius, Agrippa, Paracelsus, Bruno and, in England, John Dee. This is true to the extent that this was how these magicians saw themselves and how they were seen by the relatively small number of people who symphatized with the idea of a legitimate white magic. But, as we shall see, in the eyes of the vast majority of their contemporaries the very figures that Prospero has been related to were regarded as adepts in black magic. To bring out the nature of these two opposed ways of regarding Renaissance magic, I would like first to give an example of an educated contemporary of Shakespeare sympathetic to the sort of magic practised by Prospero, and then follow this with an account of the more widespread hostile attitude to such magic.

There is in the British Library manuscript collections a volume of magical treatises by different hands ranging in date from the middle of the sixteenth century to the middle of the seventeenth century.[26] One of its owners was Edmund Spenser's friend and mentor, Gabriel Harvey, and the first four items in this volume contain his marginalia. The first item is "The Book of King Solomon called the Key of Knowledge". The second is a "torne" book containing the "secret writings" of Dr Caius, founder of Caius College, Cambridge, inherited from him by Dr Legge who passed it on to Mr Fletcher, described as "a learned artist for his time", that is, a skilled alchemist. In the margin of this tract of secret writings Harvey has written: "The best skill, that Mr Butler physician had in nigromancie, with Agrippas Occulta philosophia". In 1612 William Butler was physician to Prince Henry, and as we learn from John Aubrey's *Brief Lives* he practised alchemy and was celebrated for his startling medical methods. The third item that came into Gabriel Harvey's possession was, interestingly, Simon Forman's "An excellent booke of the arte of Magicke, first begoone the xxii[th] of Marche Anno Domini 1567". As we have seen, Forman was the teacher of the Paracelsan physician and alchemist, Richard Napier. Napier in his turn was a friend of the alchemical Bishop of Worcester, John Thornborough, and of John Dee. The fourth item is "Certaine straung visions . . . A notable Journal of an Experimental Magitian", dealing with the visions or appari-

---

[26] B.M. Add. MS. 36674. This important collection of manuscripts dating from the mid-sixteenth to mid-seventeenth centuries constitutes a compendium of goetic magic as practised in England during Shakespeare's lifetime. It contains detailed instructions on the ceremonial invocation, control and dismissal of spirits. A list of names on f. 21 of owners or authors of some of the documents includes John Dee, Richard Napier and Elias Ashmole. A description of the first four items is given in Virginia F. Stern, *Gabriel Harvey: A Study of His Life, Marginalia and Library* (Oxford: Clarendom Press, 1979), p. 242.

tions seen by a certain H. G. and his scryer. The marginalia in these manuscripts appear to have been made by Harvey from about 1577 onwards. What a fascinating glimpse they provide of the clandestine reading of a learned Cambridge don, a follower of Sidney and Leicester, known for the excellence of his Latin verse, the butt of Nashe's merciless satire, and intimate friend of the author of the *Faerie Queene*. His wide intellectual interest stretched to all forms of magic: alchemy, necromancy based on Agrippa's standard work on the subject, and communication with spirits of the sort also practised by John Dee with his scryer, Edward Kelley. As we saw these manuscripts were passed on from one artist to the next, torn and tattered by use, and highly secret. Great caution was necessary, and the need for caution increased as the sixteenth century drew to a close.

No matter how much Harvey and people like him thought of magic as white and allowable if performed with the right motives, there were many others who classed all magic and all traffic with spirits irrespective of motive as black. To the average Englishman in the sixteenth century, "Tritheim, Agrippa, Paracelsus and Nostradamus were much more famous than Faustus and enjoyed an equally sinister reputation", and for them Germany "was famous only as a land of magicians and conjurers."[27] The same Agrippa whom Dr Butler consulted on "nigromancie" and who has been seen as the prototype of Prospero, was widely thought to be a black magician. "It became part of the attack on Agrippa to class him with Faustus, as is done for example by the Jesuit Martin del Rio in his attack on Renaissance magic published in 1599".[28] Frances Yates has made the interesting suggestion that the association of Faustus with Agrippa in Marlowe's *Doctor Faustus* is central to the play, and is "part of its general denigration of Renaissance magic."[29] This denigration of Agrippa is one indication of that hardening of attitude towards Renaissance magic in both Protestant and Catholic countries which Frances Yates has detected from the end of the sixteenth century onwards.[30]

What is true of Agrippa is true also of another man who is sometimes claimed to be the original of Prospero. This is Dr John Dee. Despite the protection he enjoyed from Queen Elizabeth, Dee was popularly regarded as a black magician. In 1584 a mob destroyed the equipment in his alchemical laboratory at Mortlake in the belief that they were the instruments of black

---

[27] C. H. Herford, *Studies in the Literary Relations of England and Germany* (Cambridge: University Press, 1886), p. 143 and 165.
[28] Yates, *Occult Philosophy*, pp. 116.
[29] Yates, p. 116.
[30] Yates, *Giordano Bruno*, p. 157.

magic. But during Elizabeth's reign, Dee was relatively safe. With the accession of James I in 1603 his situation changed for the worse. In July, 1604, James forced a revised version of the old Elizabethan Statute against Witchcraft through Parliament, making witchcraft a capital offence on the second charge, all in an effort to "uproot the monstrous evil of enchanters". Dee felt compelled to appeal to James personally to put him on trial to see if "the said name of *Conjurer*, or *Caller*, or *Invocator* of Divels, or damned Spirites can be proved".[31] James ignored the appeal. In 1605 Dee was obliged to resign his wardenship of Christ's College, Manchester. In 1608 he died in poverty. As Frances Yates has commented, "James sincerely disliked Dee and feared anything savouring of magic".[32]

James' neglect of John Dee, in such contrast to the favours that Elizabeth had extended to him, is an example of that hardening of attitude towards hermetic magic referred to by Frances Yates. It was to this hermetic, magical tradition that Dee indubitably belonged. "Agrippa's magic formed the framework in which a late-Renaissance magus like Dee operated and his library contained several copies of his extremely influential *De occulta philosophia* and one copy of the equally important *De incertitudine & vanitate scientiarum*".[33] Like Agrippa, Dee, with his fervent Christian spirituality everywhere in evidence in his Diaries, saw himself as practising an allowable form of beneficent magic. In his own eyes he was a white magician; in the eyes of his contemporaries he was regarded as a "conjurer" of devils and evil spirits. This view of him was shared by James I. It is important to emphasize this because Prospero has been likened both to James himself and to John Dee. Frances Yates, somewhat inconsequentially, has claimed that "the white magician Doctor Dee is defended in Prospero, the good and learned conjurer".[34] It is hard to believe that Shakespeare would have defended John Dee before James I, aware as he would have been of the King's dislike of Dee and of the King's views on the sort of hermetic magic with which Dee was closely associated. But what Shakespeare might well have done is to present Prospero as a magus of the Dee or Agrippa type who finally comes to abjure his magic. This would not only account for the resemblances to Dee, but also to Agrippa. As Frank Kermode has noted, Ariel is the name of one of the spirits in Agrippa's *De occulta philosophia*; in using such a spirit Prospero "exactly resembles white magicians like

---

[31] French, *John Dee*, p. 19.
[32] Yates, *Occult Philosophy*, p. 161.
[33] French, *John Dee*, p. 52, where it is also pointed out that Dee possessed probably the largest collection of Paracelsan writings in England.
[34] Yates, *Occult Philosophy*, p. 160.

Agrippa himself".[35] But whether or not Agrippa was a white magician is the crucial point.

We must now consider how James who was present in the Whitehall at the first performance of *The Tempest* would have reacted to the character of Prospero. Would he have seen himself in the figure of the royal mage, raising tempests that did no harm, commanding spirits to carry out his behests, conjuring up spectacles that then vanish into thin air, using magic on his former enemies? Was he flattered? Did he approve or not approve of the sort of magic practised by Prospero? Although we do not possess a record of how James reacted on that occasion, we do possess a full record of his view on magic in general. This is his *Daemonologie, In Forme of a Dialogue*, written and printed when he was King of Scotland in 1597. There is no reason to believe that James radically changed his views on the subject in later years.

Running through James's little treatise is a distinction between the more sophisticated practises of "Magie or Necromancie" and the more popular and widespread ones of "Sorcerie or Witchcraft".[36] It is among the first type that the magic of Agrippa would have been classed by his opponents, and this is where James himself places it in his Preface to the Reader: if the reader wishes to "knowe what are the particular rites, curiosities of these black arts (which is both unnecessarie and perilous) he will find it in the fourth book of Cornelius Agrippa (p. xv). Agrippa's *De occulta philosophia* is here treated as a textbook of the black arts.

According to James the besetting sin of the magician or necromancer is curiosity, and it is on this weakness that Satan works, leading such a person in his pursuit of knowledge to the point where he takes up "that black and unlawfull science of Magie". He finally enters into a contract with the Devil who acts as his servant the more easily to lead him into deeper evil. The Devil then teaches him the arts and sciences of magic, how to carry news from any part of the world, how to make castles and forts appear, "juglerie trickes . . . to deceive mennes senses thereby" (p. 21—2). This black magic is based on illusion and has no objective reality. In this respect it differs fundamentally from the miracles of God, James says. The illusions created by the Devil "are but impressions in the aire, easilie gathered by a spirite, drawing so

---

[35] Kermode, App. B in the Arden *Tempest*, pp. 142—3. It can be added that Johannes Reuchlin in his standard work on Renaissance magical cabalism, *De arte cabalistica* (1517; 1561 ed., p. 517) includes Ariel in a list of seventy-two powerful angelic spirits that could be invoked cabalistically.
[36] James I, *Daemonologie* (1597), rpt. in *Elizabethan and Jacobean Quartos*, ed. G. B. Harrison (Edinburgh: University Press, 1966), p. 7.

neare to that substance him selfe;" (p. 22), they are "but deluding of the senses, and no waies true in substance" (p. 22). Speaking of how such magicians should be treated, James condemns "diverse Christian Princes" who allow magicians to live in their realms, and "even delight in their practises" (p. 24). Such Princes "sinne heavelie against their office in that poynt" (p. 25). It is James's view that magicians and necromancers deserve even greater punishment than sorcerers or witches since their sin is the greater and arises from profounder knowledge (p. 26).

It seems to me beyond question that on the strength of these views on the practise of magic or necromancy James would have condemned all traffic with spirits for magical purposes. This condemnation would include even magic carried out with the object of doing good. This is specifically stated at the end of the section dealing with magicians:

neither is it lawful to use so unlawfull instruments, were it never for so good a purpose: for the axiom in theology is most certaine and infallible: *Numquam faciendum est malum ut bonum inde eveniat.*[37]

Evil is never to be committed in order that good may come of it, such is James's concluding theological axiom. Judged by this axiom, the hermetic magic of the Renaissance that used spirits stood condemned, and so too do such practitioners of "white magic" as Agrippa or Dee, no matter how morally pure their motives may have been. This is because the instruments they use are unlawful. By the same axiom, Prospero stands condemned. His Art like that of Agrippa is black, and, as James wrote, "unnecessarie and perilous."[38] We are thus forced to the conclusion that to describe Prospero's magic as white is misleading. It was white only to its practitioners. To James—and his was the official and legal view in 1611—Prospero's magic carried out by Ariel and his meaner ministers was black, "were it never for so good a purpose". Like the rest of James's subjects, Shakespeare would certainly have known the sovereign's views on this subject, and no matter

---

[37] James, p. 26. A similar condemnation of ceremonial magic involving the invocation of spirits is made by Francis Bacon in *The Advancement of Learning* (1605). In his discussion of *fascination*, he condemns the excessive status given by "the school of Paracelsus" to the power of the imagination, and suggests that "herein comes in crookedly and dangerously a palliation of a great part of Ceremonial Magic." He states that ceremonies used to fortify the imagination, even if "they be used sincerely and intentionally for that purpose," are yet unlawful. In the Latin version of this passage Bacon speaks of physical remedies achieved through the use of ceremonial invocation as being illicit. See Francis Bacon, *The Advancement of Learning*, ed. G. W. Kitchin (London: Dent and Sons, 1973), pp. 119—20 and p. 109, for Bacon's hostile attitude to "Paracelsus and the alchemists." The attitudes of Bacon, Shakespeare and James I in this matter appear to be identical.

[38] James, p. xv.

what his own private views may have been, it is impossible to believe that he would have presented at Court before the King a play in commendation of the sort of magic that James had condemned. It is for this reason, if for no other, that I believe Prospero's speech of abjuration at the beginning of Act V must be taken as just that—a solemn abjuration of the magic he has been practising in the play.[39]

We are now in a better position to understand why Shakespeare associates the magic practised by Prospero and which James I would have condemned with the magic of Medea. But as we shall shortly see this unfavourable association was also used by Shakespeare in a way that enables us to identify the particular form of goetic magic that Prospero abjures.

In comparing Prospero's magic to that of Medea by echoing her speech of invocation in Book VII of the *Metamorphoses*, Shakespeare enables his audience to understand the nature of the "rough magic" he finally abjures. Medea's invocation is made as a preliminary to the magical act of rejuvenating Jason's aged father, Aeson. She invokes Night and Earth, "the source of the magician's powerful herbs", and "all spirits of the groves and night" to aid her in gathering the herbal essences that are required to make Aeson young again. Ovid then describes her long journey on a magical chariot to gather the needed herbs, and her preparation of them in a boiling cauldron together with other strange ingredients that recall those brewed by the Witches in *Macbeth*. When the potion is ready, she drains Aeson's veins of all blood, and in what is probably the first medical transfusion in history refills them with the potion. Aeson grows young again. Now what we first notice about this act of magic is that unlike Medea's later acts of witchcraft, this one is beneficent in its effects. She is administering an elixir derived mainly from plants in order to bring about rejuvenation. It is possible that Shakespeare, as T. W. Baldwin has suggested, was aware of the distinction made by Raphael Regius in his allegorizing commentary on Ovid's *Metamorphoses* published in 1497 between black and white aspects in Medea's magic.[40] Her rejuvenation of Aeson is an act of beneficent magic comparable to Prospero's attempt to regenerate the Three Men of Sin. But as

---

[39] The fact that Shakespeare renders Ovid's 'dii omnes noctis' as 'elves of hills' in Prospero's speech of abjuration in no way makes them more innocuous in character. In his *Daemonologie* (p. 57), James specifically refers to "Fayrie" as a kind of evil spirit used by black magicians, and dismisses the superstition of "a King and Queene of Phairie" as a Papist illusion created by the devil to mislead simple people into believing that "they saw and harde such thinges as were nothing indeed" (p. 74).

[40] T. W. Baldwin, *Shakespeare's Small Latine and Lesse Greeke* (Urbana: University of Illinois Press, 1944), II, 443—52.

we have seen, any form of magic, even beneficent magic, was culpable in the view of James I. To repeat his theological maxim, good ends do not justify evil means.

The "rough magic" that Prospero abjures, then, is allusively associated with the herbal and goetic magic of Medea. It is "rough" not only in the sense of crude but also of violent in action. We saw earlier that an obsolete sense of this word relates it to the violence of a purgative medicine, and we were reminded of the violent purgative cures that were particularly associated with Paracelsan medicine in which poisons were administered (sometimes with fatal results as its critics pointed out) in order to combat the poison of the disease on the principle that like cures like. We saw also that among the medicines concocted in the laboratories of Paracelsan physicians were a variety of elixirs that were believed to rejuvenate a person or ensure long life. These elixirs, like Medea's, were alchemically extracted from plants and minerals by a process of boiling. Medea in some respects, therefore, resembles the Paracelsan alchemist of Shakespeare's time, and here perhaps lies Shakespeare's motive in relating Prospero to Medea.

We have already suggested that Jonson's *The Alchemist* performed late in 1610 by Shakespeare's own company is important for an understanding of *The Tempest*. Shakespeare's play can be seen as a more serious treatment of the Paracelsan medical alchemy that Jonson brilliantly and savagely ridicules. Both plays present a magician of the Dee type, Jonson as a charlatan, Shakespeare as an idealist. The two plays are further linked by the association of the main characters with Medea. In Act II, Scene i of *The Alchemist*, Mammon, the dupe of the play, is given a speech describing how the alchemists use the classical myths as "abstract riddles of our stone" (II.i. 104). One of these "riddles" is the legend of Jason and the Golden Fleece and of Medea's magic:

> I have a piece of Jason's fleece, too,
> Which was no other, than a book of alchemy,
> Writ in large sheepskin, a good fat ram-vellum.
> Such was Pythagoras' thigh, Pandora's tub,
> And all that fable of Medea's charms,
> The manner of our work.
> (II.i. 89—94).

Jonson's sources have been traced by the editors of Jonson's works, C. H. Herford and P. and E. Simpson. The reference to the Golden Fleece as a book of alchemy occurs in Agrippa's own work of abjuration, *De incertitudine et vanitate scientiarum* (Ch xc, 1609 ed.), and is mentioned in Thomas Nashe's *Lenten Stuffe*:

Cornelius Agrippa maketh mention of some Philosophers that held the skin of the sheep that bare the golden fleece to be nothing but a book of alcumy written upon it.[41]

It has been suggested that Jonson derived his information about the alchemical nature of Medea's charms from the alchemical work, *De veritate et antiquitate artis chemiae* (1561) of Robertus Vallensis, later included in the *Theatrum Chemicum* (1602). There he writes:

Eustathius, Suidas and other grave authors interpret the fable of Medea who is said to have restored youth to Aeson, the son [sic] of Jason, as referring to the Chemical Art.[42]

More recently Jonson's probable source has been discovered in a collection of alchemical treatises entitled *De Alchemia*, with a Preface by Chrysogonus Polydorus, printed in 1541 and 1545.[43] In this Preface Jason's quest for the Golden Fleece is given a full alchemical interpretation. The fire-breathing Bulls in the Field of Mars at Colchis are alchemical furnaces. The Dragon is alchemical argent-vive. The Dragon's teeth constitute mercury sublimate, and Jason's helm in which they are kept is the glass vessel or alembic. Concerning Medea, Chrysogonus writes:

Formerly, because this same philosopher's stone was said to cure all human bodies even then and preserve them healthy and unimpaired down to extreme old age, Medea was on this account feigned to have restored youth to Jason's father.[44]

This passage in the Preface to the *De Alchemia* enables us to solve the riddle of why Shakespeare evokes Medea's speech of invocation in Prospero's own speech of abjuration. It tells us that the rough magic he is abjuring is alchemy. Thus from a somewhat unexpected quarter we find further confirmation that *The Tempest* contains an allegory of alchemical regeneration. As we have seen, when Shakespeare wrote this play, alchemical regeneration equated with Medea's magical rejuvenation was closely associated with the medical alchemy of Paracelsus and his followers. Its founder, as we shall now see, was regarded as a black magician.

As in the case of Dee and Agrippa, Paracelsus too was consistently attacked as a practiser of black magic. His reputation and that of his followers is indicated in a letter written by the physician, Conrad Gessner and

[41] Nashe, *Lenten Stuffe*, in *Works*, ed. McKerrow, III, 221.

[42] Translated from the Latin given in Jonson, *Works*, ed. Herford and Simpson, X, 72, note to II.i. 101—4, *The Alchemist*.

[43] Supriya Chaudari, "Jason's Fleece: The Source of Sir Epicure Mammon's Allegory," *Review of English Studies*, N.S. 34, No. 137 (1984), 72.

[44] Translated from the Latin quotation in Chaudari's article, "Jason's Fleece," p. 72.

published in his *Epistolarum medicinalium Conradi Gessneri* (1577). There he refers to strange tales of Paracelsus' "intercourse with demons", and relates that it was from Paracelsus' school of medicine that "arose the wandering scholars, as they are now commonly called. The most famous of these was Faust, who died not so long ago . . . Theophrastus has assuredly been an impious man and a sorcerer (*magus*), and has had intercourse with demons."[45] It is Carl Jung's opinion that "Paracelsus was the prototype of Faust."[46] The earliest and most sustained attack on the medicine of Paracelsus was made by the Swiss physician, Thomas Erastus in his *Disputationes de Medica Nova*, 1572—3. This work, which was highly influential in England, contains a refutation both of the theory and the practise of the new medicine. Erastus accuses Paracelsus of associating with the Devil, and of "heresie, conjurations, lacke of learning."[47] Thomas Moffett, the Paracelsan physician and alchemist in the employ of William, third Earl of Pembroke, defended Paracelsus in his *De Jure et Praestantia Chemicorum Medicamentorum* (1584, 1602), against the charge of being "a drunkard, magician, imposter, beggar, market attender, worker of the hidden arts of heaven and earth". He denied that Paracelsus was "a magician and an imposter who had dealings with demons."[48] The same charges were directed at those who supported the new medicine. Robert Fludd was accused by a clergyman of diabolical practices deriving from Paracelsus whom he regarded as a monstrous conjurer working outside the bounds of nature.[49] In his long controversy with Fludd in the 1620's the Jesuit, Marin Mersenne, attacked him as the modern representative of Renaissance hermetic magic and as in line of descent from such arch-magicians as Trithemius, Agrippa, Giorgi, Bruno and Campanella.[50] Inspiring these attacks was the belief that alchemy was a branch of illicit magic, and that, like James's magician, alchemists had been drawn to it by a dangerous curiosity or pride. In the view of one opponent, the alchemists displayed "some spice of that spirit of pride which first sublimated physics into magic."[51]

---

[45] Conrad Gessner, *Epistolarum medicinalium Conradi Gessneri* (1577), fol. 1^v, cited by Jung, *Alchemical Studies*, p. 119.
[46] Jung, *Alchemical Studies*, p. 118.
[47] Debus, *The English Paracelsians*, p. 63. For a discussion of the view in the sixteenth and seventeenth centuries that magic and witchcraft were heresies, see Keith Thomas, *Religion and the Decline of Magic*, pp. 521 ff.
[48] Debus, p. 75.
[49] Thomas, *Religion and the Decline of Magic*, p. 304 and 319.
[50] Yates, *Giordano Bruno*, pp. 405 ff.
[51] Thomas Jackson, *A Treatise Containing the Originall of Unbeliefe* (1625), cited Thomas, *Religion and the Decline of Magic*, p. 321.

Behind the fierce controversy about the new Paracelsan medicine with its theory of alchemical purgation and its dependence on astral spirits we can also detect the larger issue of whether magic was allowable if the motives were pure. Had the followers of Paracelsus limited themselves to distillation of plants and chemicals for purely medical purposes it is possible that the attacks on them would not have been so fierce. But it was part and parcel of the teaching of Paracelsus that the alchemical process was universal in its character and that the work of achieving the Stone was none other than the establishment of the Age of Gold.[52] It is this millenarian element in his teaching, fostered by his followers and taken over by the Rosicrucians, that constituted a threat to established authority, for to achieve the new society the old one must be dissolved. To those who preferred the *status quo*, the teachings of Paracelsus contained something subversive and the centre of this subversive, millenarian alchemy during the early years of the seventeenth century was, as I have suggested, Rudolfine Prague. It was there in Golden Lane where Rudolf's alchemists dwelt and in the Hradschin with its laboratories and occult collections that the Paracelsan dream of a transmuted Europe took shape. It is this same dream that gave rise to Rudolf's abortive Society of Peace, and that explains the visionary quality of those strange Christmas-cards that the Emperor's secretary, Michael Maier, Paracelsan physician and alchemical allegorist, sent to James I and Prince Henry shortly after the first performance of *The Tempest*. The same dream of an alchemically purged Europe is present in the Rosicrucian manifestoes with their call for a General Reformation expressed in both millenarian and alchemical terms and with Paracelsus gratefully mentioned. There was dynamite in this dream. It raised the possibility that through the practice of magic and the invocation of spiritual beings an alchemical purgation of the world could be actively undertaken. Human beings, even without their knowledge or permission, could be subjected to experiences that would hasten their enlightenment and purge them of their sins in an alchemical furnace of affliction. The days of Antichrist would be shortened, and the wonders of the Sixth Age would more rapidly lead to the joys of the final Sabbath. That such a dream haunted the minds of various individuals at this time and was recognized by those who opposed it is indicated by the words of the satirical print attacking the Elector Palatine and Elizabeth that have already been cited:

---

[52] The alchemical nature of the coming Millennium was stressed in Paracelsus' widely disseminated prophecy that it would be heralded by the appearance of "Elias the Artist" or alchemist, fifty-eight years after his death which was either in 1541 or 1543. See McIntosh, *The Rosy Cross Unveiled*, p. 39.

> The round ball represents the world
> To which the Bohemians married the Palatine,
> They expected to teach the world,
> And to reform all schools, churches, and law courts,
> And to bring everything to the state
> In which Adam found it,
> And even to my state, Saturn's,
> And this was called the golden time.
> To that end the high society of the Rosicrucians
> Wish to turn all the mountains into gold for their own good.[53]

This is a description of the dream that haunted Europe during the first two decades of the seventeenth century, made after it had dissolved irrevocably into the chaos of the Thirty Years' War. The restoration of the Golden Age under Frederick and Elizabeth, the establishment of a just society and the magical alchemy of the Rosicrucians are all mockingly lumped together in this satire. Its mockery recalls the gibes of Antonio and Sebastian in *The Tempest* when Gonzalo presents his vision of the second Golden Age.

The link between the political programme of Frederick and Elizabeth and the more esoteric goals of the Rosicrucians seems to have been made at an early date. In 1616 the chemist, Andreas Libavius, published his *Well-meaning Observations on the Fame and Confessio of the Brotherhood of the Rosicrucians*. In this work Libavius is strongly critical of the magical element in Paracelsus' teaching, regarding it as derived from the hermetic magic of Agrippa and Trithemius. He particularly attacks Oswald Croll whose work, *De signaturis internis rerum*, as we saw, may have been known to Shakespeare. But it is above all the connection between Paracelsan magic and politics that Libavius finds objectionable. He discovers in the Rosicrucian *Fama* an allusion to

Some 'Paracelsist Lion' who will ally himself to the Turk and seek to overthrow the 'Romische Reich' and substitute for it a world government based on magic spells.[54]

It is this mystical alchemy aiming at no less than "a world government based on magic spells" that Libavius pinpoints as the goal of the Paracelsians working in alliance with some "Paracelsist Lion", who can be no other than the Lion of the Palatinate, Frederick V. A similar connection is made between Paracelsan medicine and the reform of the world at an even earlier date. In his *Wunderbuch*, published shortly after the turn of the century, Julius Sperber, subsequently a defender of the Rosicrucians, prophesied the

---

[53] Cited Yates, *The Rosicrucian Enlightenment*, p. 88.
[54] Yates, p. 85, paraphrasing Libavius.

coming of the Joachite Third Age when the Golden Age would be restored. The work of preparation had been carried out between 1500 and 1600 by Luther and Paracelsus among others. With the establishment of the New Jerusalem under the aegis of the Holy Spirit, democracy would flourish, the meaning of the Scriptures would be openly revealed, and the new medicine of the Golden Age would be spagyric, that is, Paracelsan.[55] A similar apocalyptic role is accorded Paracelsan medicine in the work of a Protestant German pastor, Heinrich Vogel, *Offenbarung der Geheymnissen der Alchimy* (Revelation of the Secrets of Alchemy), published in 1605. There Vogel states that the Antichrist would be revealed and the Last Days announced when the Gospel and alchemy appeared together. A sign that the Last Days were upon them, according to Vogel, was the work of Paracelsus and other philosophers in purifying alchemy.[56] In 1615, Julius Sperber published his *Echo der von Gott hocherleuchteten Fraternitet* (Echo of the God-illumined Fraternity), and there speaks of the Rosicrucians as in line of descent from Agrippa, Johannes Reuchlin the Cabalist, Ficino and Pico Mirandola the Platonists, and Aegidius Guttmann, that is, as the inheritors of the magical and cabalistic tradition of the Renaissance.[57] As we have seen, it was to the same figures and the same hermetic tradition that Prospero belongs, but this tradition gained from about 1600 onwards a new political dimension. It became actively revolutionary. The focus of its political goals from 1610 onwards was Frederick, the Elector Palatine and Elizabeth Stuart. It was they who would implement a new world government and a second Golden Age, based as their enemies claimed on magical spells and on the esoteric alchemy of Paracelsus.

We have now been able to identify Prospero's "rough magic" as that of the Renaissance hermetic tradition represented by Agrippa, Paracelsus and John Dee. More particularly, it is the astral and alchemical medicine of Paracelsus and his followers, widely regarded as we have seen as a heresy and as a form of demonic conjuration. It is for this reason that when Prospero finally understands the nature of the "rough magic" he has been practising he "abjures" it. Shakespeare is carefully using a word that suggests ritual renunciation of a practise now seen as reprehensible. We have also established that the echo of Medea's speech of invocation in Prospero's speech of abjuration makes sense once it is realized that Medea's rejuvenation of Aeson was a well-known symbol for alchemy, and that it is referred

---

[55] McIntosh, *The Rosy Cross Unveiled*, pp. 38—9.
[56] McIntosh, p. 38.
[57] McIntosh, p. 53—4.

to in Jonson's *The Alchemist* in connection with Paracelsan alchemy. Finally we have suggested that Prospero's experiment in the alchemical regeneration of the Three Men of Sin can be understood as the equivalent of the contemporary dream of Paracelsians and Rosicrucians of an alchemically purged Europe with the figures of Miranda and Ferdinand standing for the new society of the Golden Age and reflecting in the realm of fiction the millenarian roles assigned in real life to Elizabeth and Frederick. *The Tempest*, in other words, is both an allegory of this millenarian dream and a judgement on the means to be used for its realization. It is an adverse judgment, and it comes as a shock at the close of the play. It is one of Shakespeare's most brilliant reversals of expectation, and we miss it totally if we do not grasp that in the last act of the play Prospero is disenchanted in all senses of the word. He does not so much complete his project, as abandon it the moment he has hastily brought his victims back to their senses. He does not quietly and with a sigh of satisfaction at a job well done give up magic, but emphatically abjures it as rough.

This view of Prospero at the end of the play as a disenchanted mage goes far, I believe, to explain some puzzling features of Prospero's character and behaviour in the play that have long been noted. Throughout the entire action of the play he is presented not as the serene and philosophical magus we might have expected, but as someone on edge, given to hasty changes of mood and not completely in control of himself or of the events he is engineering. There is some truth in Lytton Strachey's witty characterization of him as "an unpleasantly crusty personage, in whom a twelve years' monopoly of the conversation had developed an inordinate propensity for talking". Strachey continues:

It is sufficient to point out, that if Prospero is wise, he is also self-opinionated and sour, that his gravity is often another name for pedantic severity, and that there is no character in the play to whom, during some part of it, he is not studiously disagreeable.[58]

Lytton Strachey's purpose was to destroy the picture of Prospero as "an embodiment of that wise benevolence which is supposed to have thrown a halo over Shakespeare's later life." He succeeded, and Prospero's less pleasant traits of character are now fully recognized. But the image of "wise benevolence" has survived in another form: in the picture of him as a white magician seeking to improve a largely corrupt world. So powerful is this image of wise benevolence in this new form that it has prevented critics of the

---

[58] Lytton Strachey, *Shakespeare's Final Period* (1922), rpt. in *Twentieth Century Interpretations of The Tempest*, p. 90.

play, as we have seen, from facing the full implications of Prospero's speech of abjuration. If my interpretation of this speech is correct, Prospero's crustiness and lack of balance in the play are seen in a different light. They grow from an increasing awareness of his own imperfections as a human being and from a dawning realization that he is playing God with his fellow human beings. This gradual insight begins with the Revels speech in Act IV and culminates with his appeal for forgiveness in the final Epilogue.

As was suggested earlier, the Revels speech that marks the abrupt termination of the betrothal masque and arises from Prospero's realization that he has forgotten the plot of the Three Drunkards against him, is a speech of disillusionment. In it, for the first time, Prospero begins to take stock of his magical practises, their nature and their scope. He is deeply disturbed, "touch'd with anger, distemper'd" (IV.i. 143—5), as Miranda and Ferdinand notice, and when the Revels speech is ended, Prospero confesses to being "vex'd", "troubl'd", "disturb'd." One source of this profound disturbance is the realization that he is no longer fully in control, that his memory is humanly imperfect. But coupled with this is the realization that he is a worker of illusions that possess no real substance. The vision that he has created is "baseless", and the pageant that the lovers have just witnessed is "insubstantial". To understand why this realization so disturbs Prospero, we return to James' *Daemonologie*. There, as we saw, James explained that the difference between God's miracles and those of the Devil lies in the insubstantiality of the latter. They are brought about by a "deluding of the senses", and are "no waies true in substance". The Devil can teach magicians to conjure "faire banquets and daintie dishes", "castles and fortes", but these are only "impressions in the aire, easilie gathered by a spirite, drawing so near to that substance himself."[59] The same is true of the banquet conjured up by Prospero before the King's Party, and of the towers, palaces and temples with which he regales the lovers. These too lack substance, and have been created out of air by an airy spirit. The Revels speech, therefore, expresses in language close to that used in James' *Daemonologie* Prospero's dawning realization that he is a trafficker in illusions.

If the Revels speech marks the onset of this realization, it is carried a stage further at the beginning of Act V just before Prospero makes his speech of abjuration. It is initiated by Ariel's description of the state of the Three Men of Sin:

> Your charms so strongly works 'em,
> That if you now beheld them, your affections

---

[59] James I, *Daemonologie*, p. 22.

160

            Would become tender.
Pro.   Dost thou think so, spirit?
Ari. Mine would, sir, were I human.
Pro.   And mine shall.
    Hast thou, which art but air, a touch, a feeling
    Of their afflictions, and shall not myself,
    One of their kind, that relish all as sharply,
    Passion as they, be kindlier mov'd than thou art?
                    (V.i. 17—24)

Here we witness a profound change taking place in Prospero. At first preoc-
cupied only with the state of the experiment, he is pulled up sharply by the
compassion of Ariel, a non-human spirit, for the subjects of his experiment.
It is Ariel who compels his master to recognize his essential kinship with his
former enemies and acknowledge his shared humanity with them. He is "one
of their kind."[60] His decision to "myself present / As I was sometime
Milan", to dress so that he will be recognized by his fellow human beings
completes his return to ordinary humanity. This crucial insight into the fact
that he is not above the castaways but on a level with them leads to the decision to abandon vengeance for virtue and to terminate a project that has been
inspired more by "fury" than by "nobler reason":

    Though with their high wrongs I am struck to th' quick,
    Yet with my nobler reason 'gainst my fury
    Do I take part: the rarer action is
    In virtue than in vengeance: they being penitent,
    The sole drift of my purpose doth extend
    Not a frown further. Go release them, Ariel:
    My charms I'll break, their senses I'll restore,
    And they shall be themselves.
                    (V.i. 25—32)

The speech of abjuration inevitably follows from this recognition that fury
and vengeance have also motivated his treatment of his former enemies. As
I have suggested, Prospero does not so much quietly complete his project,
as terminate it in haste.
    Finally, having restored the Men of Sin to their senses and brought the
separated parties on his island together, he stands alone and speaks the
Epilogue. It ends with these words:

---

[60] This growing sense of kinship with the castaways is conveyed in his subsequent language:
his eyes, "sociable" to Gonzalo's, weep "fellowly tears" (V.i. 63—4); relationship is stressed
in the phrases "my daughter", "my brother", "Flesh and blood", "You, brother mine" (V.i.
72, 73, 74—5).

> Now I want
> Spirits to enforce, Arts to enchant;
> And my ending is despair,
> Unless I be reliev'd by prayer,
> Which pierces so, that it assaults
> Mercy itself, and frees all faults.
>> As you from crimes would pardon'd be,
>> Let your indulgence set me free.
>>> (*Epilogue*, 13—20)

These words with their "weighty allusions to Christian mercy and the Lord's Prayer"[61] can, it seems to me, only be interpreted as the traditional appeal for mercy of the repentant magician who has come to see the evil of his magical practises. This suggestion was made as early as the eighteenth century by Bishop Warburton who related these words to the appeal of Faustus for prayers to save him from damnation. Frank Kermode has objected to this interpretation on the grounds that since Prospero has been persented as a theurgist (i.e. white magician) throughout the play, "to turn him into a Faustian goetist at this point is to invite confusion."[62] But there is no confusion. The appeal for mercy follows his decision to abjure his rough magic, and this decision followed from his recognition that he had set himself over the other human beings in his power and had used magical ilusions in order to take vengeance on them. These are the "crimes" mentioned in the *Epilogue* for which he seeks pardon. For if Prospero is regarded as a benevolently wise magician practising only white magic, there are no crimes to be pardoned. But if he is seen as someone who initially regarded himself as a white magician but came to see that good ends do not justify the use of evil means, his abjuration and his appeal for indulgence makes sense. The indulgence he appeals for is not only forbearance or tolerance, but also includes "a remission of punishment which is still due to sin after sacramental absolution."[63]

The Epilogue, then, is spoken by Prospero as the traditional despairing necromancer appealing for mercy, but Shakespeare uses this traditional end of a magician's career with a difference. He is no Faustus faced by imminent damnation, nor is he bound by any contract with the Devil. For a parallel to Prospero and to his state of mind at the end of the play we can turn to England's most famous magician, the thirteenth century Franciscan monk,

---

[61] Kermode, Arden *Tempest*, note on Epilogue, p. 134.

[62] Kermode, Arden *Tempest*, note to l. 16 of the Epilogue.

[63] See *N.E.D.* under "indulgence", II 3, citing *I Henry VI*, I.iii. 35: "Thou that giv'st whores indulgence to sinne."

Roger Bacon. Bacon's scientific achievements are now fully recognized, but like John Dee after him he was regarded by his contemporaries as a magician.[64] It was largely due to Dee that Roger Bacon's manuscripts were rescued and preserved, and that continuity with the Oxford scientific tradition was maintained into the sixteenth and seventeenth centuries. At the same time Bacon's reputation as a magician lived on, and crystallized in the sixteenth century in *The Famous Historie of Fryar Bacon*. Here is the description of Friar Bacon's final abjuration of his magic:

I have unlocked the secrets of art and nature, and let the world see those things, that have layen hid since the death of Hermes, that rare and profound philosopher . . . yet all this knowledge of mine I esteeme so lightly, that I wish that I were ignorant, and knew nothing: for the knowledge of these things (as I have truly found) serveth not to better a man in goodnesse, but only to make him proud and thinke too well of himselfe. What hath all my knowledge of natures secrets gained me? Onely this, the losse of a better knowledge, the losse of divine studies . . . but I will remove the cause, which are these books: which I do purpose here before you all to burne.[65]

Having burnt his books, the Friar retired to a cell in a church wall, and spent his time "in prayer, meditation, and such divine exercises, and did seke by all means to dissuade men from the study of magicke". It is in the same mood, I suggest, that Prospero abjures his own magic and turns to prayer. He is in line of descent from the scientist and alchemist and reputed magician, Roger Bacon. Bacon's influence mediated above all by John Dee extended to Robert Fludd in England and to the Paracelsans of Rudolfine Prague.[66] Shakespeare in *The Tempest* sides finally with those who regarded the hermetic tradition of goetic magic inherited by Paracelsus and his followers as bordering on the dangerous and illicit. At the end of *The Tempest* Prospero is shown recognizing the dangers and limitations of his earlier vaunted powers. Using the titles of Agrippa's two major works, it can be said that Prospero after a lifetime spent in the study of occult philosophy had come to the realization of the uncertainty and vanity of human knowledge.

[64] See William R. Newbold, *The Cipher of Roger Bacon* (Philadelphia: Univ. of Philadelphia Press, 1928), p. 11.

[65] See E. M. Butler, *The Myth of the Magus* (Cambridge: Cambridge Univ. Press, 1948), p. 152, citing *The Famous Historie of Fryar Bacon*.

[66] For the influence of Roger Bacon on Fludd and the Rosicrucian movement, see Yates, *The Rosicrucian Enlightenment*, pp. 76 and 110. Concerning Dee's extensive collection of Bacon manuscripts and his presentation to Rudolf II of the Voynich Manuscript written in cipher by Roger Bacon, see Newbold, *The Cipher of Roger Bacon*, pp. 29 ff. Newbold's outstanding achievement in deciphering this manuscript has yet to receive the recognition it deserves.

What effect does this interpretation of Prospero as a practiser of illicit magic which he finally abjures have on the interpretation of his project offered in the previous chapters of this study? Are they in conflict or can they be reconciled? I have already suggested that a distinction should be made between Prospero's Dream and the means he employs for realizing it. This Dream of a regenerated society from which human selfishness has been eliminated is evoked in *The Tempest* with all the richness of allusion that has been traced in the previous chapters. The imagery of Paracelsan alchemy, ritual initiation and the Platonic mysteries of love, the august Christian rite of adult baptism, millenarian regeneration on a universal scale, all contribute to the haunting contrapuntal music of the play. It was in these terms, as we have seen, that Shakespeare's contemporaries viewed the climactic events of their day. The ultimate struggle was taking place between the forces of evil and good. Out of the suffering of the Last Days, the gaudy days of the Thousand Years of Peace would arise. This was the Dream that had long haunted Europe, and once again in the early years of the seventeenth century it seemed that the Dream was in process of taking root in reality. All the signs pointed that way. The discovery of the New World, the spread of the Gospel facilitated by the invention of printing, the reformation of a corrupt Church, the auspicious conjunction of Saturn and Jupiter in the fiery constellations of the zodiac, the portentous appearance of two new stars in the otherwise immutable heavens, even the intensified persecution of the faithful, all indicated that the brief reign of Antichrist had commenced but also that the Millennium was imminent. These signs were the *Miranda sextae aetatis* proclaimed by the Rosicrucians, the wonders of the sixth age, and of these wonders the most significant was the appearance of the Woman of Revelation 12. The appearance of this heavenly wonder, her persecution by Antichrist, her flight to a place prepared of God in the wilderness, and her emergence to lead in the Millennium became, as we saw, the symbol of a new regenerated human society being born from the ashes of the old.

Shakespeare does not in *The Tempest* condemn this potent Dream. On the contrary, he evokes it with all the beauty and learning at his command. At the same time he does not underestimate the difficulties in achieving it. The Dream is in the charge of good but imperfect people. Gonzalo with his vision of a second Golden Age, with his undeviating loyalty and his deep conviction that all their hardships will turn out well, is nevertheless no match for the cynicism and malice of Antonio and Sebastian. Miranda and Ferdinand, responsible for establishing the new society in Machiavellian Italy, are young, innocent and naive. How will their idealism fare in the real world that awaits them? There is too the problem of the masses, the Trinculos and Stephanos of the world, easily swayed, befuddled, disordered. And there are

164

the Calibans of the world, sometimes presented as preserving traces of the original innocence of the Golden Age but also as bestial. In such hands and against such malice and ignorance, the noble Dream of a regenerated world is made to appear fragile and insecure. To ensure its realization, something more, it seemed, was needed. How could the good people of the world be aided and how could the power of the evil-minded be broken, so that the Golden Age could be more rapidly inaugurated?

The answer for Prospero was to employ magic and so tip the balance in favour of the Gonzalos of the world. The evil-minded, without their knowledge but for their own ultimate good, would be magically coerced into improvement. This corresponds, as I have suggested, to the project conceived in Rudolfine Prague early in the seventeenth century of a magically and alchemically purged mankind. This project was to be carried out behind the scenes, and in the case of the Rosicrucians by a group of unknown people operating from an Invisible College. In the words of Libavius, their object was to establish "a world government based on magic spells". It was by these magical means that the Dream was to be realized. I have argued that in the case of *The Tempest*, Prospero's use of such means to bring about regeneration is condemned by Shakespeare in the final act of the play. It follows from this that the same condemnation also extends to the magical means advocated by Rudolf and the hermetic circle of Paracelsan physicians and scholars that he had gathered round himself in Prague as well as those in sympathy with them in other countries including England. The play that James I watched on November 1, 1611, therefore dealt with the most crucial issue of the day: by what means was the longed-for era of universal peace and brotherhood to be brought about? *The Tempest* dramatizes the specific question of whether magic could be legitimately employed to achieve this end. Shakespeare's answer to this question, implicit in Prospero's final abjuration of his rough magic, is no, and it is in line with the views expressed by James in his *Daemonologie*. We saw that James condemned Christian Princes "who allow magicians to live in their realms", and "even delight in their practises." Such Princes, he wrote, "sinne heavilie against their office in that poynt." Of such Princes the most notorious example in the late sixteenth century and early seventeenth century was Rudolf II. James would also have condemned any Prince who advocated the use of magic to bring about the Millennium, for, to cite James' words, yet again, "the axiom in theology is most certaine and infallible: *Numquam faciendum est malum ut bonum inde eveniat*"—no evil should be done in order that good may eventuate. In this matter, it seems, James I and his liveried servant, William Shakespeare, were of one mind.

I would like to conclude with a few personal remarks on the nature of the crime for which Prospero asks pardon in the Epilogue. In the widest sense, his crime consists in the infringement of the free will of other human beings. He manipulates those who come under his control without their knowing and without their permission. They are being improved without their consent. In doing this, Prospero has succumbed to a temptation that faces all idealists who have a vision of how things should be and are confronted by the indifference or blindness or hostility of those they earnestly wish to help. The temptation is to compel them to change for their own ultimate good. This may well involve a temporary loss of freedom and the imposition of salutary restraints. To those undergoing involuntary improvement, however, the loss of their liberty may not seem to be compensated for by the promise of a future state when men of their own accord, without the need of law, will live together in trust and right relationship. As experience shows, the beneficent State does not willingly wither, and idealistic governors do not surrender office easily. The idealist is not perfect, and mingled with the virtue of his high dream there may well be elements of vindictiveness and unacknowledged anger. It seems to me that in *The Tempest*, Shakespeare has meditated deeply, even agonized, over the problem of the right exercise of influence over another human being. Whether this influence is exercised through the magic of the written or spoken word or by the magic of wand and conjuring book, in a theatre or pulpit, at a political gathering or in the lecture-hall, there always arises the problem of whether we are coercing or liberating those we are addressing. *The Tempest* deals profoundly with this problem, showing us the mode of coercion in the first four acts and the way of liberation in the final act. The last word of the play is "free". With that word, Shakespeare comes down on the side of a prime human freedom: the freedom to be imperfect, to make mistakes and to learn by self-chosen experience. Coercion never made a man better.

166

Bibliography

Primary Sources and Texts

A. Editions of *The Tempest* and other plays by Shakespeare

Shakespeare, William. *The Tempest*. Ed. Frank Kermode. The Arden Shakespeare. 1964; rpt. London: Methuen, 1972.
— *The Tempest*. Ed. H. H. Furness, Jr. A New Variorum Edition. New York: Dover Publications, 1964.
— *The Tempest*. Ed. A.Quiller-Couch and J. Dover-Wilson. The New Shakespeare. Cambridge: Cambridge Univ. Press, 1921.
— *The Tempest*. Ed. Northrop Frye. The Penguin Shakespeare. Harmondsworth: Penguin Books, 1959.
— *The Tempest*. Ed. J. R. Sutherland. The New Clarendon Edition. Oxford: Clarendon Press, 1939.
— *Cymbeline*. Ed. J. M. Nosworthy. The Arden Shakespeare. London: Methuen, 1955.
— *Henry VIII*. Ed. R. A. Foakes. The Arden Shakespeare. London: Methuen, 1957.
— *The Winter's Tale*. Ed. J. H. Pafford. The Arden Shakespeare. London: Methuen, 1963.

B. Other Contemporary Sources and Texts
(unless otherwise stated, place of publication is London)

Agrippa, Cornelius. *De occulta philosophia*. Cologne, 1533; trans. J. F. (John French?), *Three Books of Occult Philosophy*.1651.
— *De incertitudine et vanitate scientiarum*. Antwerp, 1530.
Andreae, Johan Valentin. *Chymische Hochzeit Christiani Rosenkreutz*. 1616; trans. Ezekiel Foxcroft, *The Hermetic Romance, or The Chymical Wedding*. 1690; rpt. in *A Christian Rosenkreutz Anthology* (Blauvelt: Rudolf Steiner Publications, 1968), pp. 67—162.
— *Christianopolis*. Strasburg, 1620.
Aubrey, John. *Aubrey's Brief Lives*. Ed. O. L. Dick. London: Secker and Warburg, 1949.
Artis Auriferae quam chemicam vocant. 2 Vols. Basle, 1593.
Aurelia Occulta. Vol. IV of *Theatrum Chemicum*. 1613.
Aurora Consurgens. In *Artis Auriferae*. 1593.
Bale, John. *The Image of bothe Churches*. 1545.
— *A Comedy concerning three laws*. 1531.
Barnaud, Nicholas. *Commentariolum in aenigmaticum*. Leiden, 1597.
Beaumont, Francis. *Philotas*. c. 1610; rpt. in Revels Plays, ed. Andrew Gurr. Manchester: Manchester Univ. Press, 1969.
— *The Masque of the Inner Temple and Gray's Inn*. 1613; rpt. in *A Book of Masques: In Honour of Allardyce Nicoll*. Cambridge: Cambridge Univ. Press, 1967, pp. 127—148.

B.M. Kings MSS. 17 c xxxv. A contemporary description, with illustrations, of the fireworks display on the Thames during the wedding festivities of Princess Elizabeth and the Elector Palatine in February, 1613.

B.M. Royal MS. 14 B xvi. A vellum roll of Latin verses, anagrams and rebuses sent during the Christmas of 1611 to Henry, Prince of Wales, by Michael Maier.

Boccaccio, Giovanni. *Genealogia deorum gentilium*. Venice, 1472.

Brightman, Thomas. *A revelation of revelation*. 1609.

Broughton, Hugh. *A Revelation of the Holy Apocalypse*. 1610.

Calendar of State Papers, Domestic Series, 1611—1618. Ed. M.A.E. Green. London, 1856.

Calendar of State Papers, Venetian,1 610—13. Ed. H. F. Brown. London: H. M. Stationary Office, 1905).

Casaubon, Isaac. *Exercitationes de rebus sacris et ecclesiasticis*. 1614.

Castellanus, Petrus. *De Festis Graecorum Syntagma in que plurima Antiquititatis ritus illustratur*. Antwerp, 1617.

Chapman, George. *The Masque of the Inner Temple and Lincoln's Inn*. 1613; rpt. Nichols, *The Progresses of King James*. Vol. II, pp. 566—586.

Chrysogonus, Polydorus, *De Alchimia*. Nuremberg, 1541.

Confessio Fraternitatis. Cassel, 1615; rpt. in *A Christian Rosenkreutz Anthology*, 1968, pp. 180—190.

Comes (Conti), Natalis. *Mythologiae*. Venice, 1568.

Croll, Oswald. *Basilica chymica*. Frankfurt, 1609.

— *Tractatus de signaturis rerum*. Prague, 1608.

Digby, Kenelm. "Concerning Spenser that I wrote at Mr Day's Desire." Before 1628; rpt. in *Spenser: The Critical Heritage*. Ed. R. M. Cummings. London: Routledge and Kegan Paul, 1971, pp. 147—50.

Dorn, Gerard. *Philosophia chemica*. In Vol. I of *Theatrum Chemicum*. 1602.

— *Physica Trismegisti*. In Vol. I of *Theatrum Chemicum*. 1602.

Erastus, Thomas. *Disputationes de Medica Nova Paracelsi*. Basle, 1572—3.

Fama Fraternitatis. Cassel, 1614; rpt. in *A Christian Rosenkreutz Anthology*, 1968, pp. 164—180.

Ficino, Marsilio. *Opera*. Basle, 1576.

Fludd, Robert. *Anatomiae Amphitheatrum*. 1623.

— *Mosaicall Philosophy*. 1659.

— *The Philosophicall Key*. c. 1618; rpt. in *Robert Fludd and the Philosophicall Key*. Ed. Allen G. Debus. New York: Science and History Publications, 1979.

— *Tractatus Apologeticus*. Leiden, 1617.

— *Utriusque Cosmi Historia*. Oppenheim, 1617—1619.

Fulgentius. *De expositione Virgilianae continentia*. Heidelberg, 1589.

Fuller, Thomas. *The Worthies of England*. 16; rpt. 1840. 3 Vols. Ed. P. Austin Nuttall.

Giraldi (Gyraldus), Lilio Gregorio. *De deis gentium*. Basle, 1548.

Harrington, John. *Preface to Orlando Furioso*. 1599; rpt. in *Elizabethan Critical Essays*. Vol. II. Ed. G. Greogry Smith. Oxford: Oxford Univ. Press, 1904, pp. 194—222.

Harvey, Richard. *Astrological Discourse upon the great and notable Coniunction of the superiour Planets, SATURNE & JUPITER, which shall happen the 28 day of April*. 1584.

Jackson, Thomas. *A Treatise Containing the Originall of Unbeliefe*. 1625.

168

James VI and I. "A Fruitfull Meditation containing a Plaine and easie exposition, or laying open of the VII, VIII, IX, X Verses of the 20 Chapter of the Revelation in forme and manner of a Sermon." 1588; rpt. in *Works of King James*. 1616.

— *Daemonologie*. 1597; rpt. in *Elizabethan and Jacobean Quartos*. Ed. J. B. Harrison. Edinburgh: University Press, 1966.

Jewel, John. *A Treatise of the Sacraments*. 1583, 1603, 1609, 1611.

Jonson, Ben. *The Alchemist*. 1610; rpt. in *The Revels Plays*. Ed. F. H. Mares. London: Methuen, 1967.

— *Bartholomew Fayre*. 1614; rpt. in *Works*. Vol. VI. Ed. C. H. Herford and Percy and Evelyn Simpson. Oxford: Clarendon Press, pp. 1—141.

Kepler, Johan. *De Stella Nova*. Prague, 1606.

Khunrath, Heinrich. *Amphitheatrum sapientiae aeternae*. Hanover, 1609.

Landino, Cristofero. *Quaestiones Camaldulenses*. c. 1480; rpt. in *Cristofero Landino's Allegorization of the Aeneid: Books III and IV of the Camaldolese Disputations*. Trans. and introd. S. J. Stahel. Diss. Johns Hopkins, 1968.

Libavius, Andreas. *Wohlmeinendes Bedenken der Fama und Confession der Bruderschaft des Rosenkretuzes*. Frankfurt, 1616.

Lilly, William. *The History of His Life and Times*. 1774.

Lodge, Thomas. *A Defence of Poetry*. 1579; rpt. in *Elizabethan Critical Essays*, I, 61—86.

Maier, Michael. *Arcana arcanissima*. Oppenheim, c. 1614.

— *Silentium post clamores*. Frankfurt, 1617.

— (see under B.M. Royal MS 14 B xvi.)

Marlowe, Christopher. *Doctor Faustus*. 1604; rpt in *The Revels Plays*. Ed. John D. Jump. London: Methuen, 1968.

Meres, Francis. "Palladis Tamia." 1598; rpt. in *Elizabethan Critical Essays*, II, 308—324.

Meursius, Johannes. *Eleusinia, sive de Cereris Eleusinia Sacra*. Louvian, 1619.

Michaelspacher, Steffan. *Cabala, Spiegel der Kunst und Natur*. 1616.

Moffett, Thomas. *De Jure et Praestantia Chemicorum Medicamentorum*. 1584. In Vol. II of *Theatrum Chemicum*, 1602.

Napier, John. *A Plaine Discovery*. 1593.

Nashe, Thomas. *A General Censure*. 1589; rpt. in *Elizabethan Critical Essays*, I, 307—337.

— *Lenten Stuffe*. 1599; rpt. in *Works*. Ed. R. B. McKerrow. Vol. III, pp. 220 ff.

Nichols, J. *The Progresses of King James*. 1828. 4 Vols.

Nollius, Henricus F. *Systema Medecinae Hermeticae Generale*. Frankfurt, 1613.

Ogilby, John. *The Accurate Description of Africa*. 1670.

Osborne, Francis. *Traditional Memoires on the reigns of Queen Elizabeth and King James*. 1658.

Paracelsus. *The Archidoxes of Magic*. Trnsl. R. Turner (1656); rpt. London: Askin, 1975.

Puttenham, George. "Of Ornament". In *The Arte of English Poesie*. 1589. Rpt. in *Elizabethan Critical Essays*, II, 142—193.

R. N. E. (Richard Napier?). *A Revelation of the Secret Spirit declaring the most concealed secrets of Alchymie*. 1623.

Rabelais, François. *Oeuvres Completes*. Ed. J. Plattard. Paris: Editions Fernand Roches, 1929.

Schweighardt, Theophilus. *Speculum Sophicum Rhodo-Stauroticum?*, 1618.

Siebacher, J. A. *Hydrolithus sophicus, seu Aquarium sapientum*. Frankfurt, 1619; rpt. in *Musaeum Hermeticum*. 1678, pp. 73—144.

Sperber, Julius. *Wunderbuch?*, c. 1600.

Studion, Simon. *Naometria*. 1604. Ms. Cod. theol. 4 23, 24, in Wurtemberg Landesbibliotek, Stuttgart.

Taylor, John ("The Water Poet"). *Heaven's Blessing and Earth's Joy* 1613, rpt. in Nichols, *The Progresses of King James*, II, 529 ff.

Theatrum Chemicum. 6 Vols. Strasburg, 1602—1661.

Tymme, Thomas. *A Dialogue Philosophicall*. 1612.

Trismosin, Salomon. *Splendor Solis*. 1598.

Vallensis, Robertus. *De veritate et antiquitate artis chemiae*. Paris, 1561; rpt. 1602 in *Theatrum Chemicum*.

Vaughan, Thomas. *Lumen de Lumine*. 1651.

Visio Arislei (full title: *Aenigmata ex visione Arislei philosophi, et allegoriis sapientum*). 1593 in *Artis Auriferae*, II, 146—54.

Vogel, Heinrich. *Offenbarung der Gehymnissen der Alchimy?*, 1605.

Wotton, Sir Henry. *Sir Henry Wotton: Life and Letters*. Ed. L. Pearsall Smith. Oxford: Clarendon Press, 1907.

Secondary Sources and Texts

A Book of Masques: In Honour of Allardyce Nicoll. Cambridge: Cambridge Univ. Press, 1967.

A Christian Rosenkreutz Anthology. Ed. P. M. Allen. Blauvelt: Rudolf Steiner Publications, 1968.

Aristophanes. *The Frogs and Other Plays*. Transl. D. Barrett. Harmondsworth: Penguin Books, 1964.

Aston, Margaret B. "The Fiery Trigon Conjunction: An Elizabethan Astrological Prediction." In *Isis*, 61 (1970), 159—187.

Baldwin, T. W. *Shakespeare's Small Latine and Lesse Greek*. 2 Vols. Urbana: Univ. of Illinois Press, 1966.

Bennett, Josephine Waters. *The Evolution of the Faerie Queene*. Chicago: Univ. of Chicago Press, 1942.

— *Measure for Measure as Royal Entertainment*. New York and London: Columbia Univ. Press, 1942.

Binns, J. W. "Shakespeare's Latin Citations: The Editorial Problem." In *Shakespeare Survey*, 35 (Cambridge Univ. Press, 1982), pp. 119—128.

Bolton, Henry Carrington. *The Follies of Science at the Court of Rudolf II, 1576—1612*. Milwaukee: Pharmaceutical Review Publishing Co., 1904.

Brooks, Harold F. "Richard III: Antecedents of Clarence's Dream." In *Shakespeare Survey*, 32 (1979), 145—150.

Butler, E. M. *The Myth of the Magus*. Cambridge: Cambridge Univ. Press, 1948.

Chambers, E. K. *William Shakespeare*, 2 Vols. Oxford: Clarendon Press, 1930.

Chaudhuri, Supriya. "Jason's Fleece: The Source of Sir Epicure Mammon's Allegory". In *Review of English Studies*, N.S. 137 (Feb., 1984), p. 72.

Clark, Melville. *Murder Under Trust: The Topical Macbeth and Other Jacobean Matters*. Edinburgh: Scottish Academic Press, 1981.

Clasen, Claus-Peter. *Anabaptism A Social History, 1525—1618.* Ithaca: Cornell Univ. Press, 1972.

Coffin, C. M. *John Donne and the New Philosophy.* Diss. in *Studies in English and Comparative Literature,* No. 126. New York: Columbia Univ. Press, 1937.

Cohn, Norman. *In Pursuit of the Millennium.* London: Paladin Books, 1970.

Coulter, A. C. *The Literary Microcosm: Theories of Interpretation of the Later Platonists.* Leiden: Brill, 1976.

Coudert, Alison. *Alchemy: The Philosopher's Stone.* London: Wildwood House Ltd., 1980.

Cyril of Jerusalem. *Catéchèses Mystagogiques.* Ed. A Piedangel. Paris, 1966.

— *St Cyril of Jerusalem's Lectures on the Christian Sacraments.* Ed. F. L. Cross. London, S.P.C.K.F., 1951.

D'Alviella, Goblet. *The Mysteries of Eleusis.* Wellingborough: The Aquarian Press, 1981.

Daniélou, Jean. *Bible et Liturgie.* Paris: 1951.

Debus, Allen G. *The Chemical Philosophy: Paracelsan Science and Medicine in the Sixteenth and Seventeenth Centuries.* 2 Vols. New York: Science and History Publications, 1977.

— *The English Paracelsians.* London: Oldbourne, 1965.

— *Robert Fludd and the Philosophicall Key.* New York: Science and History Publications, 1979.

Dionysius the Pseudo-Areopagite. *The Ecclesiastical Hierarchy.* Ed. Rev. T. L. Campbell. *The Catholic University of America Studies in Sacred Theology,* Ser. 2, No. 83 (Washington, 1955).

Edwards, Philip. "Shakespeare's Romances: 1900—1957". *Shakespeare Survey,* 11, (1958), 1—18.

Elizabethan Critical Essays. 2 Vols. Ed. G. Gregory Smith. Oxford: Oxford Univ. Press, 1904.

Firth, Catherine R. *The Apocalyptic Tradition in Reformation Britain.* Oxford: Oxford Univ. Press, 1978.

Fletcher, Angus. *The Prophetic Moment: An Essay on Spenser.* Chicago and London: Univ. of Chicago Press, 1971.

Fowler, Alistair. *Spenser and the Number of Time.* London: Routledge and Kegan Paul, 1964.

French, Peter J. *John Dee: The World of an Elizabethan Magus.* London: Routledge and Kegan Paul, 1972.

Friedlander, Paul. *Plato: An Introduction.* Bollingen Series 59:1. Princeton: Princeton Univ. Press, 1969.

Grant, Patrick. "The Magic of Charity: A Background to Prospero". In *Review of English Studies,* 27 (1976), 1—16.

Grant, R. M. *The Letter and the Spirit.* London: Macmillan, 1957.

Gombrich, E. H. *Symbolic Images: Studies in the Art of the Renaissance, II.* Oxford: Phaidon Press, 1972.

Hallett, Smith. "The Tempest as a Kalaidoscope." *Twentieth Century Interpretations of The Tempest,* pp. 1—11.

Hankins, John E. *Backgrounds of Shakespeare's Thought.* Hassocks: Harvester Press, 1978.

— "Spenser and the Revelation of St John." *Publications of the Modern Language Association of America,* 60 (New York: The Modern Language Association of America, 1945), 364—381.

171

Harden, Donald. *The Phoenicians.* Harmondsworth: Penguin Publications, 1971.

Herford, C. H. *Studies in the Literary Relations of England and Germany.* Cambridge: Cambridge Univ. Press, 1886.

Hill, Christopher. *Antichrist in Seventeenth-Century England.* Oxford Univ. Press, 1971.

Hoeniger, David F. "Shakespeare's Romances since 1958: A Retrospect." *Shakespeare Survey,* 29 (1976).

Holmyard, E. J. *Alchemy.* Harmondsworth: Penguin Publications, 19i57.

James, D. G. *The Dream of Prospero.* Oxford: Clarendon Press, 1967.

Jonas, Hans. *The Gnostic Religion.* Boston: Beacon Press, 1958.

Jung, Carl G. *Alchemical Studies.* Vol. 13 in *Collected Works.* London: Routledge and Kegan Paul, 1967, 1983 ed.

— *Mysterium Coniunctionis.* Bollingen Ser. XX. Princeton: Princeton Univ. Press, 1963, 1977 ed.

— *Psychology and Alchemy.* Bollingen Ser. XX. Princeton: Princeton Univ. Press, 1953.

Kermode, Frank. "The Cave of Mammon." In *Stratford-Upon-Avon Studies, 2 Elizabethan Poetry.* Ed. J. R. Brown and B. Harris. London: Edward Arnold, 1960, pp. 151—173.

Kott, Jan. *Shakespeare Our Contemporary.* London: Methuen, 1967.

Levy, G. R. *The Gate of Horn.* London: Faber and Faber, 1948.

Lindroth, Sten. *Paracelcism i Sverige till 1600-talets mitt. Lychnos-Biblikotek 7.* Uppsala: Almquist and Wiksell International, 1943.

Loughrey, Bryan and Taylor, Neil. "Ferdinand and Miranda at Chess." *Shakespeare Survey,* 35 (1982), 113—118.

Macdonald, Michael. *Mystical Bedlam: Madness, Anxiety and Healing in Seventeenth Century England.* Cambridge: Cambridge Univ. Press, 1981.

McIntosh, Christopher. *The Rosy Cross Unveiled: The History, Mythology and Rituals of an Occult Order.* Wellingborough: The Aquarian Press, 1980.

McLean, Adam. "A Rosicrucian Manuscript of Michael Maier." *The Hermetic Journal* 5 (1979), 1—7.

Montgomery, J. W. *The Cross and the Crucible: J. Andreae (1586—1654), Phoenix of the Theologians.* 2 Vols. The Hague: Nijhoff, 1972.

Moss, Jean Dietz. *"Godded with God": Henrik Niclaes and His Family of Love. Transactions of the American Philosophical Society,* 71:8. Philadelphia: The American Philosophical Society, 1981.

Murrin, Michael. *The Allegorical Epic.* Chicago and London: Univ. Press of Chicago, 1980.

— *The Veil of Allegory: Some Notes towards a Theory of Allegorical Rhetoric in the English Renaissance.* Chicago and London: Univ. Press of Chicago, 1969.

Neuse, Richard. "Book Six as Conclusion to the Faerie Queene." *Critical Essays from E.L.H.* Baltimore: Johns Hopkins Press, 1970.

Nicholl, John. *The Chemical Theatre.* London: Routledge and Kegan Paul, 1980.

Norhnberg, James. *The Analogy of the Faerie Queene.* Princeton: Princeton Univ. Press, 1976.

Nosworthy, J. M. "The Narrative Sources of *The Tempest.*" *Review of English Studies,* 24 (1948), 281—294.

Nuttall, A. D. *Two Concepts of Allegory: A Study of Shakespeare's The Tempest and the Logic of Allegorical Expression.* London: Routledge and Kegan Paul, 1967.

Otto, Walter F. "The Meaning of the Eleusinian Mysteries." *The Mysteries*, Bollingen Ser. XXX, ed. Joseph Campbell. Princeton: Princeton Univ. Press, 1955, pp. 14—31.

Ovid. *Metamorphoses*. Transl. and introd. by Mary M. Innes. Harmondsworth: Penguin Books, 1955.

Parker, Geoffrey. *Europe in Crisis, 1598—1648*. London: Fontana Peperbacks, 1979.

Parry, Graham. *The Golden Age Restor'd: The Culture of the Stuart Court, 1603—42*. Manchester: Manchester Univ. Press, 1981.

Partridge, Eric. *A Dictionary of Slang and Unconventional English*. London: Routledge and Kegan Paul, 1937.

Pettett, E. C. *Shakespeare and the Romance Tradition*. London: Staples, 1949.

Plato. *Gorgias*. Trnsl. W. Hamilton. Harmondsworth: Penguin Books, 1960.

— *Phaedo*. Ed. R. Hackforth. Cambridge: Cambridge Univ. Press, 1972.

— *Phaedrus*. Ed. R. Hackforth. Cambridge: Cambridge Univ. Press, 1952.

— *Republic*. Trnsl. H.. D. P. Lee. Harmondsworth: Penguin Books, 1955.

Quintillian. *Institutio Oratoria*. 4 Vols, Loeb ed. Transl. H.E. Butler. Cambridge, Mass., Harvard Univ. Press; London: Heinemann, 1920; rpt. 1963.

Rahner, Hugo. "The Christian Mystery and the Pagan Mysteries." *The Mysteries*. Bollingen Ser. XXX, 2 Ed. Joseph Campbell. Princeton: Princeton Univ. Press, 1955, pp. 337—401.

Reeves, Marjorie. *Joachim of Fiore and the Prophetic Future*. New York and London: Harper and Row, 1976.

— *The Influence of Prophecy in the Later Middle Ages*. Oxford: Oxford Univ. Press, 1969.

Rivers, Isabel. *Classical and Christian Ideas in English Renaissance Poetry*. London: Allen and Unwin, 1979.

Rola, Stanislas de. *The Secret Art of Alchemy*. London: Thames and Hudson, 1973.

Rowse, A.L. *Simon Forman: Sex and Society in Shakespeare's England*. London: Weidenfeld and Nicolson, 1974.

Ruskin, John. *Munera Pulveris*. 1872.

Schanzer, E. "Four Notes on Macbeth." *Modern Language Review*, 52. Cambridge: Cambridge Univ. Press, 1957, 223—227.

Servius. *Commentarii in Virgilii*. 3 Vols. Ed. G. Thilo and H. Hagen (1881—1923).

Sherwood Taylor, F. *The Alchemists*. London: Heinemann, 1952.

Silvestris, Bernard of. *The Commentary of the Six Books of the Aeneid of Virgil commonly attributed to Bernardus Silvestris*. Ed. J. W. and E. F. Evans. Lincoln: University of Nebraska Press, 1977.

Sisson, C. J. "The Magic of Prospero." *Shakespeare Survey*, 11 (1958), 70—77.

Starnes, De Witt T, and Talbot, E. W. *Classical Myth and Legends in Renaissance Dictionaries*. North Carolina: Univ. Press, 1955.

Stern, Virginia F. *Gabriel Harvey: A Study of His Life, Marginalia and Library*. Oxford: Clarendon Press, 1979.

Still, Colin. *Shakespeare's Mystery Play: A Study of The Tempest*. London: Cecil Palmer, 1921.

— *The Timeless Theme*. London: Nicholson and Watson, 1936.

Strachey, Lytton. "Shakespeare's Final Period," in *Twentieth Century Interpretations of The Tempest*, pp. 88—91.

Taylor, Thomas. *Thomas Taylor The Platonist: Selected Writings*. Ed. K. Raine and

G. M. Harper. Bollingen Ser. 88. Princeton: Princeton Univ. Press, 1969.

The Hermetic Journal. Ed. Adam McLean. Edinburgh: Megalithic Research Publications, 1979—.

The Mysteries. Bollingen Ser. XXX, 2. Ed. Joseph Campbell. Princeton: Princeton Univ. Press, 1955.

The Viking Portable Renaissance Reader. Ed. J. B. Ross and M. M. Mclaughlin. Harmondsworth: The Viking Press, 1953.

Thomas, Keith. *Religion and the Decline of Magic: Studies in Popular Beliefs in Sixteenth- and Seventeenth-Century England.* London: Weidenfeld and Nicolson, 1971; Harmondsworth: Penguin University Books, 1973.

Tillyard, E. M. W. *Shakespeare's Last Plays.* London: Chatto and Windus, 1962.

Turnbull, George. *Hartlib, Dury, and Comenius: Gleanings from Hartlib's Papers.* Liverpool: Univ. Press of Liverpool, 1947.

Twentieth Century Interpretations of The Tempest. Ed. Hallett Smith Eaglewood Cliffs: Prentice-Hall, 1969.

Virgil. *The Aeneid.* Trnsl. W. F. Jackson. Harmondsworth: Penguin Books, 1956.

Vyvyan, John. *Shakespeare and Platonic Beauty.* London: Chatto and Windus, 1961.

— *Shakespeare and the Rose of Love: A Study of the Early Plays in Relation to the Medieval Philosophy of Love.* London: Chatto and Windus, 1961.

Walker, D. P. *Spiritual and Demonic Magic from Ficino to Campanella.* Vol. 22 in *Studies of the Warburg Institute.* London: Warburg Institute, 1958.

Warburton, William. *The Divine Legation of Moses.* 2 Vols. (1765).

Weinstein, Donald. *Savanarola and Florence: Prophecy and Patriotism in the Renaissance.* Princeton: Princeton Univ. Press, 1970.

Wilson Knight, G. *The Crown of Life.* Oxford: Oxford Univ. Press, 1947.

— *The Shakespearian Tempest.* Oxford: Oxford Univ. Press, 1932.

Willson, D. H. *King James VI and I.* London: Jonathan Cape, 1963.

Wind, Edgar. *Pagan Mysteries in the Renaissance.* London: Faber and Faber, 1958.

Yates, Frances. *Astraea.* London: Routledge and Kegan Paul, 1975; Peregrine Books, 1977.

— *Giordano Bruno and the Hermetic Tradition.* Chicago: Chicago Univ. Press, 1969.

— *The Art of Memory.* London: Routledge and Kegan Paul, 1966; Peregrine Books, 1969.

— *The Occult Philosophy in the Elizabethan Age.* London: Routledge and Kegan Paul, 1979.

— *The Rosicrucian Enlightenment.* London and Boston: Routledge and Kegan Paul, 1972.

Index

Latine and Lesse Greeke, 152n

Bale, John, 96;*A Comedy concerning Three Laws*, 96; *The Image of bothe Churches*, 94

baptism, 19, 20, 34, Ch. IV *passim*; adult, 73, 76, 77; and alchemy, 73—4; and pagan mysteries, 75—6; as eschatological event, Ch. V *passim*; as marriage, 89—90; as a mystery, 79; catechumens and, 79, 80, 84—7; Chrysostomus on, 80; Cyril of Jerusalem on, 80; Dionysius on, 80; and Baptist Church of 1611, 76; ship of, 88

"badges", 69—70; as livery badges, 70; as *sphragis*, 70

Barnaud, Nicholas, physician and alchemist, 128

Baronius, *Annales*, 50, 76—7

Beaumont, Francis, *Philaster*, 14, 119, 120; *The Masque of the Inner Temple and Gray's Inn*, 137, 138n

Bennett, J. W., *The Evolution of the Faerie Queene*, 106

Bethell, S. L., 13, 17

Binns, J., 48n

Boccaccio, 9

boiling, alchemical, 35—7, 50

Bolton, alchemist, 23

Bolton, H. C., *The Follies of Science at the Court of Rudolf II*, 127n

Botticelli, Sandro, and Joachim of Fiore, 139; *Crucifixion*, 139; *Nativity*, 139

Brahe, Tycho, on *nova* of 1572, 97

Brightman, Thomas, *A Revelation of Revelation*, 95, 96

Brooks, Harold F., 55

Broughton, Hugh, *A Revelation of the Holy Apocalypse*, 136

Bruno, Giordano, 147, 155

bulls, symbolism of, 86; in alchemy, 86n

Butler, E. M., *The Myth of the Magus*, 163n

Butler, William, physician and alchemist, 147, 148

Cabalism, 21

Calendar of State Papers, Venetian, 117—8, 122n, 131n, 132n.

Caliban, 3, 4, 40—3, 108—114, 136, 165; and drunkenness, 68—70; as the Beast, 108—114; as "this thing of darkness", 108—114

Calvin, on Man of Sin, 107; on Psalm 23, 85

Campanella, Tommaso, 155

Campion, Thomas, *Songs of Mourning*, 134n; *The Lords's Masque*, 135—6

Carthage, 18, 53, 55, 84; as symbol of civic life, 56

Casaubon, Isaac, 49, 71, 76—81; *Exercitationes*, 49—50, 51n, 77—81; life of, 76—7; talks with James I, 77

Castellanus, Petrus, de *Festis Graecorum*, 49, 71

catharsis, 82

cauda pavonis, alchemical, 33

Chambers, E. K., *William Shakespeare*, 119n, 121n

Chapman, George, 12, 15, 18, 48; *The Masque of the Middle Temple and Lincoln's Inn*, 136—7

Charles V, at Tunis and Algiers, 133—4

Chaudari, Supriya, "Jason's Fleece", 154n

chess, 37—39

Chrysogonus, Polydorus, ref. to *De Alchemia*, 154

Christian of Anhalt, 29, 123

Claribel, 134

Clement of Alexandria, 76

clothes, and baptism, 87: "new-dyed", 33, 54, 83; "sustaining", 87—88

coagulation, alchemical, 37

Coffin, C. M., *John Donne and the New Philosophy*, 135n

Cohn, Norman, *In Pursuit of the Millennium*, 92

collections, alchemical: *Artis Auriferae*, 22, 32; *Theatrum Chemicum*, 22, 37n, 154

Colonna, Prospero, *Poliphili Hypnerotomachia*, 39

Comenius, 140 n. 61; and *centrum securitatis*, 129

163; and Maier, 99; on conjunction of 1603, 97; *Summum Bonum*, 41n; *Tractatus Apologeticus*, 97

Foakes, R. A., 121

Forman, Simon, physician and alchemist, 24, 25, 119, 120, 147

Fowles, John, *The Magus*, 115

Frederick V, the Elector Palatine, 14, 16, 119, 122, 123, 130, 131, 132, 140; and Ferdinand, 131; and performance of *Tempest*, 116; and Prague, 94; and Rudolf II, 102; as King of Bohemia, 138—9; as "Paracelsist lion", 157; as St George, 132—3; marriage, Ch VI *passim*; millenarian role, 90, 96, 99, 103—4, 116, 137, 138, 139, 159; negotiations for marriage with Elizabeth, 117—122

French, Peter, J., *John Dee*, 146, 149n

Frye, Northrop, 5, 142

Fuller, Thomas, 24

Furness, H. H., 34

Furnivall, F. J., 4

Galen, 21

Gessner, Conrad, physician, on Paracelsus, 154—5

Gilbert, Adrian, alchemist, 23

gnosticism, 110

Gombrich, E. H., 8, 11, 12—3

Gonzalo, 14, 18, 19, 30, 33, 53, 82, 83, 90, 105, 157, 161n, 164; role in *Tempest*, 54, 67, 82—5

Grant, Patrick, "The Magic of Charity", 5, 142, 143

Grant, R. M., 7

Guarinonius, C., physician and alchemist, 128n

Gurr, Andrew, 119

Gyraldus, L. G., *De deis gentium*, 48, 71

Hajek, T., alchemist, 128n

Hallett, Smith, "The Tempest as a Kaleidoscope", 141

handbooks, mythographic, 48—50, 71

Hankins, J. E., *Backgrounds of Shakespeare's Thought*, 61

Harden, Donald, *The Phoenicians*, 53n

Harington, John, 7, 9, 19

harpy, 45; Ariel as, 57

Harvey, Gabriel, 147—8

hell: as Underworld, 71, 81; descent into, 44, 74, 89; as Hades, 34, 56—7, 62; Harrowing of, 72, 74, 89; in baptism, 75; as Tartarus, 34, 56, 63, 70

Helwys, Thomas, Baptist, 76

Henry, Prince, 2, 15—16, 118, 122, 130, 131, 134, 136, 140; as apocalyptic figure, 95, 99, 188; death of, 120, 121, 132; Maier's Christmas card to, 52, 99—102, 130, 156

Herbert, William, third Earl of Pembroke, 23

Herford, C. H., *Studies in the Literary Relations of England and Germany*, 148

Hilary, St, 74

Hill, Christopher, *Antichrist in Seventeenth-Century England*, 94n, 107n

Hippocrates, 21

Homer, 7

Horace *Fourth Ode*, 112

incongruity, 11—12, 18—19, 88

initiation, as baptism, 81; Christian, 70, 79; platonic, 58

island, and wilderness of Rev. 12, 107; as symbol, 55—6; as Tartarus, 63, 70; in *Christianopolis*, 106

Jackson, Thomas, *A Treatise containing the Original of Unbeliefe*, 155n

James I, 2, 23, 24, 26, 120, 121, 129, 136, 139, 140, 146, 156, 165; *A Fruitfull Meditation*, 94, 138; and Algiers, 134 and n. 48; attitude to magic, 130n, 143, 150—2; *Daemonologie*, 143, 150—2, 152n, 160, 165; and Dee, 149; compared to Rudolf II, 130—1; Maier's Christmas card to, 52, 99—101, 156; *Premonition*, 124; *Tempest* and, 116

Jewel, John, *A Treatise of the Sacraments*, 87

Joachim of Fiore, 93, 106, 133, 139;